# BETWEEN TWO RIVERS

## A Memoir

Dorothy Al Khafaji

*Dorothy Al Khafaji*

PARTHIAN

Parthian
The Old Surgery
Napier Street
Cardigan
SA43 1ED

www.parthianbooks.com

First published in 2013
© Dorothy Al Khafaji 2013
All Rights Reserved

ISBN 978-1908946874

Cover by www.theundercard.co.uk
Front cover design: Chris Iliff
Typeset by Elaine Sharples
Printed and bound by Gomer Press, Llandysul, Wales

Published with the financial support of the Welsh
Books Council

British Library Cataloguing in Publication Data

A cataloguing record for this book is available from
the British Library.

# Introduction

The first car I ever drove was a Mercedes: it was the most luxurious car I had ever seen – a large cream saloon with bench seats upholstered in leather and a lot of chrome around the bumper. I wish I still had it because it would probably be a collector's dream nowadays, but the truth is it never belonged to me. The whole thing came about because of a chance meeting and a series of coincidences. I suppose you could call it fate.

Many Eastern cultures believe in fate, that our destiny, or 'Kisma', is written on our foreheads on the day we are born. Of course, most people try to do a bit of wheeling and dealing along the way, trying to make the best of the path that they have been placed on, but that basic path is inescapable. They would definitely say that it was fate that I agreed to go to a dance with my sister and her friends on a cold, wet winter's evening when all I wanted to do was go to bed. My sister begged me to go so that she would have someone to walk home with from the late night transport drop-off point, because her friends were going home on a different bus. I went very reluctantly and perhaps my reluctance showed on my face, because for once I was the wall flower, the girl nobody asked to dance. Whilst I was sitting at a table waiting for the others a very thin, olive skinned young man sat down beside me and struck up a conversation. His name was Zane and he was an Iraqi engineering student. His chat up line was highly original – within minutes he was asking me about my educational qualifications, which he appeared to find highly impressive, even though I only possessed a few 'O' levels in those days. At any rate, we hit it off immediately and almost before I knew it we were married with a baby on the way.

1

That's how it came about that in the autumn of 1962, six months after my eldest daughter was born, I was literally on the road to Baghdad.

Over the years, I've often been told that I should write about my experiences in Baghdad. It wasn't that I was unwilling, but I kept putting it off, partly because I always had something else to do but also because I couldn't decide on a style or genre. First of all, I wanted to write an allegorical novel of a monster (Saddam Hussein, obviously) but by the time I got around to it, the world had already found out for itself about his atrocities. Later, I wanted to write a serious study of the events which were unfolding in Iraq, but they became such an important factor in international politics, almost overnight it seemed, that professional political commentators were falling over themselves to produce books which I didn't feel qualified to compete with.

I tried once or twice, but I never got beyond the first few pages. Meanwhile the situation in Iraq veered inexorably from bad to worse until finally the powers that be lost patience and a so-called coalition invaded, allegedly looking for weapons of mass destruction. There was saturation coverage of the campaign of course, but there seemed to be something wrong with the daily TV news bulletins. The women all looked old and care-worn and most of them appeared to have gone back in time, covering their hair and wearing very conservative clothes. Men I remembered as being dapper, with immaculately pressed suits and shirts, now looked scruffy and unshaven, with crumpled clothing and dusty, unpolished shoes. Most of all, the whole country looked like a barren dust bowl. Where were the carefully tended gardens, bright with flowers and green, green grass shaded by palms and citrus trees?

As the catastrophe unfolded, I got really cheesed off with so-called experts appearing on television to argue that Iraqis 'had been dying to have a civil war for ages', not to mention slippery American politicians who, as the country descended into chaos, showed an increasing tendency to criticise the Iraqi government for lapses such as 'not reinstating the electricity system quickly enough', conveniently forgetting that it worked fine before they crippled the country with sanctions, causing the bulk of the professional classes to leave, and then bombed its infrastructure out of existence for good measure. The final straw came one day when I was watching a news bulletin about the prison at Abu Ghraib. It showed a group of people, mostly women and old men, crowded around the barbed wire outside the prison as they tried to get news of missing relatives. As the size of the group increased, the young soldier who was on guard duty tried to move them on, indicating with his rifle that they should go. Some people did move away, but one tiny woman remained and even moved forward towards the guard. He raised his weapon slightly as he towered over her but she stood her ground. 'Don't you tell me to leave; who gave you the right to tell me to leave? This is my country and I'm staying here until I find out what you've done with my son', she shouted at the guard. He almost certainly didn't understand precisely what she was saying, but he got the message loud and clear. He backed off, rather sheepishly I felt, at the same time turning away from her so that it didn't seem like a retreat as he moved towards another group of relatives. I wondered what her story was; there were so many stories, every Iraqi family had either experienced tragedy or witnessed it first-hand. I think that was the moment when I knew that it was time to start writing.

Iraq and its people have been irrevocably altered by the events of the past 40 years. Self-interested governments at home and abroad have shown an incredible disregard for moral considerations or the well-being of the people, forcing them to weather many storms and hardships. Sadly, these have taken their toll on the spontaneity and charm which was one of their most striking features. Like a Middle Eastern 'Gone with the Wind', Iraq's story is of a society which has been changed forever. In telling my own personal story, I want to give the reader an idea of what life used to be like, in the days before Iraq became a player on the international stage and most Europeans didn't even know where Baghdad was.

# Chapter One

In the late fifties and sixties, young Iraqis flocked abroad to get a university education; the newly created republic was eager to plough back some it its oil wealth into development, so engineering was a popular choice of subject. Many of these students ended up in our local college, where they formed a lively group, drawn together by their shared language and experience and making the most of their unaccustomed freedom. Thousands of miles away from parental supervision and the strict rules of behaviour they expected of them, they slept, woke, ate and got together whenever they felt like it, regardless of the time of day or night. Zane had dabbled with a career at the port of Basra before coming to Britain, so he was already well into his twenties when we met. I suppose the laid back lifestyle he enjoyed with his friends must have seemed very glamorous and bohemian to an inexperienced young girl like me. They were different from anyone I had met before, direct to the point of rudeness – they never hesitated to say what they thought – and I quickly learnt that they always meant what they said, even when they were chatting up a girl, for they were enthusiastic chasers of women to a man.

Although I couldn't understand Arabic then, it was clear that any attractive girl who passed their way was a subject for discussion, and they always seemed to end up with the prettiest ones. I think this may have caused some resentment among the local lads – it certainly earned them a reputation, and I know for a fact that at least one institute of higher education routinely warned new female students of the dangers involved in going out with Iraqis. Naturally, this only added to the attraction for nubile young women, and there are a surprisingly high number of 50-year-old marriages still going strong as a result. It wasn't very long after we met that Zane declared that he thought we should get married; since I happened to agree with him, we did.

He always made it clear that he intended to return to Iraq as soon as he had qualified and I had absolutely no qualms about going with him. I wasn't put off in the least by a visit from one of Zane's friends with his English wife. They had just returned from Iraq and at the first opportunity she took me off to the kitchen where she told me in a hushed voice, 'Don't go there – they don't even have English biscuits'. Since I wasn't in the habit of eating biscuits in those days, her words fell on deaf ears. Similarly, my father had an old pub mate who had served in the Middle East in the war; we bumped into him one night whilst out for a drink with my parents. When he heard we intended to go to Baghdad at the earliest opportunity, he turned to me in horror: 'Why do you want to go there? They all live in mud huts, you know'. I had the feeling that my father was just slightly perturbed by this, because apart from visiting the USA as a young man he had never been outside Europe, but I brushed his worries aside with a laugh. Sometimes, when one of my grandchildren is behaving in an annoying and typically mindless teenage way, I remind myself how thoughtless I was at their age and try to keep my mouth shut.

Anyway, once Zane had passed his final exams and become a fully-fledged civil engineer, he was anxious to start his new career, and there was never any question that he wanted to start it in Baghdad. Unfortunately, he didn't have the money for his own plane fare, let alone mine. He had written to his family asking for money and so we moved in with my parents while we were waiting to hear from them. Every day he would make the long bus journey to the house where we had been living in the hope that he would find a reply to his letter. When it came, it wasn't quite what he expected. Instead of money for his journey, he received a request from his eldest brother to collect a Mercedes from Germany on his behalf and drive it to

Baghdad. This happened to be rather convenient as it meant that we could take our baby daughter, Summer, and travel to Iraq together. Not only would it cost very little more for the three of us than if he travelled alone but I also welcomed the idea as a wonderful opportunity to see a bit of the world.

He didn't tell me that he had never taken a driving test. He applied for a visitor's licence, which any overseas student could obtain from a police station in those days without taking a test. He also had no insurance and the only other documentation he obtained was the Green Card which was essential at border controls when driving abroad. He had learned the basics of driving off-road in the residential compound at Basra before he came to the UK, but had never actually driven on busy roads before. Armed with this experience, he went to Hamburg to collect his brother's car and drove it back to Britain.

Before we could leave, we had to make several trips to London to apply for the visas we would need along the way, as we would be travelling through Holland, Germany, Austria, Bulgaria, Yugoslavia, Turkey, Jordan, and Syria to reach Baghdad. It was quite unusual to see a Mercedes on British roads in those days, but as we drove up the A3 from Hampshire to London we occasionally passed one heading in the opposite direction. Invariably, its driver would toot his horn and flash his lights and Zane would toot a little fanfare in response, as if we were members of some elite club.

I found it all tremendously exciting. Some of the countries we would pass through were satellites of the Soviet Union, while others were said to be crawling with bandits, so we were given all sorts of advice about the potential problems we might meet along the way as we went from embassy to embassy. Most of it we disregarded but we never forgot the warnings not to leave any luggage on the roof of the car overnight, since it was unlikely to be still there in the morning, particularly when travelling through Turkey. During the journey, we faithfully unloaded the two large cases from the roof-rack every night, no matter how tired we were. This was mainly because I did not wish to arrive in Baghdad without my wardrobe, sparse as it was by today's standards. At last, after several trips to the capital, all our visas had been issued except one – my Iraqi visa. I can't remember why I left without it – I only know that I thought it best not to tell my parents that I didn't have one, since there was a strong possibility that I would be refused entry into the country if I didn't have a visa by the time I arrived at the Iraqi border.

Of course, there was also the slight problem of driving 4000 miles with a 6-month-old baby, particularly as a large part of the journey would take us through countries which were just coming to terms with the modern world. The 'Mothercare' chain had not yet been launched and few of the aids to motherhood which modern Mums take for granted, such as wet-wipes, were available. Paper nappies had just been invented but were not in general use. I managed to track some down – they were huge and looked rather like the incontinence pads which are used by the elderly today. I had never heard of Milton liquid – boiling was still the usual method of sterilizing babies' bottles – but I was as fanatical about hygiene as most new mothers and I was determined not to let my standards slip during the journey.

I put together a baby-care kit, trying to cover every eventuality as carefully as if I was a member of the SAS preparing for a special operation. First and foremost came a generous supply of the huge paper nappies, which extended from below Summer's knees to her armpits. I also bought several bottles of baby lotion and cotton wool which I planned to use as a substitute for water if I was faced with the problem of a dirty nappy while we were on the road. Like any soldier on the move she was going to need food, so I bought enough ready-prepared baby food to last for a month, backed up with several thermos flasks for hot water. Every evening after I rinsed her bottles in a hotel bathroom, Zane would instruct the hotel staff to immerse both bottles and teats into boiling water. Whenever I doubted his orders were going to be carried out, I would insist that Zane accompany some hapless waiter into the kitchen to ensure that it was done correctly. The following morning, we would fill up our flasks with boiling water so that we could make up the bottles as needed along the way. I was determined that Summer would not suffer any discomfort and she never missed her evening bath throughout the journey, though it usually took place in the hotel wash basin. She was a very contented, smiley baby who took to the road quite happily, propped up in her pram which we dismantled so that the top could be wedged onto the back seat. She usually dropped off to sleep after a few miles, but when she was not sleeping she sat on my lap – there were no seat belts or car seats, of course.

In those days, for a small fee, the AA would plan a route for its members anywhere in the world, complete with directions and maps. My brother had requested a route for us and it proved to be so clear and accurate that we only lost our way once.

Once our paperwork and other preparations were complete, we did the rounds saying goodbye to relatives and friends. Zane's eldest brother had arrived in Britain on business and was visiting his in-laws in Southampton. Just before we went to show him his new car, Zane told him for the first time that we were married. I was as surprised to find out that my in-laws didn't know that Zane had a wife and child as they probably were to learn that he did, particularly as he had visited Iraq the previous year to announce the news. I was the second foreign wife in the family – eventually there were to be five – so I couldn't understand why he had kept us a secret. I was yet to learn how strong the pull of tradition and the need to please the family was for Iraqis, no matter how 'westernised' they might appear. Zane's brother, Omar, was so much older that he might have been his father, and he certainly acted like one. Although he was meticulously polite and friendly to me, he never missed an opportunity to 'have a go' at Zane over past mistakes he may or may not have made. I found this a very inappropriate, not to say mean way of behaving, particularly as we had just met. My family would never behave like that.

The brother was tall, distinguished and well-dressed, obviously an experienced man of the world, but when we first met I thought him arrogant and opinionated. Later I came to understand that, because he was the first boy born to the family, he had been spoiled and deferred to all his life. No doubt his commanding personality was partly owing to this. But he was a good brother and did a lot to help his younger siblings, so long as they did exactly as they were told in return! He had travelled the world regularly from the age of 16, and at one stage was a student in Scotland. He still spoke English with a slight Scottish accent, and I found this both amusing and fascinating – this was before Britain went multi-cultural and regional accents could be heard emanating from virtually every ethnic minority.

At any rate, after he had satisfied himself that he had given us enough instructions about caring for his precious car, and what he considered to be sufficient money (a tiny amount) to get us to Baghdad, he was on his way. He refused an invitation to meet my family – he obviously had other fish to fry. My mother was very disappointed: she regularly asked me whether my in-laws had made any attempt to 'recognise me' as though I were the newly formed government of some African state. Direct-dialled international phone calls were still some years away and most international communication was by letter, so I always replied that they could not write to me directly as they could not write in English. In fact, Zane received very few letters from Iraq. I was later to learn that this was because he never bothered to answer when he did; the fact that he had written to me a couple of times when he visited Iraq the previous year made those letters quite unique: I wish I had kept them.

There was now nothing stopping us from leaving. We had the

necessary transport and enough money provided nothing went wrong on the way. My brother in law had solved the problem of my Iraqi visa by promising to 'put in a word with a friend' – an expression I was to become only too familiar with – and arrange for a visa to be waiting for me at the Iraqi consulate in Damascus. The weather was already cold, wet and foggy in Britain, even though we were still in September and all of a sudden I just wanted to go. So, just two weeks after my twentieth birthday, we set off at dawn, leaving my mother in tears and the rest of my family yawning and dazed. I had never gone further than Scotland before, but I was young and foolish and eager for adventure. Years later, my sister told me that my mother thought she would never see me again, but I left as thoughtlessly as if we were going on a picnic. My beautiful baby daughter was safely asleep in her baby carriage and I felt that our life with our own little family was just beginning. I wonder if I would have started down that road at all if I had known what lay ahead of us. At any rate, off we went, heading towards Dover and the Ferry which would take me outside of the UK for the first time in my life.

I can't remember the first part of the journey at all; I was probably sick a lot on the ferry from Dover to the Netherlands, because I only had to get on the ferry from Portsmouth to the Isle of Wight to start feeling queasy. In fact, I had suffered terribly from travel sickness all my life, apart from when I travelled by train. Every day trip to the seaside or to Bristol zoo, every school outing, was misery for me, so I think I must have started to remember the journey from about the time that I became acclimatised to the road, which was in Germany. On the other hand, it may be that our first experience of driving on an autobahn was so memorable that it forced me to pay more attention.

An autobahn would have been a novelty for most British drivers in those days, let alone an inexperienced one like Zane, bearing in mind that the M1 had only just been completed and most roads were still single carriageways. It was late at night and very dark; it seemed that winter had come early right across Europe that year. As we travelled through the darkness the car was transformed into a family sized, warm little cocoon – we might have been in a space capsule catapulting towards our unknown future on an eastern trajectory. Although outwardly rash and incautious, I did sometimes feel that we were heading towards a place as alien as outer space, yet for those few moments I was surrounded by warmth and affection and there was no dread in my anticipation. Zane reached over and took my hand, squeezing and stroking my fingers in a rare display of affection. He was rarely tactile or outwardly demonstrative, except with Summer, and this gesture seemed to me to be an indication of how our future life would be – more relaxed and affectionate, more of a couple at last. So when he put his hand on my knees, pulling them nearer so that they rested against his, I naturally snuggled closer so that I could lean my head on his shoulder. We might have travelled all night in this warm, companionable silence if a pair of headlights had not suddenly appeared, heading straight towards us, accompanied by the continuous blare of a horn. As Zane swerved to avoid the car we both became aware of two things at the same time. First, that there was suddenly a lot more traffic on the road, all of it heading towards us, and second, yes – we were travelling along the wrong side of the autobahn.

I don't know how Zane managed to keep swerving from lane to lane between the oncoming cars and still avoid a collision, but he did; it was like a police chase in a movie with us as the stars. As he drove he displayed a coolness under pressure and an ability to make split-second decisions that was quite unexpected. After what seemed forever, but was probably only a few moments, he spotted a gap in the traffic; like all good movie stars, he put his foot down hard and bumped the car over the central reservation (luckily it wasn't very high) setting us down on the right side of the road. Miraculously we were still heading in the right direction, so we continued on our way with hardly any reduction in speed.

I think this incident woke me from the torpor I had struggled with for months – nowadays I would probably have been diagnosed as suffering from post-natal depression – but there was hardly any recognition of the condition at the time. Whatever the reason, my awareness of the journey seems to have sharpened after this near mishap and I remember that I spent the rest of that night reflecting on our brief time together.

I don't think I've ever told anyone that the first day of our marriage was a great disappointment. We had rented a flat on the ground floor of a Victorian end-of-terrace and planned to spend our wedding night there. Zane did not want to miss any lectures after our wedding because he had spent three months in hospital following an accident on a moped and had failed his exams as a result. He was very anxious to make up for lost time and graduate as soon as possible, which seemed reasonable to me, so our honeymoon was going to be exactly two days. Naturally, I expected that we would wake up lazily on the first morning, perhaps have breakfast in bed and snuggle up for a while, so I was rather disappointed when Zane shook me awake to ask: 'It's nearly nine o'clock, aren't you going to get up?'

I stretched, yawned and asked what the hurry was in what I imagined to be a beguiling manner, but he became more insistent: 'Come on, don't be so lazy, you need to get dressed.' His tone did not suggest that he had some wonderful surprise planned for me once I jumped out of bed so I was beginning to get very annoyed. I sat up, wondering why on earth I needed to get dressed, just as somebody started tapping on our bedroom window. The window faced directly onto the pavement where a group of Zane's friends had gathered – they had come from all over the country to attend our wedding. He jumped out of bed and rushed to open the front door while I lay there listening to the loud conversation which was taking place in Arabic.

After a few minutes he came back to the bedroom and began throwing on his clothes before tearing out of the house with a 'see you later'. 'Later' turned out to be after seven in the evening, when the sound of a car stopping outside to the accompaniment of more loud Arabic alerted me to my new husband's return. By this time the romantic meal I had planned, shopped for and prepared was dried out and unappetising while I was wound up, hurt and ready for a row. I didn't get one; he hardly appeared to notice my stony silence as he ate the meal in the business-like way in which he always approaches food, then said he was going to bed. I felt as if I had been slapped in the face. I know I was foolish and full of romantic ideas in those days, but I think any woman would have expected a bit more of an effort on the first day of a marriage.

Yet that day set the pattern for those that followed. Zane rarely ate breakfast or even drank a cup of coffee in the morning. He would get up at the last possible moment, dress hastily and set off alone to college. If he had only got up half an hour earlier, we could have gone to town together, as the college was only three or four minutes' walk from where I worked, but he never would. After lectures he joined his friends at a coffee bar near the engineering department – they always made up the largest and noisiest group of students there. Coffee bars were a relatively new innovation into British cultural life; they had been welcomed enthusiastically by Britain's teenagers as somewhere they could get together and enjoy themselves away from the eyes of a disapproving older generation. Their popularity with young people was somehow seen as proof that they fostered bad behaviour, and many parents regarded them as dens of iniquity. Zane was one of those people; although he continued to hang out with his friends after we were married, he made it clear that he did not want me hanging around the coffee bar, as "only cheap girls went there", so I always went straight home from work, stopping to buy something for our evening meal on the way.

By the time he came home, I would have dinner ready and then he would start studying whilst I did the dishes. It was a very lonely and monotonous routine, in sharp contrast to the good natured teasing and lively banter of our family home, and I think that was probably when I really began to appreciate my family. Although I was trying hard to be a good little housewife, I certainly didn't suffer in silence, particularly as Zane would go out at weekends to see his friends rather than spend time with me. There were also other problems. We were always chronically short of money because Zane had fallen out with his family after failing his exams. They wanted him to return home so they stopped sending him money as an incentive, but he was determined to stay until he qualified. As a result, his only income came from a brother who lived and worked in Denmark and who sent him a little money every month. The tiny amount I earned just about covered the rent, so we had to manage on what his brother could afford to send him. We were always hiding from the milkman, or asking the landlady if it would be OK to pay late and these unpleasant duties were left entirely to me. I didn't expect to be rolling in money when we got married, but I hadn't expected this. Because we were always broke Zane couldn't afford to buy text books, so he borrowed books from his friends. Obviously he couldn't hold on to them for long, so he would ask me to read them and summarise them for him, which I did. So it came about that, although I was pathetic at maths and found physics mind-bogglingly boring, I took on the role of interpreting, summarising and sometimes even explaining the principles of civil engineering to Zane. It never occurred to me to tell him that he could do the summaries for himself or that he would probably learn much more if he did. I think I quite enjoyed doing it – I had always been good at précis during English lessons at school and found the engineering books a challenge.

Zane, like many Iraqis, was brilliant at maths and had an unerring ability to memorise facts, but as I got to know him better, I learned that he hated reading and rarely read anything but newspaper articles. He would get really wound up and irritable when he had to read something of importance or fill out a form and would invariably go over it several times to make sure that he had understood. In later years, faced with the fact that we have more than one dyslexic in the family, I began to wonder whether they inherited this condition from him and whether this was the real reason for his dislike of reading and writing letters.

But he was never averse to hard work, so once he had graduated he couldn't wait to return to Baghdad and start to earn some money. I would like to be able to say that this was because he was keen to start supporting us, but the truth was that he seemed more anxious to return to his family and carry out what he considered to be his duty to them. I think he also felt guilty, not only because he had married before he had a chance to do this but also because he was bringing another English girl into the family, despite his mother's specific request that he should not. So as we drove onwards towards his homeland, he probably had just as many anxieties as I did: we were both unsure of the welcome we would receive, but for different reasons. For the moment we were in limbo, neither in his world nor mine; with no outside influences we were free to be ourselves.

# Chapter Two

Yugoslavia under Tito was a dark, threatening place where everyone seemed surly and unhelpful. Even the bread was dark grey and so hard it nearly broke your teeth. It was there that we got lost; we ended up in the mountains on roads that were so narrow and scary that in the end we decided to stop and spend the night in the car. As soon as we found a stretch of road which was wide enough we pulled over, parking the car well away from the steep drop at the edge of the road. We made ourselves as comfortable as we could – we couldn't move the backrests much because of Summer's pram on the seat behind us – and gradually settled down to a restless doze in the cramped front of the car. I drifted in and out of sleep for the next few hours until something woke me very early the next morning. Feeling stiff and cold, I turned round to check on Summer, who was warmly wrapped and still sleeping, then I began wiping the inside of the windscreen which had steamed up during the night. Once I had cleared a patch of glass I could see that the morning was grey and misty, while the road was little more than a bumpy track.

After that I started to de-mist the window nearest me, rubbing it with the sleeve of my jacket in the hope of catching sight of the main road somewhere below. Instead, I found myself face-to-face with some ugly-looking characters who were leaning forward to stare at my shocked expression as the window cleared. They peered into the car, probably wondering what on earth we were doing there. I leaned over and tugged at Zane's jumper, urging him to wake up, and trying a tentative smile through the window in the meantime. Their expressions did not change but they seemed to move closer together, all leaning in towards the car at the same time. It dawned on me that the car was surrounded on three sides by these rough-looking men; they looked anything but friendly so I began shaking Zane much more violently, urging him to wake up.

I was just thankful that we had locked the car before settling down for the night, but as soon as Zane was alert enough to take in the situation he opened his door and jumped out of the car. He spoke to the men in English, then in his fragmentary German but they did not seem to understand but stood there wordlessly staring, or possibly glaring, back at us. They varied in age from late middle age to quite young teenagers, but they were all similar in that they were swarthy, unshaven, unsmiling and silent. I wished that he had stayed inside the car because the situation did not look at all promising, but instead Zane leaned over and poked his head inside, taking out our maps and spreading them on the bonnet. He tried to convey through mime that we were lost, inviting them to indicate our whereabouts on the map with smiles and self-deprecating shrugs. It did not work; they continued to stand in silence until one of them muttered something in guttural tones, upon which they turned as one man and moved back to a spot a few yards from us, where they stood huddled and silent, shivering in the early morning mist. As we were now freezing ourselves and it was obvious that no assistance would be forthcoming from them, we started the car and went further down the road until we found a spot where we could turn. Later I was to understand why they behaved as they did, but at the time the incident just hardened my impression of Yugoslavia as the most unpleasant of the countries we passed through.

We eventually got on the road to Sarajevo and by the time we reached the city the weather started to warm up at last. I remember it as being very beautiful, with wide avenues and squares which were crowded with people, many of whom looked like gypsies or beggars. Whilst we were having a look around I took off Summer's cardigan and tights so that she would get some sun on her plump little legs; they used to turn brown really quickly when she was a baby, which I thought was very cute. However, one of the women passing by obviously did not agree. She waved her arms and pointed at Summer's legs while she harangued me, then pointed towards her own layers of clothing. It was obvious that I did not speak her language so in the end she gave up and walked away in disgust snorting something about 'tourista' as she went. I think she was trying to tell me that the baby would catch a cold and, although I wasn't at all worried that she would, I felt that her advice was kindly meant and took it as a sign that we were entering more civilised territory, a place where foreigners had actually been sighted before.

Thank heavens they had, for a few miles outside of Sarajevo we had a puncture, which shouldn't have been too much of a problem except that Zane had no idea how to change a tyre. Neither of us realised this straight away because we had to unload most of our luggage to get at the spare. Once we had removed everything from the boot and set the spare tyre on the ground, Zane jacked up the car in a purposeful manner then tried to loosen the bolts. The wheel whizzed round at an impressive speed but the nuts holding the tyre in place didn't budge. He tried again but they stood firm; for a moment we stood looking at them, trying to come up with ways of loosening them. We tried to do it together, with my hands gripping the iron while Zane gripped mine, then I had a go alone. I tried to hold the wheel steady by straddling it and gripping it with my knees in order to give Zane more purchase on the tyre iron, but nothing worked – the wheel simply spun around when he tried to loosen the nuts. We didn't exactly scratch our heads but we might as well have done because neither of us had a clue as to what to do next. In the end, Zane decided to go for help and set off down the road in the direction of the nearest village, as shown on the map, leaving the car jacked up. I settled down by the roadside to wait with Summer on my knee, trying to keep her amused with her rattle and occasionally tickling her with a long blade of grass for variety. Zane was back in a surprisingly short space of time, about an hour or so I think, and although he was still alone he looked much happier. 'Don't worry, I know what to do now'. As he spoke he proceeded to lower the car to its normal position, then picked up a couple of large stones from the side of the road. Once he had placed them in front of the back wheels he seized the tyre iron again in a noticeably more confident manner. This time the nuts moved immediately and once he had loosened them all, he jacked up the car once again and changed the tyre in what must have been record time for a first attempt.

As soon as the car was safely back on the ground Zane began gathering up his tools with the pleased expression of a man who has done a good job, but sadly my confidence in his car maintenance proficiency had been severely dented by the incident. I had visions of the wheel falling off while we were driving along so I insisted that he tested the nuts several times before I would agree to re-pack the boot and get back into the car. Later, while we were on our way to the village he told me how lucky we had been to have our puncture in that spot because it turned out that there was a small mechanic's shop attached to the petrol station. Amazingly, the mechanic spoke quite reasonable English and, although he refused to accompany Zane back, saying that he could not leave his business, he managed to explain to him exactly how one went about changing a tyre. He even gave him a glass of tea before sending him off to do the job. Once we arrived, the young mechanic expertly repaired the puncture, charging a tiny amount of money for this service. Once he had been paid he shook hands with Zane, slapping him on the shoulder as he wished him goodbye. I had been totally ignored while all this was going on; I might as well have been invisible as I fussed around, waiting for the puncture to be repaired. I think this was probably my first encounter with the etiquette of the Eastern male, which makes it impolite to pay too much attention to another man's wife.

Once we crossed into Bulgaria the sun really started shining. The countryside was flat and green and everywhere there were colourfully dressed women working in the fields, smiling and calling out to each other as we passed. That was where I learnt to drive. We rarely passed another vehicle as we drove eastwards along those country roads, so it seemed a good opportunity for me to learn the rudiments of driving. Once I had mastered the skill of releasing the clutch whilst accelerating without causing the car to jerk up and down like a bucking bronco, Zane sat back in his seat and relaxed, leaving me to do the driving. And what a wonderful feeling that was, the heady excitement of being young in a strange country with the sun shining on me as I sat behind the wheel of a flash car, speeding towards the unknown. Nowadays I rarely tell people that the first car I ever drove was a Mercedes, unless they are very good friends: I know it sounds pretentious. In the past when I have mentioned it, I could almost hear people thinking 'stuck up bitch', but that was just how it was.

Although I visited the country again later under less happy circumstances, I'll always think of Bulgaria as a golden place because that is how I remember it from this first visit, even though things did not go at all smoothly for us there. The problem was that the car started playing up. It began by stalling on the rare occasions when we needed to slow down; Zane naturally thought it was my driving and took over the wheel, but it happened a couple of times after that, much to my secret relief because I already felt something of an expert, before it stopped completely and refused to start again. He lifted the bonnet to look at what lay beneath, opening screw caps and peering at the engine, but I knew enough by now to realise that he would not be able to solve the problem, whatever it was. In the end, he decided that what was needed was a good push, so he showed me how to engage the gear at the last moment once he had got the car moving and we tried to bump start it. The engine fired a couple of times but I was hopeless at keeping it going: by the time I had slowed down to allow Zane to catch up and jump into the passenger seat it stalled again.

It was obvious that I was going to have to push or we would be stuck there forever, so we swapped places and I gave it a go. I don't know whether you have ever pushed a heavy vehicle like a 1960s built Mercedes saloon single handed, but it is very hard work, particularly when it is loaded with most of one family's possessions. Eventually I managed to get moving and Zane bump started the engine, but that wasn't the end of the problem. At the next town we were unable to find a mechanic who could help us, or even one who could understand us, but the car seemed to be running smoothly by then so we hoped that it was just a temporary blip. Since we had wasted quite a lot of driving time by then and it was already late in the afternoon, we decided to go no further that day but to look for a hotel and have an early night. The food was so much better than in Yugoslavia and the hotel staff so pleasant and eager to please that we were glad that we had stopped early for once. We had been really pushing ourselves to cover as much ground as possible up till then, partly out of worries that Summer would be affected in some way by the journey and partly because we wanted to arrive before our money ran out, so we allowed ourselves to relax and linger in the dining room that evening. If I remember correctly I think we even sampled the delicious Bulgarian wine.

At any rate, over the next few days I was glad that we gave ourselves this respite because we didn't get much peace after that. Next morning the car engine purred into life at the first attempt, much to our relief. Summer was beginning to weary of the road and once she became bored, no amount of jiggling on my knee or shaking of toys could stop her becoming fretful. During the first part of the journey, the motion of the car usually sent her off to sleep quite quickly, but there is after all a limit to how much a six-month-old baby can sleep, even one who loved to sleep as much as she did. So when the car's engine died again as soon as we were in the middle of nowhere, our hearts sank and our tempers frayed very quickly. Zane only let me try the bump start solution once before ordering me out of the car and taking over the wheel, yelling at me to push. I heaved and strained but it was hopeless; the car seemed even heavier than yesterday – it hardly moved and the engine was even more reluctant to turn over. In the end, he pulled the bonnet lever and jumped out of the car, lighting a cigarette at the same time – always the first thing he turned to in times of trouble. I hovered around, staring into the engine in the vain hope that some divine inspiration would show me what was wrong, and tried to pacify Summer. The weather was getting hotter, and she was getting uncharacteristically crosser now that there was no car fan blowing cool air in her direction.

Once again, Zane went through his routine of unscrewing caps and peering at the liquids inside, then poking leads and fittings to see if they were loose, but by now I knew that he didn't have a clue what the problem was, let alone how to fix it. I was afraid that we would be stranded there for days, so I took out the map to try to work out how far he would have to walk this time. It wasn't easy, as Summer, red-faced and screaming by then, was waving her arms around and snatching at the map, creasing it so that it became even more difficult to read. I re-folded it and used it to fan her for a few moments before getting down onto my knees so that I could spread it in front of me out of her reach. I tried to hold her still with one arm whilst leaning forward and trying to work out our location at the same time. I've never been the world's best map reader and this wasn't the best time to try and improve that skill; I was so intent on the map that it didn't immediately dawn on me that I could hear something which sounded very much like the hum of an approaching motor vehicle – surely it was wishful thinking.

Thankfully, it wasn't and as I struggled to my feet with the baby under one arm and the map flapping in the other I saw that not only was there a car slowing down as it approached us but that it was another Mercedes. Zane had begun waving his arms at the driver as soon as he was near enough to see but it wasn't really necessary because as soon as he could see us clearly he began to slow down, pulling in neatly behind us at the side of the road.

The new arrival was a black Lebanese businessman who was on his way back to Beirut, accompanied by his Finnish wife and little boy. He had a brisk, jovial manner and was rather short and stocky, so she was much taller than him; I remember thinking that she had a rather old fashioned hair-style for such a young woman. Both of them spoke excellent English and her Arabic also sounded pretty good to me. Their little boy was about three or four and he was very handsome. He spoke only Arabic and was fascinated by the fact that Summer had no teeth. He was so amused by her toothless state and mentioned it so often that I managed to arrive in Baghdad already knowing how to say 'she hasn't got any teeth' in Arabic. I'm ashamed to say that I can't remember any of their names, but the husband seemed to have a good working knowledge of mechanics and diagnosed the problem as a loose fan belt. I think he managed to tighten it a bit; at any rate he got the car going and we set off in convoy, travelling east and hoping to find a mechanic who would be able to provide a permanent replacement somewhere along the way. Later, after we arrived in Baghdad, Omar was to comment that Zane should have had enough sense to take a spare fan belt with us, but this advice would have been more helpful if it had been given before the event rather than afterwards, particularly as he was a mechanical engineer and Zane was not. At any rate, we couldn't find anyone to fix the problem before it started to get dark. Because the battery was not charging properly, our car lights wouldn't work, so our new Lebanese friend switched on his headlights and told Zane to keep very close behind and follow him until we found somewhere to stay for the night. With our new friends lighting our way, we drove on until we eventually found a hotel where we all checked in. We spent a pleasant evening in the bar and whilst the men chatted about I don't know what the wife gave me valuable insights into the kind of life I could expect as a foreigner married to an Arab and living in an Arab country.

We all set off together the next morning, but it turned out to be a frustrating day as our car stopped two or three times more before we found someone who could fix it. Despite this the couple were unfailingly cheerful, kind and helpful to us even though we must have held them up considerably. At one point, their car speeded up the road away from us and we thought that they had finally had enough and abandoned us. Zane shrugged and said 'you can't blame them', but I felt like a child whose parents have disappeared. My heart sank and only lifted again when we saw them patiently waiting for us a few miles further on. Perhaps they had intended to leave us to sort out our own problems and then thought better of it. The important thing was that they did not – they stayed with us until they had made sure that our engine problem had been properly repaired so that we could go on our way with confidence. They were truly good Samaritans, and we were quite sad when it was time for us to go our separate ways. In the years when the troubles in Lebanon were at their worst we would sometimes remember them, wondering whether they had stayed in the Lebanon and hoping that they had all survived unscathed.

Once we had entered Turkey I experienced the Middle Eastern heat for the first time, even though it was now October. There was no escaping it; the air itself was hot. It enveloped you like a warm body wrap, inducing loose limbs and slow, energy-conserving movement. I remember the bustling chaos which was Istanbul, with its stalls piled high with goods and every type of fruit and vegetable; at the time I was appalled at the smells which emanated from the dried out gullies of the drainage system, the dust and the rubbish rotting on the ground around the refuse bins, but of course I was seeing everything through my ignorant, small town girl eyes.

I remember that we asked the way to some famous historical site from a young passer-by who beckoned to us to follow him, indicating that he would show us the quickest way. We followed him through dingy side streets which grew narrower and narrower until it became obvious that we were not going in the right direction. Zane thought that the boy got us lost deliberately because the Turks hated Arabs ever since the days of the Turkish Empire, and especially since they fought on opposite sides during the First World War. I tended towards the opinion that he simply wanted to take us to a lonely spot where he could relieve us of all our possessions, especially those loaded on the roof of the car. Whatever the truth, we didn't hang about but drove away from him and within a few minutes were heading back towards the city centre. We would have loved to spend a few days sight-seeing in Istanbul but the baby was feeling the unaccustomed heat more every day and I was worried that she would pick up some germ or other. So we kept on going until the highway ended at the strait which links the Sea of Marmara with the Mediterranean, where we had to take the ferry. As we queued for the boat which sets off from Europe on one side and deposits you in Asia on the other I must admit that I felt a fluttering in my stomach as it finally dawned on me that there was no going back now.

Once we had boarded the rather dilapidated ferry and parked the car we went on deck to admire the fantastic view of Istanbul from the water. Most of our fellow passengers had the same idea, so we were soon joined by a throng of people who were nearly as fascinating to watch as the view. There were smartly-dressed businessmen with shiny briefcases, trendy students and Turkish house wives mingling with people dressed in probably the biggest variety of national costumes I'll ever see in one place. I've no idea where they all came from – it was like the Arabian Nights, Hollywood style.

The morning after we left Istanbul I awoke to the heaviest period I had ever experienced. Pads alone were not enough to keep it under control, so I stopped at a pharmacy in the suburbs to buy a box of tampons. There were none visible on the shelves, so I asked the male pharmacist who had come forward to serve me whether he had any in stock. I had to repeat my request several times, but the pharmacist obviously had no idea what I was looking for. Nevertheless he was eager to help, and kept asking me to explain what my symptoms or illness was. 'Do you have a headache? A back-ache?' He wrinkled his forehead in distress as he scanned my obviously embarrassed face, searching for clues to my condition. Suddenly it hit him: 'Ah, do you have vomiting and diarrhoea by any chance?' By this time I had quite an interested audience, all waiting to find out what ailed this foreigner who had unexpectedly appeared on their doorstep. The pharmacist's female assistant had been called from a room at the back and they were all discussing the matter in Turkish. I had no idea whether Turkish women used tampons at that time, and didn't think it advisable to try to mime how they would be used in front of a mixed audience. I tried again, 'tampons – for periods'. I didn't mind mentioning the dreaded word in front of strangers – I knew that most of my audience would probably not understand me anyway. In the end I gave up, told the kind-hearted pharmacist not to worry and left. I assumed the unusually heavy bleeding was the result of pushing the car, but because of my failure to find tampons, I ruined several pairs of trousers in the next few days.

The countryside in Turkey was amazing; I had never seen such beautiful beaches. Driving along the narrow, winding roads which spiralled upwards by means of a succession of hair-pin bends we would suddenly catch a glimpse of the sparkling blue water below us. Every so often it was fringed with a wide strip of the whitest sand I had ever seen, but the beaches were always deserted because mass tourism had not yet arrived in Turkey and the locals did not appear to be interested in sunbathing. This seemed such a waste to me. I would have loved to have stopped at one of the beaches for a swim, but Zane told me that it was out of the question in rural areas, adding that we would probably be mobbed or attacked if we put on swim suits.

Breath-taking as these beaches were, the mountains were even more spectacular. Just as I thought the road could not possibly rise any higher, relieved that we were at last descending, it would begin to climb again as another peak came into view. The roads themselves were narrow and poorly surfaced, sometimes little more than dirt tracks, often with no barrier to prevent vehicles from plunging down the side of the mountain. I've never been very good with heights and this was definitely the most hair-raising part of the journey for me. After a while I could bear it no longer, but sat frozen with my hands gripping the sides of the seat, staring straight in front of me, too scared to look either up or down at the twists and turns in the road. I'm sure Zane was almost as scared as me but he would never admit it and anyway he needed to devote all his attention to just staying safely on the road.

There was a lighter moment though before we reached what felt like safer ground; it happened just as we were ascending what seemed like one of the highest points on the road. We could see a lorry ahead of us. It was not moving and appeared to be parked just before the next bend, which was obviously a sharp one as we could not see the road ahead after that. As we got closer we realised that there was something lying on the road beside the lorry which gradually took on the shape of a man. It was clear that he was not moving, and we began to fear that he was ill or worse, we certainly did not expect him to be asleep. But asleep he was, with 2 large boulders propped in front of each of the back wheels and his head propped up on his arm, motionless and relaxed as a baby. The reason soon became clear – he wasn't going anywhere for the simple reason that the front wheels of his lorry had over-shot the road so that the front of the vehicle jutted out over the edge of the mountain-side. It was swaying slightly in the breeze but it was counter-balanced by the heavy load it was carrying, and kept in place with the help of the bricks which prevented it from sliding.

Since we had no equipment which would be of any use and we were certain that he would not leave his lorry, nor would we be able to understand anything he said, we simply left him there, sleeping peacefully while he waited for someone to miss him and send out a search party. I knew that his laid back (I can't actually find the right word to describe it) response to the accident was born out of familiarity with the hazards of those mountain roads, but his total acceptance of his situation somehow communicated itself to me and I was able to relax a little for the rest of that mountain drive.

I was to get used to the easterner's ability to lie down and sleep when faced with a situation over which they have no control. Perhaps it is fatalism, but I've often noticed that, when faced with an impossible situation they pragmatically accept the fact that they can't do anything about it, and just take the opportunity for a nap. My first experience of this was while Summer was being born. At the time I was deeply hurt and would have been lost for words had I not already been rendered speechless by labour pains. For years afterwards, I missed no opportunity to tell the story, which goes like this: the flat we lived in at the time was on the ground floor of an end of terrace Victorian house. At the front was a large bedroom, next to which was a small sitting room sparsely furnished with a couple of uncomfortable armchairs. Behind this, was a tiny kitchen and bathroom, but the toilet was outside in the yard, which was not ideal for a pregnant woman, especially as we had a lot of snow that winter. Anyway, the reason the sitting room was so small was that a section was partitioned – off to form a small second bedroom. We never used this room as it had no window and showed very obvious signs of damp. We didn't even use it for storage because it was already pretty full of cardboard boxes and other items left behind by the grown-up children of our landlady, including a sagging old single bed. The only means of heating the flat was one electric fire with two meagre bars which added some grudging heat to the sitting room. There was also an open fireplace in the main bedroom.

I was having a home birth, not out of choice but because I was told that there would not be a bed for me at the local hospital. I often wondered how they knew that, as it seemed to me that it must be pretty hard to know exactly how many maternity beds would be needed at any one time and, as it happened, Summer was born three weeks late anyway. Those three weeks seemed almost as long to me as the entire pregnancy, and I had several false alarms before I went into labour. Not too many homes had a telephone installed in those days and cheap rented flats almost never did, so once I was certain that this was actually the real thing, I sent Zane off to call the mid-wife from a phone box.

It seemed as though it took hours for the mid-wife to arrive, although it was probably more like one. She turned up at last with a trainee in tow and they set to work lighting a fire in the bedroom grate. They also used this fire later to destroy all the gruesome evidence of the birth, reserving the placenta for examination at the local hospital. Only when they were satisfied that the fire was well established and beginning to warm up the bedroom did they make a start on all the embarrassing and uncomfortable examinations and procedures which were considered as essential preparations for labour in those days.

Once they were over, the drill was essentially that you lay in bed on your back and made as little fuss as possible. The mid-wife did give me an injection which she said would dull the pain, but it made no noticeable difference. I was also offered gas and air by means of a little portable machine which they had brought with them, but the first time I tried it I decided immediately that I preferred the pain to the disgusting taste of the gas and the light-headed feeling it induced. As a matter of fact, I was never able to use a gas and air machine and so went on to have four children through perfectly natural labour, in the sense that I did not use any pain killers at all.

The early stages of labour seemed to go on forever and I think I even dozed occasionally between pains. The mid-wives settled down with the newspapers that I had been instructed to have ready: they were to be used to wrap the debris ready for disposal after the baby was born and my mother had been collecting them for weeks. As they skimmed the papers they chatted to each other from time to time as though I wasn't there. Apparently I was quite organised as it was not unknown for them to go to a mother-to-be only to find that there were none of the essentials to labour, such as soap, in the house. I couldn't help feeling that they were surprised to find me so well prepared. Because I was so young and already living in grotty rented accommodation, I think they had also mentally categorised me as feckless. There was just something in their tone, nothing tangible, but they definitely gave me the impression that they approached what was the most momentous experience of my life with a resigned expectation that I would somehow be lacking. At one point the trainee mentioned a delivery she had just attended which only lasted a very short time, but as the mid-wife pointed out, unlike me she was an 'experienced pusher'.

The senior mid-wife was typical of her time, unmarried and childless and therefore not very disposed to be sympathetic. I did learn something interesting from her though, something I had never heard of before: she told me about female circumcision. I listened in horror as she described the practice, which she had become aware of through delivering babies to Sudanese women. She described how agonisingly difficult labour is for a circumcised woman and spoke of the dreadful tears it causes, until I almost began to believe that she was human after all. She rather spoiled the effect, though, as she went on to talk about delivering a baby to a woman who was left with a horrifying, ragged opening in place of a normal vagina after her baby was born: 'It was horrific – I didn't know what to do about it, so I just left it as it was'.

Anyway, there I was lying on my back and the pains were getting really bad now. The mid-wives were also getting restive and one of them wondered out loud whether 'anyone in this house' had ever heard of 'any newspaper other than the *News of the World* and the *Daily Mirror*' – my father's favourites. Feeling this to be a slur on my position as the wife of a prospective civil engineer, I managed to grit my teeth between pains long enough to inform her that we rarely bought any newspapers and so had been forced to collect them from friends and relatives.

The pains were really bad now and I began to realise just why people made so much fuss about child-birth. Senior mid-wife might have been a touch insensitive but she could spot the different stages of labour without even looking under the sheet. 'Right, it's time to phone for the doctor', she said, 'where's your husband?' I hadn't given Zane a thought for quite some time as my mind had been completely focused on the waves of pain which came and went. Frankly, I often feel that current ideas about husbands, partners or other children being present when babies are born are very misguided. I remember that all you want to do is get that baby out and you don't want any distractions from the task. Nevertheless, her words were very welcome because I knew they meant that my baby would be born soon.

At that time NHS rules stated that a GP would only be paid for the delivery of a baby to one of his patients if he was present at the birth so, provided there were no complications, it was common practice for him to arrive just before that was likely to happen. I told the mid-wife that Zane was probably in the sitting room, so off she went to take a look. She was familiar with the layout of the flat as she had visited to inspect it a few weeks before, but she came back without my husband. She hadn't found him in the sitting room, kitchen or bathroom. She had even gone out to the yard to check that he wasn't being sick with nerves in the toilet. 'I think he's gone out', she looked at me as she said this as if it was my fault. The trainee volunteered to go and have a look and came back within minutes with a horrified expression on her face to announce that she had found him asleep in the 'store room' – the unusable room off the sitting room.

Zane duly woke himself up and came into the bedroom to receive instructions as to what he was to say to the doctor. He was careful not to look in my direction as he turned to leave the room, whether from fear of what he might see or embarrassment at being caught napping at such a moment I'm not sure. As I lay there trying to co-operate with the midwife's instructions not to push, more out of consideration for the doctor than myself, I felt, she entertained us by repeatedly telling us how 'never in all her years of experience had she known a husband to go to sleep while his wife was in labour'. She was also to repeat this regularly during her post natal visits and it was her parting shot to Zane as she took her leave of us for the last time.

Anyway, we travelled through Turkey without further incident and crossed over into Syria around noon. A Syrian friend of Zane had told me that I would love Damascus because it was very beautiful. It certainly did have shady, tree-lined avenues with imposing colonial style buildings along both sides, often ending in unexpected squares cooled by fountains. What interested me, though, was the way the women of Damascus were dressed. Many of them wore black veils of some light-weight silky material which covered the whole of their heads and reached down to waist level, or just below. They were rather like a circular table cloth and they certainly safeguarded a women's modesty from the waist up. Below that was another story, though, for the unveiled lower part of the body often revealed surprisingly modern clothes, so that shapely legs and trim ankles could be seen stepping out on stiletto heels, and many a curvaceous bottom in a tight pencil slim skirt was on view to the appreciative male audience. This was my first glimpse of the contradictions which permeated Arab society at that time: those women managed to conform to a local code of propriety whilst still having the satisfaction of drawing admiration from the opposite sex.

We found the Iraqi embassy without difficulty and my passport was duly stamped with the necessary visa which would allow me entry into Iraq. The staff were very jolly and friendly, cooing and clucking over Summer, who accepted all the admiration with condescending smiles. Whilst we were standing there telling them about our journey, two young Englishmen arrived in shorts and hiking boots to enquire after their visas, which they had apparently been awaiting for some time. They told us that they had been on a walking holiday and were now looking forward to the highlight, which was to be a tour of Iraq. Whilst we were chatting one of the consular staff muttered something in Arabic which made the others grin and it was obvious to me that they were enjoying a joke at the visitors' expense. After we left, Zane explained to me that the Iraqis found it hilarious that the men went out in shorts – they considered it both silly and impolite for men to reveal their legs in public. Apparently there was also no chance of the men being given entry visas, but the staff were not authorised to tell them that. The policy then was to keep people hanging on until they simply tired of waiting and gave up. Experience has led me to believe that this policy has now been adopted by utility companies in the west, proving that we can still learn something from the Arab world.

We didn't hang around once I had received my visa; in addition to the ever-rising temperature our money was rapidly running out, so we set off on the road to Jordan without further delay, arriving at the border in the heat of the afternoon. It was there that we encountered men from the Arab Legion, Bedouins formerly led by the famous Glubb Pasha, and I felt afraid for the first time since we started on our journey. I don't know what it was about them that inspired fear – it's true they were grim and unsmiling beneath their chequered head-dresses, but it was more than that. They rode up as we were showing our papers to the border guards, seemingly appearing out of nowhere, the four of them taking over from the uniformed guards without a word. I think it was that which made them so scary; the guards handing over to them without a word. They sat effortlessly astride their horses, each one with rifles and ammunition criss-crossed on their chests, knives and swords hanging from their belts. The abundance of their weapons did nothing to reassure me as they led Zane away to a wooden hut, leaving me and the baby waiting in the car.

I felt numb – what would I do if Zane didn't return? My brain had ceased to function and I sat there frozen, trying to formulate a plan of action. I couldn't imagine that help was likely to be found anywhere near-by, although I thought the guards must have a phone and might let me use it if the worst came to the worst. But who would I phone? I didn't even have my in-laws' telephone number. My anxiety communicated itself to Summer and she sat uncharacteristically still and quiet for what seemed an age until Zane reappeared alone, the grin on his face signalling his relief. Don't worry, they only asked me a few questions – everything's fine.' He fended off my questions as he slid behind the wheel and started the engine. A surge of relief flooded through me, loosening my limbs and I realised that I was squeezing Summer far too tightly. No wonder she was quiet.

I don't know whether that was the usual routine when entering Jordan at that time, but the men had a collective persona which was very intimidating; I still remember the effect they had on me. I wasn't to see so much weaponry carried by one man until I encountered Kurdish tribesmen in the north of Iraq several years later.

A few miles into Jordan, we stopped so that I could prepare a bottle for Summer. The terrain was stark and sandy, not exactly desert as I had expected it to be, but different to anything that I had ever seen before. I was sitting in the shade of a prickly tree giving Summer her bottle while Zane re-arranged our possessions when two men arrived on camels. They dismounted and came over to chat to Zane. From their clothing I guessed that they were poor, but within minutes they were cutting open a deliciously cool water melon and urging us to eat. This was the famous Arab generosity which I had heard so much about. They seemed to be very interested in Summer, and whatever they were saying was obviously amusing as Zane was laughing as he took out his cigarettes and offered them to the men. They lit up and stood there smoking and watching Summer as I held out a slice of the melon for her. She obviously enjoyed it and sucked the juice enthusiastically until there was only the rind left. The men mirrored her action, sucking on the cigarettes until they burned right down to the cork tips then grinding the butts into the sand before re-mounting and riding off into the desert. 'What was that all about? What were they saying about the baby?' 'They've never seen a baby fed with a bottle before; they couldn't understand what was going on. After I told them, one of them asked: "Hasn't she got any breasts, then?"'

I did not immediately see the funny side – I was too conscious of my short-comings in the boob department – and there was more to come. As we gathered up our possessions ready to leave, a group of women approached, obviously alerted by the men to the presence of an 'Ingleesia' in their neighbourhood. They wore traditional Abiyas on their heads but they were pushed back over their shoulders to reveal brightly coloured dresses underneath. Long ear-rings dangled from their ears and their wrists and ankles were loaded with heavy bracelets. Some of them also wore nose rings, with lines tattooed on their foreheads joining their eyebrows together. Those country girls obviously made only a token observance of the local conventions of modesty. They all carried water pots on their heads and had probably been going to a well for water since they were small. As a result, they walked with an erect, graceful glide seldom seen in the west outside of a cat-walk. They turned their heads to stare at me as they passed, tittering and whispering behind their hands. I found this very irritating. 'What the hell are they grinning at? I think *they're* funny; I should be laughing at them, not the other way round'. I was very childish in those days and Zane often spoke to me as though I were a child. 'Don't be silly, they're just curious. Come on, get your things together; let's go'. He was not about to undermine his fellow countrywomen to me even when they were strangers, a trait I was to become familiar with in the years to come.

Jordan still looked like I imagined it would look in those days, with little flat-roofed houses which might have come straight off a Christmas card. In fact, for years I found it the only country in the region which matched my expectations of the Middle East and I loved it for that. As we drove on we passed a sign-post to Jerusalem. Zane offered to turn off and take me there, saying that it would only add a few hours to our journey. The temptation was very strong. I would have loved to have kept going to Jerusalem, but Summer really needed to get back to some sort of normality by that time, so we agreed that we would come back for a visit as soon as we could. We were not to know that within a few years the Israelis would roll their tanks into Jerusalem and occupy the city, making us persona non grata as residents of an Arab country.

# Chapter Three

I don't remember the moment that I first entered Iraq, but somewhere along the dusty highway between Jordan and Iraq a huge pipe-line appeared. It ran along the side of the road, dominating the landscape in both directions and was impossible to ignore, carrying the oil that was to have such a crucial impact on our lives and the lives of the 12 million other Iraqis who then inhabited Iraq. I do remember the date, though. I arrived in Baghdad on a scorching hot afternoon on Tuesday 10 October 1962. But first we stopped off at a guest house just outside the city where we ordered Pepsi Colas which we drank very cold whilst we waited for our kebab to arrive. It was the first time I had tasted Iraqi kebab, which is made with a mixture of minced lamb and beef, mildly spiced and served with Nejef pickles. We ate it with crispy flat bread, hot from the oven and that meal was delicious. The Welsh say that their lamb is the best in the world but I would have to disagree, it is the second best. Or it used to be when I lived in Iraq and lamb was so tender and tasty that it literally melted in your mouth. Flocks of sheep were escorted by their little shepherds from pasture to pasture, their huge fat tails evidence of the richness of the meat which they were to provide. Sadly, the years of wars and bombing have created an environmental catastrophe and I can't imagine that the countryside provides much nourishment for any sheep still surviving there.

Anyway, we took our time over lunch, which was served by smiling waiters who probably didn't have many opportunities to wait on foreigners then. Zane usually wolfed down his food and hated lingering at the dining table, so I think he was putting off the moment of truth which would come when we arrived at the family home and found out exactly what our reception was going to be. When the meal was eventually over, I took Summer to the toilets so that we could both freshen up. I changed her into her prettiest dress, discarding the huge paper nappy and redressing her in the more usual terry nappy, covered by frilly pink plastic-lined pants – the latest in fashion accessories for baby girls. The days of travelling along those sunny roads had turned her chubby little arms and legs a delicious golden brown and her firm cheeks were flushed a dusky pink. She looked adorable – my mother-in-law used to say 'like a Persian apple'.

As we set off on the last leg of our journey, the weather was hotter than anything we had experienced so far – opening the car windows just made things worse as the air was so hot. It became impossible to calm Summer at all. She was red-faced and screaming, stiffening her body in protest and waving her arms about so much that in the end I took off all her clothes, apart from her nappy. I would have preferred to arrive at my in-laws with all of us looking at our best, but the combination of the heat and Zane's increasing tension made this impossible. We were all hot and bothered, my carefully teased bee-hive had collapsed to one side and after a while I was past caring – I just wanted to get out of that car.

Unlike Jordan, Baghdad wasn't what I expected at all. It was undeniably foreign with its shady palm trees and flat roofed houses but it was also unmistakably a modern city as well. Of course, I had not yet seen the old part of Baghdad, with its covered souqs and ancient streets with narrow lanes running between the shuttered houses. The roads we drove through were wide and bordered by large houses. They all seemed to have shiny tiled patios at the front and wide gardens. Many of the streets had central reservations planted with shrubs and trees and there were modern-looking shops along the way. As we made a turn at an intersection between one of these, a little girl in a school uniform ran across the road causing Zane to brake sharply. He stuck his head out of the window and cursed her, making a spitting sound at the same time. I was deeply shocked: in the time that I had known him he had been unfailingly sweet and charming to every child we had ever met – now he seemed to be changing into another person before my eyes.

The intersection took us onto Liberty Square and I knew we were nearly there, which probably explained why Zane lost it with the little girl. Sure enough, after leaving the square and turning into a long road which led to the river Tigris, we pulled up in front of a house which I recognised from photos as belonging to Zane's parents. I opened the car door but Summer was still screaming, so I sat with one leg already out of the car and took a minute to try and calm her. As I did, a young girl of around 12 years old with long dark hair in a pony- tail and a pretty summer dress dashed out of the house and grabbed Summer. Without a word to either of us, she turned, ponytail swinging, and carried the baby back towards the house, where another girl of similar age but quite a bit taller was waiting for her. They went inside together, leaving me feeling a bit light-headed and nauseous and Zane chuckling nervously at the way his sister had ignored us both. The walk across the patio into the welcome coolness of the porch felt like slow motion and we probably looked like a couple of idiots. 'Kiss my mother and my sisters' he instructed out of the corner of his mouth as several members of his family came towards us, all smiling hugely. Everything was a bit of a blur for a while after that. The baby was being passed around from one person to another and someone was demanding clothes for her as it was so cool inside the house.

I felt dreadful by now so I stood up and asked for the toilet just as Zane's elder brother arrived. He was a medical student so when I said 'I feel sick' he started to ask me about my symptoms. 'I feel sick' I repeated, pushing past him and opening one door after another until I found one which mercifully led to an eastern 'hole in the floor' toilet. I promptly covered it in vomit. I had food poisoning, probably from the kebab which I was later to learn should never be eaten from an unfamiliar restaurant.

That night Zane's mother took Summer to sleep with her in her bedroom downstairs. It was kindly meant, but I had heard stories about Eastern parents taking control of their grandchildren, preventing the mother from rearing her own children, so I was not happy about this. I protested weakly, but felt too ill to do much about it – I just wanted to sleep. Fortunately, Summer would not settle in her grandparents' room. She cried so much that before long they were more than happy to return her to us, so it was fortunate that I had given in without too much fuss.

I was pretty much recovered by the next afternoon and woke to find that Zane's elder sister had carried off all the dirty clothes which we had accumulated on our journey for washing. I was mortified, remembering the pile of blood-stained clothing which I had stuffed into a bag. I was not even sure whether I would be able to wear the trousers again, because they were so badly soiled. A couple of days later she was helping me to unpack the rest of our things. We were beginning to understand each other by then through a combination of her scant English phrases – mostly baby related – and the few Arabic words I had learned from Zane and his friends. As she pulled out Summer's things, admiring the pretty, smocked dresses and lacy tights, she came across the last of the giant paper nappies. She pulled one out, her eyes widening as she opened it up, her expression becoming increasingly horrified. As her gaze shifted from the nappy to me and back again it took me a few seconds to understand the reason for her horror – of course, she thought they were sanitary towels. Since she must have seen the stains on my clothes when she took them away to be washed, I suppose it was a logical conclusion.

Fortunately, a few months later, when my Arabic had progressed to the point where I could communicate effectively, the subject of menstruation came up. I tried to reassure her that English women did not generally need giant-sized sanitary protection, but she had seen the evidence and it took me some time to persuade her that we were pretty much like other women in that respect.

There were still three unmarried sisters and one brother, the medical student, living at home with my parents-in-law when we arrived. Their house was spacious with a large lounge and dining room, a family sitting room and four large bedrooms. The two upstairs bedrooms were separated by a large tiled landing which had ornately worked metal banisters. There was also a western style bathroom, complete with bidet, tiles and a shower fitted over the bath. We had almost exclusive use of this because most of the family preferred to use the oriental bathroom downstairs. There was also a large interior lobby leading to the two downstairs bedrooms, the staircase and the rear patio and gardens. The three girls shared one of these bedrooms because they enjoyed each other's company and liked to chat in bed at night and at siesta time. It was furnished with both a single and a huge double bed as well as the usual bedroom furniture. The other bedroom belonged to Zane's parents. It also contained two beds – one was the intricate cast iron bed which had been part of my mother in law's original marriage furniture: she still slept in it, alone now. It was in its original pale green and decorated with painted roses. It was pretty much in mint condition and would have fetched a good price at a British auction. The other bed was a leather upholstered chaise longue type affair which my father in law now slept on.

The medical student, Emir, had the other upstairs bedroom. It doubled as a study with a large desk and bookcases to one side. He even had his own artificial skeleton for anatomy. Apparently, when he first went to university he had brought home genuine human bones to study, but his father had been outraged and refused to allow them in the house, saying it was sacrilege that a human being had not been given a proper burial. Dear Emir, he was an outspoken idealist with a heart of gold and a temper to match his deep auburn hair; it had already got him into trouble with the authorities.

My mother in law had prepared the largest bedroom for us, with new bedding which included a gold satin quilt and a cot for Summer. Someone in England had given her a candlewick cot throw and once this had been unpacked and placed on her cot she resumed her former sleeping patterns. From that day on we had no more problems getting her to sleep, so long as the throw was in place, and her grandparents were quite happy to leave it that way.

In the next few weeks it seemed that I was constantly on display. All the neighbours, relatives and friends wanted to see the new addition to the family, meaning me – babies were always welcome but a foreign daughter-in-law was much more interesting. As soon as lunch was over I would have to go and smarten up so that I would look my best for that day's visitors, who would invariably be women and children. My in-laws did not practise segregation of the sexes, either at home or when visiting, but it would not have been deemed proper for men to come and look me over (apart from close relatives). Visitors who spoke English made the most of the opportunity to practise this skill, sometimes asking surprisingly personal questions. They were fascinated by every aspect of my life in Britain and wanted to know every detail about my family; the fact that I came from a large family appeared to go down well and it didn't take me long to realise that one's family background was of extreme importance in that society. For the most part though, the visitors who didn't speak English would sit and stare at me whilst drinking tea with cakes and biscuits or white cheese. Much of the time I suspected that they were talking about me and in a surprisingly short time I began to understand what they were saying. I was right, they were.

They would talk about my appearance, my hair, my clothes.

Sometimes they would be complimentary, sometimes not, but they were never deterred by the fact that I was in the room. They would ask my sisters in law what they thought of me and ask how I behaved at home. Ditto. They usually brought presents with them, sets of china and similar gifts which were intended as belated wedding presents. My mother in law would pack them away in her large sideboard, saying simply that 'they owe us a present'. When she in turn went on a visit which required a present she would select one from the sideboard and off she would go.

Things gradually settled down and I became accustomed to the routine of Iraqi family life. The street where we lived contained a varied collection of families – Moslem and Christian families, Turkoman and Kurds all lived next door to each other quite happily. The guy next door to us was married to a Turkish girl who had once hidden Emir under her bed when the police were looking for him. Unfortunately, they left soon after we arrived so I didn't really get to know her. On the other side lived a young couple of Iranian origin who spoke Persian at home. They both came from rather wealthy families and were always very smart and fashionably dressed. I remember Zane's youngest sister, Nadia in particular was very friendly with them. No-one asked who was Shia or Sunni, it was quite irrelevant, and my mother in law often reminisced sadly about the Jewish neighbours who had fled after the creation of Israel. Apparently, she always went to switch on their lights on Sabbath evenings and they did little favours in return. At the end of the street was a large corner plot where two large houses were occupied by the co-wives of an elderly man. Unusually, they kept themselves to themselves and were rarely seen at local gatherings, but they were the only family I knew where the husband had two wives, apart from Zane's eldest sister.

Most of the neighbours worked in commerce, importing goods and acting as wholesalers or operating retail outlets of one kind or another. On the whole, their adult children were emerging as professionals, so I suppose it could be described as a lower middle class area, except that Iraqis never discussed people in terms of class. At that time, people were either 'good folk', meaning honest and honourable with no taint of scandal attached to the family, or they weren't. True, they might be good folk who were also rich, good folk who were highly educated or good folk who were very pious, but the emphasis was always on coming from a family who were good folk. In addition to this, a man born and bred in Karrada was likely to be described as 'a good lad' by others from the same neighbourhood simply because there could be no hidden skeletons in his cupboard. I suspect that this was true of people who had always lived in other areas too.

I soon got to know the immediate neighbours and those which my in-laws were most friendly with. The tall girl who had been with my sister in law when we first arrived was Zabiya, eldest daughter of the neighbours opposite. They were a shia family from Nejef – of course I didn't know that then; the father was a businessman in the souq and they had six children ranging from a teenage son to a little boy, Zaid, who was the same age as Summer. They were to become inseparable friends and as they grew older Zaid would climb up onto their flat roof and yell Summer-aaaah to let her know he wanted to play. Their children were always in our house, they never seemed to want to go home and my in-laws rarely tired of them. They would casually join in meals and family conversation and Sophia would spend hours in the bedroom with my youngest sister in law, Nadia, poring over the latest fashion magazines and trying out new hairstyles on their beautiful long hair. Her father had just bought a brand new British made car although he didn't drive. His young son, Sami, acted as his chauffeur, driving him to and from work and using the car himself in between. He was immensely useful to my in-laws, driving Nadia to school with Sophia and going off to the shops for fresh bread or whatever else was needed in a hurry.

Layla was the eldest sister living at home. She was small, like all the women in the family, with rather masculine features and very thick curly hair which she wore in a plait. Although she was quite stout her body was strong and firm and on the rare occasions when she bothered to change her shapeless house dress for something more formal she revealed a surprisingly shapely figure. She was responsible for most of the housework, a full time job in that climate. She would rope in the other girls, including Sophia, to help her out when they were at home. Sajida, the third sister was a PE teacher so she was often out of the house, but Nadia went to a local school which meant that she only had about four hours tuition a day, so she was most often called on to help. If she didn't jump to it, an argument would inevitably follow; Layla would start to shout, her voice gradually rising until she was screaming like a fishwife with Nadia responding in kind. She usually cited homework or up and upcoming exams as an excuse, calling on whoever was present to back her up. The arguments often ended with Layla chasing her around the house with the palm tree branch which she used to sweep the dust off the patios. Nadia would run around the house, dodging behind one adult after another, hair swinging wildly as she begged for help until finally she gave in and did the chore. If she was present, Sophia would often come in for equal punishment, sometimes in front of her mother, a plump little woman called Oom Sami who my mother in law treated as an additional daughter. She never took offence when Layla was on the rampage, but would stand, her little round body shaking with laughter as she offered her moral support for the disciplining of her children: 'that's it, that'll teach her, let her make herself useful,' she would egg Layla on before adding: 'They're killing me; they don't listen to me either'

One afternoon quite soon after we arrived in Baghdad I was ironing on the shady rear patio, enjoying the autumn sunshine. Zaid's older brother was with me and he chattered away to me all the time I was ironing. It must have been quite soon after we arrived in Baghdad, because I couldn't understand a word he said but I found his chatter an excellent accompaniment to my ironing. Somehow we established a rapport and became firm friends even before we could talk to each other. Years later, when I heard that he had been taken a prisoner of war by the Iranian army and Zaid had been killed in battle I felt as though I had been punched in the solar plexus; even though I hadn't seen them for years, I still remembered them as smiling, fresh-faced children and the grief was acute.

Another family whom I came to know well was that of Oom Fatin, who lived two streets away, about five minutes' walk. She also had several children and an unmarried sister who lived with her and helped out around the house. This sister was a special friend of Layla, probably because they shared the same ambiguous position in their respective households. They were both well past the age when they were likely to be married, were both indispensable at home and carried out the lion's share of the household tasks, yet they had no real means of supporting themselves financially and so were dependent on the goodwill of others for all their needs. As far as I know they never discussed this: they acted willingly as surrogate mothers to the children in the family and were influential within the home. Indeed, the neighbour was so involved in the personal lives of her sister's family that people used to joke that the husband shared the services of the sisters to such an extent that he probably slept with them both as well.

Layla was not above complaining about her lot when there was no-one else at home, though. She was always moaning that she had devoted her life to bringing up her younger brothers, passing up her chances for a family of her own. She constantly bewailed what she saw as their ingratitude as brother after brother left to pursue a career and marriage rather than spend the rest of their days pampering her. She often told me that I had snapped Zane up too early, before he had a chance to repay her and her mother for their care of him. There is no doubt that she played an important part in bringing up this large and turbulent family, but from what I gathered her only offer of marriage had been from an elderly widower, so it seemed likely that she had wisely decided that she was better off where she was. Although she was largely dependent on the family to provide for her, she did make a little money by taking in sewing for the neighbours, just house dresses, pyjamas for their children and that sort of thing usually. When she learned that I could hem and sew buttonholes – a legacy of my post war grammar school education which considered it necessary to encourage traditional pursuits for girls in case the education didn't work out – she used to pass most of the garments she made to me for finishing off. I didn't mind doing it as it gave me something to do and her sewing tended to be called for only on a seasonal basis anyway. Because of the extremes of the Iraqi climate, people would have completely separate wardrobes for summer and winter, so she would be particularly busy when her clients were changing from summer to winter clothes or vice versa.

The other neighbours I should mention lived near to Oom Sami. Their household consisted of a married couple, their four daughters and the man's mother and sisters, three of them if I remember correctly. God knows how the head of the household felt surrounded by all those women. He was the proprietor of a busy pharmacy and seemed to spend little time with his family; whether this was because of the pressures of business or because it was more peaceful than at home who can say? All the females in the family from the mother in law down were very good humoured and always smiling. They came to see me a couple of days after I arrived and chatted to me in their admirable English – the sisters were all university students at the time. Before we left the UK Zane had lectured me on how Iraqi girls led very sheltered lives and conformed to strict rules of propriety; he told me I must follow suit otherwise people would think I was fast. I was never to refer to any subject which might be considered to have sexual connotations and I was not to laugh too much in public.

Because of these lectures I was sometimes rather tongue-tied when meeting new people, afraid that my answer would offend someone. Consequently, when I first met this family I was astonished when one of the sisters suddenly asked me what protection I used. I looked to Sajida for confirmation of what she meant. Yes, she was asking me what method of contraception I favoured, a very popular subject for female chat I was to learn, but more usually among married women. This family were eventually blessed with a son who was notably lacking in the good humour of the rest of the family. In fact, he was a spoiled brat who was always throwing stones and picking fights with neighbouring kids. Years later, when my youngest daughter was a student in London, they met again and he made a formal request for her hand in marriage. She promptly and emphatically refused and Layla has never really forgiven her for that.

My preconceived notions on acceptable behaviour for young women were frequently turned upside down during those first weeks. Although I didn't really smoke then I had puffed at a cigarette in an effort to look sophisticated from time to time. Zane had told me that I wouldn't be able to smoke in Baghdad as it was considered improper for women to smoke, so I was rather surprised to see his mother passing her cigarettes around to all her friends when they came to visit. When I asked him about this he replied impatiently 'she's an old lady'. Similarly, I had been told that love matches were still frowned upon and marriages mostly arranged, yet within days of our arrival Emir turned up at the house with his girlfriend, a law student who was obviously well known to the family. She sat chatting and drinking tea and biscuits for several hours before driving off in her little car. When I asked about this the answer was 'that's different, her family are rich and she's political'.

It was becoming clear to me that this was a much more complex society than I had expected. Cultural rules and roles were blurring, much as they were in Europe, but in their own unique Arabic way. This was evident in the television programmes we watched, many of them from Egypt. A popular soap opera of the time, roughly translated as 'daughter of the meadows' followed the story of a beautiful young village girl and the strategies she used to evade the dishonourable intentions of the local sheik. A few years ago he would have had little difficulty in having his wicked way with her and everyone used to look forward to the weekly episodes, mentally cheering her on as she tried to negotiate a way out of the abuses of her traditional background.

Although there were plenty of Iraqi programmes, most people seemed to prefer the Egyptian ones which were far more sophisticated and sparkled with wit and humour. There were also frequent musical programmes where the singer would be supported by dancers, or some romantic situation would be played out in the background. I suppose these were the precursers of the pop video; some of the performers were regarded as classical singers and idolised just as much as Maria Callas or Mario Lanzo in the west. My Arabic was coming along nicely by now, but I really struggled with the Egyptian vernacular, which is very different to Iraqi Arabic. Because of this, it took me a while to catch on to the fact that one song, performed enthusiastically by a chorus of girls and boys who danced around a wooden-looking army officer was in fact a satirical version of the Iraqi president, General Abdul Karim Kassim. The chorus of the song went 'welcome, welcome dear potty general' and it was played nearly every night on Baghdad television. There had been a war of words going on between him and the Egyptian president, Nasser, for the past few years so bearing in mind that all broadcasting, newspapers and books were heavily censored I could only presume that General Kassim had a sense of humour.

Egyptian films of the period often contained the germ of a women's rights movement. The most popular actress of the time was Faten Hamama, wife of Omar Sharif; she would be seen defying her family and refusing to be married off to some old man when all she wanted was a university education. There were films showing how Egyptian men cast off faithful elderly wives, exchanging them for younger models and leaving their first wives destitute and living in abject poverty. Sometimes phrases from a film were taken up by the public and became embedded in everyday speech. One film I particularly remembered was about a poor girl struggling to put herself through university. She meets and falls in love with a young man from a wealthy family but inevitably her secret – that she works part time as a maid – is exposed. When he finds out he extends his arm like an outraged Victorian father, pointing an accusing finger at her as he repulses her in disgust and the end of the film shows her sobbing hysterically as she rushes out of the house crying, 'yes, I'm a maid, a maid'. The reason I remember it is because the children incorporated this scene into their games so that the youngest child present would invariably be ordered out of the house with horrified shouts of 'you're a maid? A MAID?' Unfortunately, within a few years the growth of the Moslem Brotherhood in Egypt put the brakes on these moves towards female emancipation. They also paved the way for other extremist groups which have sprung up in recent years.

Although I enjoyed the Arabic programmes, I always made a point of watching the news in English which was broadcast daily in the early evening. The news features mainly consisted of reports of what the president had done that day and which foreign dignitaries he had received, but the fact that it was in English made it feel like a link with home. The newsreader was a pretty girl with shiny dark hair and big blue eyes. Zane and I always used to laugh when a particular word came up because of the way she pronounced it. The word featured regularly in news bulletins and we used to wait for it to come then say it with her, chuckling as we dragged out every vowel. Years later, when I worked with her at the British Council, I realised that she had probably been using the Irish pronunciation: oddly, I can never remember the word but the name of the newsreader was Margaret Zane.

From the first day of our arrival, my in-laws encouraged me to feel like one of the family; they asked me to call them by the Iraqi equivalent of 'Mum' and 'Dad' and since I always did so I shall call them this for the remainder of this book. For their part, it was easier for them to call me 'Dot' which actually sounded quite attractive with their long drawn out Arabic vowels. Dad never managed to get it right, however, and the nearest he got can best be described as 'Dodge' which he called me until the day he died.

I suppose this would be a good place to explain the customary way of addressing other people. Once women had a child it was considered polite to address them as Oom, meaning mother of, followed by the name of that child. If it was a girl, it would be replaced by the name of the first son in due course. When speaking to strangers, it was polite to call them 'Aunty' or 'Uncle', or if they were younger 'brother' or 'sister'. Of course there were more formal methods of address which were used on more formal occasions – this was just the traditional way which came naturally to people in everyday life.

Within a very few weeks, Zane had fallen out with his eldest brother, Omar, who had suggested that we go and live with him and his wife when we first arrived. Their house was certainly much larger than my in-laws, but I'm sure he also felt that I would feel more comfortable living with his English wife, who apparently was looking forward to having another English girl in the family. Unfortunately, Zane turned the offer down without consulting me, stating rather pompously that he intended to 'look after his family' as if setting up a separate household was somehow a betrayal. This caused a great deal of bad feeling between the brothers which soon erupted into a series of violent rows. These frequently took place in the garden, where we often sat to drink afternoon tea in the milder months, making it easier for the neighbours to watch from their roofs, which they did with great enjoyment.

I used to be horrified by these family rows, which would erupt as suddenly and unexpectedly as an earthquake. It wasn't that I had never bickered with my brothers and sisters, of course I had, but I had never witnessed such passion and anger in a family argument. It would start with verbal daggers inserted into the conversation which would be countered with outright accusations. Suddenly there would be shouting and waving of arms and everyone present would surge backwards and forwards as the sisters tried to prevent their brothers from coming to blows, shrieking hysterically all the while. To be fair to them, they never did actually hit each other, although cups of tea might be smashed or furniture overturned. It was more like a ritual skirmish, with all the participants determined to play their part as fiercely as possible. I couldn't stand them, so as soon as it was obvious that a row was on its way I used to pick Summer up and take her up to our room. Once there I would occupy her with stories and nursery rhymes until peace descended on the household and I felt it was safe to venture back downstairs.

Before the revolution which ousted the Iraqi royal family and turned the country into a republic, Omar had worked as an engineer in the port of Basra. At the time it was British run and he was one of only two Iraqis to be promoted to senior positions. There was widespread dissatisfaction in the country with the government's close relationship with Britain, which was generally believed to benefit from Iraqi oil far more than the majority of Iraqis did. Some unions were strongly influenced by communist thinking, unlike Omar who believed in democracy and the rule of law. Like the rest of the family, he was a perfectionist and expected the same high standards from everyone he worked with. If you added this to the fact that his wife was English it wasn't surprising that he wasn't very popular with workers at the port, so after the revolution many of them called for him to be fired. It was a time of great social tension, so the port authorities played safe and asked Omar for his resignation. He was forced to take his family to Baghdad and move in with my in-laws until he secured a new job as manager of a privately owned pipe factory.

The move proved to be a blessing in disguise. The factory was located on the outskirts of the city on the banks of the Tigris and came with a large house, a chauffeur-driven car and a manservant who did most of the housework and cooking. My sister in law, Alice, needed all the help she could get with four little boys to look after and another one on the way. Alice was easy to get along with, calm and matter of fact and I enjoyed visiting her. They would send the car for me early in the morning; no matter how early it was I would be ready, waiting with Summer all dressed up in my arms, so that I could go to spend the day with her. Sometimes she invited other women whose husbands worked at the factory to join us for coffee and cake. They were mostly English or American and these visits were a welcome respite from the constant strain of trying to understand what was being said at home. At first I did not notice that, although her husband was a frequent visitor to his parents' house, Alice never came with him.

The first time we went there we were greeted by three excited and very striking little boys, all of them with a thick thatch of bright blond hair and blue eyes. They were followed by their mother, heavily pregnant and carrying the fourth little boy who was a month or two older than Summer. Almost the first words spoken by the eldest, very proudly, were 'I'm getting my willy cut next week'. 'He means they're being circumcised next week,' Alice laughed as she came forward to shake my hand. I was becoming accustomed to straight talking by this time, although I was rather surprised that they were looking forward to it. Alice was not averse to straight talking herself, and was soon telling me how easily she became pregnant – apparently trousers coming down would do the trick. She also told me of her concern that she was almost 30 and still having babies. I felt so sorry for her: although she didn't look it, 30 seemed very old to me then.

She was much more circumspect when speaking to her husband though. If she said anything to annoy him he would fly off the handle and yell at her, much like he did with his brothers, and he was very easy to annoy. He also constantly talked down to her even though she had a degree in English and was obviously very bright. He wouldn't tolerate any disrespect towards her from anyone else though as this would have constituted disrespect to himself. Sadly, as relations between the brothers deteriorated our visits decreased correspondingly until eventually they ceased entirely, so Alice and I never became as close as we might have done.

It was hard to believe that it was nearly Christmas, mainly because life was so different now and also because the autumn weather in Baghdad was so beautiful it was impossible to feel that winter was nearly here. Summer was thriving, terribly spoilt by everyone and already beginning to talk. Her candlewick bedspread had been christened 'lulloowa' because of all the lullabies which were sung to her when it was time for bed. So long as she had this to tickle her cheek while she sucked her thumb she was happy. Zane, however, was not happy. He was still trying to find a permanent job; he had been given three months' work experience by a friend of his eldest brother but had not yet been paid for this, and he blamed his brother for not making it clear that he expected payment at the end. Obviously, the addition of three more mouths to feed was a burden on his parents, who were not wealthy people. Whenever I needed something, my mother in law would say: 'Why don't you ask Alice, she's got plenty', underlining the tensions which were obvious beneath the surface of what Zane had always assured me was a very happy family.

I was constantly up-tight because of the interference in the way I did things, well-intentioned though it undoubtedly was.

It started almost as soon as we arrived; my mother in law was horrified to see that Summer slept without a pillow and lost no time in going out and buying one. I quietly put it away but often when I went to check on her after she had been put to sleep I'd find that someone had replaced the pillow, even though I had explained to everyone that she might suffocate. 'Why do you use one then?' was the invariable reply.

If she was slow to go to sleep I was told it was because I refused to wrap her in swaddling, a large triangular piece of cloth. This would be wrapped tightly around a baby's shoulders so that the arms and legs were more or less immobile, then tied tightly at the ankles so that the baby resembled a little triangular stick. As it grew older it was used less, but always at bedtime because it was thought to induce sleep. Apparently there was some scientific basis for this as the immobility lowered the blood pressure and made babies drowsy, but there was no way I would subject Summer to this treatment. I was always being told that she would grow up with crooked legs and I would reply by displaying my own undeniably straight legs as proof that swaddling was not necessary.

In addition to this, getting her off to sleep became increasingly difficult as she became older because my in-laws could not accept that children should have regular bed times. Iraqi children never seemed to be put to bed, they merely fell asleep on somebody's lap, or on a settee when they were older, and were then transferred to bed by an adult. Of course, Summer soon tuned into the fact that if she cried a bit when she was put down one or other of her relatives would be only too happy to rescue her. When this happened, it was invariably to the accompaniment of 'see, I told you she's not tired.'

Her food was also a source of conflict. I tried to prepare foods which I considered suitable for a baby of her age but I was constantly pre-empted by my mother in law or Layla. Just before the carefully balanced and suitably mashed meal was ready, I would find one of them feeding her whatever had been cooked for the family, calling out 'your daughter's starving' as they crammed whole rice loaded with clarified butter, chickpeas and lumps of meat down her throat. Annoyingly, she relished any food she was given and would swallow it enthusiastically, but it often passed straight through her digestive system to reappear whole in her nappy a short time later. I was convinced that her digestion would be irrevocably damaged, but how could I explain this to her doting relatives?

All these things may seem trivial but they were a source of constant irritation to me, probably because I felt that I was losing control over how my daughter was brought up. Combined with this, the constant strain of understanding what everyone was saying, particularly when I thought they might be talking about me was taking its toll, and matters were made worse because I knew that my in-laws were often talking about Zane. Inevitably, the simmering feud between the brothers spilled over onto other members of the family, forcing them to take sides as they tried to defend one brother against the other.

Against this background, my spirits were immensely lifted when Emir came home from university one afternoon to ask me 'do you realise it's Christmas Eve tonight?' Of course I had, but being so far away from my family or anyone else who would be celebrating, it hadn't seemed important. 'Well, I'm taking you and Zane out – you can't stay in on Christmas Eve; I'll show you a bit of Baghdad.' I was so excited as this would be a proper outing, not a visit to friends of the family or relatives and I rushed off to wash my hair and get ready. We didn't do anything special; we went to the centre of Baghdad where Emir pointed out famous landmarks, then we walked along the Corniche, named after the famous poet Abu Nowas, boozing companion of the equally famous Haroun Al Rashid, founder of Baghdad. The corniche was lined with restaurants serving fish caught fresh from the nearby Tigris. The weather had suddenly turned very cold, making the night crisp and clear with stars so large and bright they were like stars on a theatre set. In the dark, with my dark hair, I barely drew a second glance, especially as foreigners were not such a novelty here in the centre of town. It was such a welcome interlude, I felt my true personality returning as we wandered along the river bank, the constraints of always trying to do and say the right thing temporarily left behind. Emir took us for a meal and drinks, probably spending most of his student allowance, then gave what was left to an old beggar who stopped us by the taxi rank.

That simple evening reminded me what life had been like before I became part of the extended family. Of course, I was grateful that we were able to live with my in-laws until such time as we had a home of our own, but I was equally grateful that I always had that to look forward to whenever I was feeling down. Very soon after the new year Zane was given a permanent job, working for a private contractor on the new international airport which was under construction. He was responsible for the runways and as the airport was just on the outskirts of the city, he would be able to come home every night.

# Chapter Four

The cost of living in Baghdad was very low compared with Europe at that time. The average monthly salary of a professional working for the government was about 50 dinars, the equivalent of £50.00 and most Iraqi families seemed to live quite comfortably on this. Food, especially meat, fresh fruit and vegetables was cheap and abundant and even the poorest families appeared to be well fed. When we drove out into the countryside, the children playing in the little mud-built hamlets were rosy and healthy-looking with perpetual smiles on their faces. Added to this, the Iraqi government was committed to full employment, so many people who worked for the state actually had very little work to do. Consequently, life was good for the majority of Iraqi citizens. You could buy a kilo of locally raised, freshly killed organic lamb or beef for less than 20p, any cut you wanted and you could also tell the butcher how much fat you wanted removed before weighing – most people liked a lot of fat on their lamb. Because of this, Baghdadis tended to be overweight and men were often pot-bellied by the time they reached middle age, so there was an unpublicised but clearly discernible campaign being waged via TV plays and other programmes to raise awareness of the need to reduce the consumption of animal fats. One afternoon Mum returned from a shopping trip in a foul mood. She was slinging things around the kitchen and muttering curses under her breath as she cut up the meat and put her shopping away. 'Whatever's the matter with your mother?' Zane tried hard to keep a straight face, but could not contain his laughter, which infuriated her even more. 'They've put the price of meat up to a quarter of a dinar a kilo – she's cursing the government'.

From the beginning, Zane had decided not to apply to any of the government departments for work, even though he would have been employed straight away. He wanted to make enough money so that we could live comfortably while still doing something to repay his family for the support they had given him during his years abroad. He was luckier than most returning students because his broken leg meant that he wouldn't have to do the normal two years of military service, so I was overjoyed to hear that not only had he got his first job, but his starting salary would be 250 dinars, an immense amount for a newly-qualified engineer. Government employees only worked from 8.30am until 2.00pm, but Zane would have to work right through the day, hence the higher pay.

At the end of the first month he came home proudly with his first salary and handed it all to his mother. She unfolded the notes and counted them, then handed two of them to me, 20 dinars if I remember rightly. I didn't mind too much, we had after all been living in their home for weeks now, but I made it clear to Zane that I expected him to give his money to me from then on, after making a contribution to the household expenses, of course. Perhaps this was a mistake because the question of money, or the fact that we had more than anyone else in the house, definitely contributed to the bad feeling that always simmered beneath the surface in his relations with his family. I don't think it was even the money itself that rankled as far as his mother was concerned, but the fact that she wasn't being accorded the respect due to her as the manager of the family finances. I should probably have waited a little to see whether she intended to insist that we keep more for ourselves in the coming months, but hindsight is a wonderful thing.

Anyway, I enjoyed spending my part of the money on presents for my family. We had not been able to send any Christmas presents, of course, so I took this opportunity to make up for it. I went with my sisters in law to the souq in central Baghdad for the first time, an experience in itself. In order to reach it you had to pass through Freedom Square, which was as big as several football pitches. At the point where the road entered the square a huge white stone fresco stretched from one side to the other, giving traffic approaching from the Karrada side a fantastic view of the black marble figures depicted on it. They represented rebels fighting to overthrow the government during the revolution in a style reminiscent of the ancient Assyrian friezes on display in the Baghdad museum. It was an impressive work and I loved it, even though it was rumoured that the artist had been placed under house arrest by Abdel Karim Kassem until he finished it.

Liberation Square was also the bustling terminus for all kinds of road transport: professional drivers constantly tooted their horns as they engaged in macho attempts to get ahead of the competition, so the din was considerable. The state-run buses which covered the whole city were very cheap and fares were fixed, but they were so overcrowded that passengers hung out of the door, sometimes clinging on desperately by their arms whilst their feet flew out behind them as the bus speeded away. There were also inter-city buses, mostly privately owned and rather battered, whose fare was at the discretion of the driver. It was a common sight to see groups of passengers standing on the pavement surrounded by piles of luggage whilst they haggled over the fare. There were also mini buses which people could board either in groups or individually; these seemed to be used mainly by young men and it always amused me to see them helping the driver by collectively sticking their arms out of the open windows to indicate the direction they intended to take. Apart from the normal taxis whizzing their way through the mayhem, there were also 'individuals'. These were taxis which would take several separate people at the same time, so long as they were going in the same direction, dropping them off at their individual destinations on the way. The driver would charge the passengers according to their number, effectively dividing the fare between them. 'Individuals' were popular with students as they were cheaper and thought to be safer, particularly by lone female students for whom travelling alone in a taxi was believed to be fraught with danger.

In the midst of all this chaos, one would occasionally see someone leading a donkey or even a camel, loaded up with produce from the countryside, wending its way through the traffic. There were also horse-drawn carriages which seemed to be popular with the people who still resided in the oldest part of Baghdad on the far side of the square. As you passed the entrances to these narrow alleys you caught glimpses of ancient, tall houses with ornately decorated balconies and latticed shutters intended to shield the women of the house from view. They were redolent of the mystery of the Orient and dated right back to the Ottoman Empire, some of them perhaps earlier.

After that came the commercial centre of Rashid Street, a rather grand road which boasted imposing marble-fronted banks and other buildings on either side, reminding pedestrians that this was, after all, an oil rich country. Traffic always speeded up once it reached Rashid Street and from then on it slowed down for no-one, so you really took your life in your hands when crossing the road. If you took one of the side streets off Rashid Street you arrived at River Street, which ran parallel with the Tigris and marked the beginning of the central Souq. At this point it was like any other shopping centre, with shops on either side selling mainly toiletries and cosmetics, clothing and shoes, some locally made and others imported. As you progressed further along the street, barrows selling cooked local delicacies, nuts, dried fruits and chilled drinks began to appear until finally you reached the souq proper. Once you entered you had to weave through throngs of people all trying to make their way down the narrow lanes which separated the shops. Some of these were properly glazed and modern-looking whilst others were hardly more than market stalls. They were grouped nto sections, each of them specialising in a specific product; there was the Fabric Souq, the Shoe Souq, the Copper Souq, street after street filled with merchants offering their goods until eventually I believe one reached Spare Part Street, although my shopping never took me that far. Large sections of the souq were covered over with some dark, heavy material which gave it an authentic Arabian Nights feel. I must confess that I always found it a little scary when I stepped inside. The vendors did not try to entice you in or persuade you to buy as they do in some countries; on the whole they maintained a rather dignified reserve, as if it was of no consequence whether they sold anything or not. However, if you did show an interest in any item they all expected you to haggle. Mum was best at this and the shop-keepers seemed to enter into negotiations with her with great enjoyment; you knew that the price was agreed when they suddenly said 'OK, wear it in good health' as they slapped the item on the counter and began wrapping it.

On this occasion I bought such trinkets and little ornaments as I thought would be easy to post. My only other purchase was a badly needed new white shirt for Zane, which after some haggling was secured for the princely sum of 1.5 dinars. It was instantly clear to me that my in-laws disapproved of my spending money on my family. How complicated everything was; they behaved as though my family were in no need of the trinkets or as if I was favouring them over my in-laws, when all I wanted to do was let them know I was thinking of them. When we had finished in the souq we went to one or two modern stores, including Orosdi-back, the Harrods of Baghdad, which sold imported goods at fixed prices. It was much less fun than haggling with the shop-keepers for locally made merchandise and also more expensive. Layla told me disapprovingly that Alice shopped at these stores; oh dear, another brownie point lost by her. Quite soon after we met, Omar told me a story about an Iraqi boy who had married an English girl then told his family that she was the daughter of King George, obviously in an effort to impress them. I had noticed that whenever Layla or Mum were in a bad mood about something they often made veiled comments about 'the daughter of King George' and it didn't take a genius to work out that they were referring to Alice, whose maiden name was in fact George. I'm sure that Omar would have been furious if he had known, and for my part I couldn't help wondering whether my father's name, which happened to be Henry, was ever going to be used in that way.

The weather continued to be very cold and the house, which was built for coolness rather than warmth, was freezing. Homes were heated with primus stoves fuelled by kerosene, which was also used to heat water for bathing. These stoves stood about two feet high, were easy to knock over and therefore potentially dangerous, so they were usually only lit when there were people in the room. My mother in law had a metal insert which was topped by a large circular tray. It could be placed into the funnel of one of these stoves so that the tea pot could be kept warm and allowed to brew on top, making the stove even more of a hazard when in use. The stoves had to be taken outside to be re-filled at least once a day and the wick also had to be trimmed daily. Cooking was mainly done on kerosene stoves which caused a thick black coating to form on the outside of saucepans. Once the pans had been emptied they had to be scrubbed with wire wool dipped in washing powder until they were bright and shining again.

The kitchen was separated from the dining room and the main part of the house by a small porch, presumably for coolness in summer. Even though my in laws were fanatical about hygiene and never left a dish unwashed in the sink, cockroaches still lurked in the kitchen drains, waiting for night-time when the lights went off. I found them repulsive and whenever I needed to go into the kitchen at night to prepare Summer's bottle, I would stand trembling in the porch, trying to muster the courage to open the kitchen door and switch on the light. Once I was sufficiently psyched up, I would throw open the door and rush into the kitchen, hoping against hope that the kettle would be still warm and not take too long to boil. The reddish brown insects, some of them huge, would scuttle back towards the drain, antennae waving. Whilst I was preparing the bottle my whole body would be tense and I would be scanning the shadows thrown by Mum's large stocks of groceries which were stored in sacks under the shelves for any lingering roaches. Once it was ready I would dash out as fast as I could, slamming the door behind me. Hard as I tried I could not overcome my revulsion and there were times when I would have tears streaming down my face by the time the bottle was ready. The family found this hugely amusing, but Zane found it childish and irritating. Despite this, I never lost my loathing for cockroaches. When we had our own home I used to pour kerosene down all the drains and man hole covers at least twice a year. The roaches would come staggering out, huge ones and little tiny ones together, and I would watch them as they died a horrible death on the garden paths, squashing any which looked likely to survive. This inhumane and probably highly dangerous method worked and we were never troubled by cockroaches at home.

Because of the long, dry summers housework was a never-ending chore. Floors were tiled in marble or ceramics, with oriental rugs laid down in winter for warmth. These tiles showed every mark or speck of dust and had to be washed down at least once a day, twice in summer. This was never done with mops, but with a cloth and bucket, squatting down and rubbing with the wet cloth until the tiles shone, preferably without a smear or smudge in sight. The patios and garden paths were also tiled and had to be hosed down daily, especially in the summer. Most Iraqis slept on their flat roofs in summer at that time; these were also tiled and so were hosed down before the family retired for the night, both to cool the air and to remove any dust which might have accumulated during the day. Dishes were washed with wire wool dipped into the locally produced washing powder. It was grayish-white in colour and hell on your hands; I soon discovered that it was also hell on babies' bottoms if you used it to wash their nappies. Summer developed her first ever nappy rash soon after we arrived and I was convinced that the washing powder was to blame. Mum always bought blocks of amber coloured washing soap to use on stubborn stains, so I took to grating this soap up to produce home- made soap flakes which I used to wash Summer's clothes. I don't know what it was made of but it was much kinder on her skin and I subsequently used this method for all my children's baby clothes.

We did have a washing machine, a top loader with rotating paddles and an electric mangle on top, but my mother in law didn't like me using it for baby clothes, especially nappies, which she thought were 'unclean'. In fact, she didn't like us using the washing machine too often at the best of times, because there was no mains drainage. Waste water drained into a septic tank which had to be emptied regularly, at what she considered to be horrendous expense – she was always in a foul mood when the tank had to be emptied. She would send one of the neighbours' boys to wait at the end of the road and flag down a passing drainage truck. These were usually owned and manned by Christians from the same village in the north, Tel-Kafe. They had a monopoly and were probably relatively wealthy, but if someone in Baghdad said a person was a Tel-Kafi it not only meant that he came from Tel-Kafe but also that he cleaned cess pits for a living. When my son was a student in Britain he met another boy who said he was from Iraq, 'from a little village in the north called Tel-Kafe'. Before he could stop himself my son blurted, 'Oh, you're a Tel-Kafi', and the boy immediately took offence and walked away, obviously interpreting the label as an insult.

As it was quite expensive to have the septic tank emptied, Mum always made sure she got her money's worth. She would stand over the men as they reversed their lorry onto the hard-standing in front of the kitchen, then she would supervise the lowering of the huge coiled hose down into the man hole. After they had emptied the cess pit, they would bring a hose and wash down the inside of the pit, then pump it out again to make sure that they had not missed anything unpleasant. This was never enough to satisfy my mother in law, though. She always insisted that one of them went down into the pit to ensure that everything was clean. They would protest and argue that the job was done, but ultimately they knew that they would not get paid until someone went down, so in the end one of them would strip to his underwear, grasp the edges of the man hole and down he would go. She would then stand at the edge calling, 'check the corners, make sure there's nothing stuck to the walls' until two strong hands gripped the edges of the hole and up he would come, hosing himself down in the freezing cold water before getting dressed again. I remember once that Emir, returning home early from university, was absolutely horrified and furious at this. 'Pay them and let them go', he stormed, 'they don't have to do that, what's wrong with you? Don't go down, uncle, you don't have to' he turned to the unfortunate operative. 'Never mind, mate, it's no trouble' and down he went anyway, wisely concluding that this was the only way he was going to get his money.

Every house had several water tanks on the roof and for most of the year the natural heat of the sun ensured that the tank water was warm enough to use for showers and washing dishes, but for the six to eight weeks when the weather was really cold and regularly dipped below freezing the kerosene hamam heaters had to be used. I could never understand why my in-laws, like most Iraqis, would shower two or three times a day most of the time, but when the weather was freezing cold and hot water was really needed, the bath water was only heated once a week. I think it was partly the danger involved in lighting it. The hamam was heated by means of a glass container filled with kerosene which was located in a concrete-lined space resembling a small cupboard. This was built under the outer wall of the hamam with a space on the top where it met the garden path. In order to ignite the hamam, a long taper wrapped in a length of kerosene soaked cloth had to be inserted into the space. It was usually my mother in law who lit ours, often after several attempts, and you knew when she had succeeded because there would be a very loud bang and sometimes a bit of a flare up. Once it got going, though, the tiled floor of the hamam would be deliciously warm and the water would be almost boiling as it foamed out of the tap. If any of Oom Sami's children were around, they would be ordered to have a bath, too, Sophia joining Nadia and sometimes Layla for a good scrub.

And what a good scrub it was. Loofas, pumice stones and large quantities of vegetable soap would be used, combined with a generous amount of elbow grease, on just about every part of the body. The soap would be rinsed off then the process repeated several times until the skin glowed and skins that were normally olive were smooth and rosy. Those bathers were the original exfoliators. Babies didn't escape and Summer would be snatched up by one of her aunties and taken off yelling into the steamy hamam. When she reappeared after a lengthy interval she would be very red in the face. 'Now she's clean, not like when you bath her'. I would contemplate this fact as I looked at my screaming but undeniably clean daughter. Girls often went into the bath together, sisters, friends or mothers and daughters, but I never saw men doing the same. I'm not sure why that was.

Unfortunately, clean or not, I could not be content to bathe only once a week, so was forced to heat water and carry it from the kitchen across the rear patio, through the rear lobby and then up the stairs to our bathroom. I also had to heat water to wash clothes and nappies, then rinse them in freezing cold water, often outside so that it would run into irrigation ditches in the garden rather than fill the septic tank and annoy my mother in law. I had two huge empty ghee cans which I used for this, one for clean water and one which I used for boiling nappies. Of course, I also heated water to bath Summer, despite being constantly warned by relatives and neighbours that it was much too cold and I would make her ill. She was a tough little thing, though, and resolutely refused to oblige them, remaining stubbornly cold-free throughout the winter.

Fortunately, the cold weather only lasted a few weeks and as the temperature began to rise it coincided with things hotting up indoors whenever Omar visited. Zane wasn't usually at home when he arrived, but if he was he refused to stay in the same room with him, which made things rather awkward for me, as I didn't want to appear disloyal. I used to compromise by staying for a short while, then making up some excuse to leave the room and then simply not return. I found it all very childish and unnecessary, though, and often told my husband so, not that it made any difference. The other reason for tension when Omar was in the house was Emir.

It took five years to complete a degree at Baghdad School of Medicine and qualify as a house officer: he did it in 10. This was not because he was stupid or lazy, it was because at exam time he was often either imprisoned for his political activities or had just come out of prison. Years later, when he was a respected consultant specialising in skin conditions, I would still occasionally meet someone who, on learning that I was related to Emir, would laugh, 'Do you know it took him ten years to graduate?'

He had joined the Baathist party as a teenager, their slogans of 'unity, freedom and socialism' appealing to his generous and idealistic nature. He soon became disillusioned as he increasingly recognised that this rhetoric, though constantly repeated in party announcements, was rarely reflected in its practice. The final straw came when the Baathists fell out with the Egyptian president, Nasser, who was Emir's life-long hero. He left the party but his belief in the right of everyone to justice and equality never wavered. These were not beliefs that were generally endorsed by Iraqi governments, which in turn were viewed as puppets of western imperialism by most of their citizens. The majority of Iraqis, being a pragmatic people, accepted this, kept their heads down and concentrated on the business of their day to day lives but not Emir. He was constantly involved in something – mysterious appointments and meetings at friends' houses, trips out of town which necessitated his missing lectures – he was adept at concealing what he was up to from his long suffering family, but not so good at hiding things from the ever vigilant security forces, and Omar had been tipped off that they had their eyes on Emir again.

It seemed to me that Baghdad was like a big village; everyone appeared to know everyone else and if they didn't, they knew his cousin. Once you knew a person, often simply because you went to school with them, you were connected and that person would feel free to ask you for a favour in time of need. These favours often consisted simply of 'putting a word in for a friend' with someone you knew who had influence in that particular situation. These favours were reciprocal, with the favour being returned on demand at some time in the future. Anyway, one of his friends had alerted Omar to the fact that Emir was involved in political activities which would put him behind bars again if he wasn't very careful. Like the good son he was, Omar hot footed it to his parents' house to warn them: unfortunately his speed was not matched by his tact as he delivered the bombshell to his mother. 'Tell your son to watch it, he's meddling again in things that don't concern him. Let him stay at home and concentrate on his studies so he can graduate and pay his way. When is he going to learn?'

The thing about Zane's family was that their tough exterior hid very soft hearts, so when there was a problem in the family where one person was obviously in the wrong, at least one family member would feel sorry for the wrongdoer and take his side. Inevitably, this would result in rows which distracted attention away from the heart of the problem, often allowing it to continue unresolved. This was the case with Emir. Zane and Layla immediately empathised with him as the underdog and jumped to his defence, leading to more rows every time Omar called, but so far as I know, Emir was never asked if there was any truth in what had been said.

For a time, life went on as usual apart from these occasional rumbles. The weather started to improve, lifting our spirits and easing my sore hands which were now rough and red from rinsing nappies out in the freezing cold. We started to spend more time out in the garden again, often with muted sounds from radios wafting on the air. It seemed that everyone in the family had a radio constantly tuned in or glued to their ear. Zane, like his father, usually listened to the radio in bed until he fell asleep; his favourite channel was the Voice of America and I was often startled out of sleep by the deep bass voice of a newsreader in the middle of the night. Layla carried out all her chores whilst listening to tips for housewives on the radio in the kitchen and Emir always had the beautiful art deco one in his bedroom switched on and belting out music by his favourite Egyptian singers whenever he was at home. They were all on first thing in the morning, so everyone knew the latest news by the time they had breakfast. That was how we learned that a military coup was under way – everyone was gathered round the radio in the family room when we went downstairs, listening to the announcements from the soldiers who had taken over the radio station at dawn.

This went on all day. There were regular updates about ministers who had been removed from their posts and announcements about who would take their place. A total curfew had been imposed, so there was really nothing else to do but listen to the bulletins and speculate about the changes they would bring. From time to time, one of the neighbours would pop across to discuss what they had heard, after ensuring that the coast was clear in the street, then return home after

71

taking the same precautions on the way back. We learnt later that Alice had gone into labour that morning, forcing Omar to leave the house and walk along the river bank until he found a jeep full of soldiers. They returned with him to the house and then took Alice to hospital in the jeep. She gave birth to a beautiful little boy later that day and finally accepted the fact that she would never have a daughter. Of course, we knew nothing of this and apart from the occasional sound of shooting or a fighter plane overhead, it was deadly quiet in our suburb, quieter than it would have been on a normal day. I did have a phone call from the British Embassy enquiring if I was all right and advising me to stay indoors, the one and only time the embassy contacted me in 18 years.

I knew nothing of politics at all but as the day wore on I could feel the family becoming increasingly sombre. It seemed that the incoming government was 'not good', the people involved in the coup were 'sons of bitches' and much worse – I think Iraqis have the best command of swear language in the world. There is nothing more frustrating and boring than being prevented from going out, even if you had not intended to. I suppose that's what prison is like. Endless cups of tea were consumed, someone would go off to take a shower or nap, leaving the rest of the family to man the radio, until eventually it was time for bed. Over the next few days the curfew restrictions were gradually reduced then eventually lifted. People began to return to their normal daily lives, although there were armed and fully manned tanks stationed at every important road junction for quite a while after that. My good friend Pauline worked at the radio station, although I didn't know her then. She later told me that when she returned to work after the coup she found blood stains sprayed all over the wall of the room she usually worked in. She was told it was the brains of General Abdul Karim Kassem, the 'potty general' of the television sketch.

The new government was controlled by the Baathist party. All I knew about Baathists was that when we lived in Britain

Zane didn't like students who were Baathists and tended to avoid them as much as possible. I soon found out why. Within weeks, there were groups of threatening young thugs, officially labelled National Guards, patrolling the streets. They wore pseudo military combats and were always stationed at the roundabout at the end of our road, where they harassed and intimidated passers-by. There was increasing tension in the air which had nothing to do with the situation at home, and growing whispers of mass arrests and summary executions of people who had been prominent under the previous regime. One afternoon Sami was returning from school when he was pulled from his car and roughed up by the guards at the roundabout. From the insults they hurled at him as they thumped him it was obvious that their only reason for stopping him was jealousy that he had a car.

Rape was a routine part of the Baathist torture procedure even then, and many girls were reported to have come out of prison either pregnant or with babies born in prison. Many of the people arrested had affiliations with the communist party, including a girl who lived right at the end of our street near to Liberty Square. Although I didn't know her, I found out later that after she came out of prison she remained hidden away at home for many years, seldom going out. It was her way of protecting her family from the shame of what had happened to her in prison. There seemed to be a tacit agreement in the neighbourhood that it was better not to mention her in order to avoid embarrassing her family. With all this going on, it was only a matter of time before they came for Emir.

Mum decided we should all go on a visit to Nejef to give thanks for the safe return of Zane from abroad. Summer had just had her first birthday and we would also take her to be blessed at the shrine of the holy saint, Ali. Oom Sami and her daughters were coming with us and we were all going off to her family's house for lunch afterwards. All women had to cover themselves with the traditional black 'Abiya' in Nejef, there was no other choice. At that time, most educated or younger women in Iraq, at least in the cities, wore modern, western-style clothing. However, when they were not perhaps looking their best and wanted to cover this up they would still resort to the abiya. I had often seen Sajida throw an abiya on over her cotton house dress because she wanted to run over to her friend's house and couldn't be bothered to change, so she was quite at ease when wearing one. Obviously I was not, however and there was much hilarity as I tried one on and attempted to walk in it. I constantly tripped over it because it kept slipping off my fine hair, which it was particularly important to keep covered. To make matters worse, I just couldn't master the way they held it around themselves to conceal the clothing underneath. In the end I resorted to pulling it right forward until it formed a peak over my forehead and clutched it under my chin.

We set off on the drive and arrived at the outskirts of Nejef well before mid-day. My first impression was that it was a barren and eerie place, mainly because of the graveyards which stretched out towards the horizon as far as the eye could see. There were simple, unadorned headstones pointing up out of the iron-red soil, mile after mile of them, their very starkness serving to increase the melancholic atmosphere. The graves had no ornaments and there were no flowers left by grieving relatives. It seemed to me that the entire site was the embodiment of the 'ashes to ashes, dust to dust' sentiment. Once we had entered the town proper I saw that most of the houses were built on much smaller plots than the average house in Baghdad. They also had much thicker walls, with cellars underneath which provided cool sanctuaries from the fierce heat of the summer, but I didn't see this until later because we went straight to the shrine. Its dome, covered with gold leaf, was the first thing you noticed once you reached the main street of the city. The square which surrounded it was heaving with visitors and pilgrims, the majority of them women, interspersed with the black and white turbans of the religious officials who cared for the shrine, rather like officials at the Vatican. Those wearing white turbans were highly educated men who spent their time studying the Koran and other religious writings. They were often highly respected and were frequently at odds with the government over policies which they considered to be un-Islamic and/or a breach of human rights. The men in the black turbans were 'Sayids' a hereditary title meaning that they were directly descended from the prophet Mohamed. Not all Sayids followed a traditional life style, and so were not instantly identifiable as they were in Nejef. The Nejef Sayids were not held in particular esteem by my in-laws, though, and I had already heard Dad describe them as a bunch of crooks and fornicators.

Nearly everyone in Nejef seemed to live off the shrine in one way or another, not least the men who ran the shoe deposit stalls. Everyone had to remove their shoes before entering the shrine and the men would pick them up on long poles and arrange them on the shelves which took up quite a long section of the square. There must have been hundreds of shoes stacked there, yet no receipts were given and when you were ready to leave they would unfailingly hand over the correct pair of shoes and take their fee. I tried to work out the system they used to achieve this but couldn't, nor could anyone else enlighten me, it was just taken for granted that they would get it right – that was their job after all. Anyway, when we were all shoe-less and ready to go we entered the shrine, with me clutching wildly at my abiya and Summer comfortably perched on her grandmother's arm. There was a table near to the entrance on which candles and narrow strips of green cloth were displayed. As we brushed past, a tall Sayid with a large, protruding belly which spoke of easy living said something I didn't understand. I ignored him and carried on but he suddenly grabbed my arm, causing my abiya to come adrift. He was obviously very put out about something. 'What's she doing here? – she's a foreigner', he berated my tiny mother in law but she wasn't having any of it. 'Why shouldn't she be here? She's a Moslem just like the rest of us.' The others gathered round and joined in the altercation, their abiyas firmly gripped under their chins, whilst I struggled desperately to keep mine on my head. Suddenly Mum delivered a telling blow: 'She has more right to be here than you, she converted. She chose to be a Moslem and here's her daughter – she's the mother of a Moslem as well'. Summer was held up in evidence at this point. It was obvious that the man was wavering in the face of the group of angry women, and by this time we were the centre of attention as people in the crowd pushed forward to get a better view. They were probably just curious, but I felt very threatened in that confined space, clutching at my abiya whilst what felt like thousands of dark eyes stared at me from under their securely anchored black robes.

'Let's just go, I begged', but we had not done what we came to do so I was over-ruled and I certainly didn't fancy going outside on my own after that. Mum had obviously bested the Sayid, so we left him and circled the shrine, which was ornate and beautiful in a delicate and unpretentious way, with gold and silver filigree and cut glass. It contrasted with the rather garish gold of the dome which I gather was added years after the original tomb was built, obviously by someone with more money than taste. Some of the more devout pilgrims were kissing the gates enclosing the shrine. We lit candles and everyone said their individual prayers before making our way outside again. Apparently the candles had been the cause of the problem; the Sayid had invited me to buy one and was outraged because I had simply ignored him and brushed past – he was annoyed because I had deprived him of some income, according to my mother in law.

The incident was told and re-told through the day with a combination of annoyance and amusement, but I was uneasy about it and could not find it funny. Years later, when I was a mature student I signed up for a module on racism. To illustrate a point, the lecturer said, 'none of us can know what it's like to be in a room in a strange place, surrounded by a sea of black faces all staring at us.' Suddenly the memory of that day in Nejef came flooding back. 'I can, I can' I wanted to yell, and that was really what it was about, the feeling of being alien and the focus of the attention of people whose expressions you can't read. Later on, Layla said that there must have been a reason why I had been picked on. 'Perhaps you were having a period and were unclean?' Strangely enough, I was. I returned to Nejef a couple of times over the years, but it changed. The last occasion was when Saddam's secretive building campaign was at its height and we were surprised to see uncovered 'Russian' women walking the streets, apparently un-harassed by passers-by. All women from the eastern bloc were assumed to be Russian, but wherever they came from it was obvious that there was a sizable construction site somewhere in the area which was important enough for the usual religious requirements to be ignored by the locals, whether by choice or as the result of duress from the government it was impossible to know.

Spring is the most beautiful time of the year in Baghdad – sunny and warm with breezes scented with blossom from the orange trees which grow so easily in suburban gardens. The orchards in the green belts dotted around the city are shady and inviting, so Baghdadis like to make the most of them on Fridays, often heading out of town with a generous picnic lunch packed in the boot of the car. The months of March and April provide a window between the extremes of winter and summer, so everyone spends as much time out of doors as possible before the summer heat drives them indoors. My father in law loved gardening and did most of the work in his garden himself. This was unusual as you could hire the services of a gardener for as little as 3 dinars a month, but he only brought someone in occasionally to help with the heavy work. He would be out in the garden before breakfast, as soon as he had completed his dawn prayers, whilst my mother in law baked the bread which she had prepared and left to rise overnight. Invariably at this time of year, when I came down to breakfast he would present me with a rose. The dew would still be on it and I knew he had selected it as being the most perfect when he did his morning round of the garden. In fact, everything in the garden seemed to respond to his loving care; he grew every kind of citrus fruit from oranges and tangerines to lemons and pomelos, but though they were the result of his daily tending, woe betide anyone who picked them before Mum had given the all clear. These citrus trees formed shady borders under which varying flowers flourished according to season. At this time of year there were large numbers of carnations nestling in the shade, their scent making Mum sneeze as she baked the morning bread.

I was fascinated to learn from my father in law that palm trees had to be pollinated by hand if they were to bear fruit. Summer and I watched in admiration as the slim, athletic-looking young man specially brought in for that purpose clipped a belt around a palm tree so that he was within its circle, then shimmied up the trunk, gripping the belt for support and moving it upwards as he went.

Summer was running around now and proving to be a very precocious talker, probably because of all the adult attention she received. She spent a lot of time in the garden with her grandfather, 'Jidu' as she called him, and he would show her his flowers and tell her stories as he worked. There were two systems of water supply in Baghdad, sweet water used for household purposes and drinking and untreated river water which was used for watering gardens; both were metered and plentiful. Most gardens had an irrigation ditch around the perimeter to hold the river water which gushed out of the huge irrigation taps, much larger than standard household taps.

One morning I went out to call Summer into the house for some reason, 'she's not with me, she went back inside.' Jidu turned his attention back to diverting the flow of water from the irrigation ditches to his flower beds. But she wasn't, so Layla and I began a search of the house, then checked she hadn't escaped out into the street. I ran over to see whether she had found her way to Oom Sami's while Layla returned again to the garden to see if she was hiding somewhere. No-one had seen her in our street and I went back to find Layla and Jidu frantically delving into the irrigation ditches. I was beside myself by then and ran to the front of the house to check the ditches which I knew were already flooded with water. Head down, kneeling and scrabbling in the mud, it hardly registered with me at first that someone was asking 'are you looking for your daughter?' I looked up to see Layla's friend, Shetha, a big smile on her face, hand in hand with Summer. Presumably bored with the gardening she had taken herself off for a walk and ended up at Oom Fatin's, where they had given her a drink and a biscuit before bringing her home. It took about eight minutes for an adult to get from our house to theirs and of course we didn't know exactly how long she had been gone, but children playing in the street had noticed her walking along and recognised her as the daughter of the 'Ingleesia' living nearby. They called Shetha, who chose to believe she had intentionally visited them because she had such a good time with their children. I was just thankful that luck had taken her in their direction that day. It was a popular belief that gipsies stole babies to train them up as dancing girls or boys – a pseudonym for rural prostitutes. I don't know how true this was, but when I first arrived in Baghdad I made the mistake of putting Summer to sleep in her pram at the front of the house on the shady patio. A few minutes later she was brought indoors by a scandalised Oom Sami, who told me in no uncertain terms that I might as well send out an invitation to the bands of travelling dancers that there was a baby available.

These were the events our lives were taken up with. Zane and I had made a few friends of our own by then and it was a relief to be able to speak English with them occasionally. There were

Selwa and Adnan, whom I had first met in England when Summer was born. When I met her Selwa, British born and christened Sylvia, had already adopted an Arabic name, wore her unfashionably long hair hanging down her back and usually had long gold earrings dangling from her ears. Apparently, she had become fascinated with the east when she was a teenager and adopted this look, which was what had attracted Adnan in the first place. His family owned large orchards and lived a traditional farming life in a very large house which accommodated the extended family just outside of Baghdad. We would go to spend the day there at this time of year and wander in the orchards, picking tangerines or oranges which were just ripening, whilst Summer played with their little daughter. Not surprisingly, Selwa had adopted the Arabic lifestyle with gusto and she was such good company, always laughing and joking, that we always enjoyed the time we spent with them. Things were not so good there in the winter, though, because the house was so huge that it was always freezing and their daughter seemed to have a perpetual cold. Another thing which made their house unusual was the full sized concrete model of a twin-engined aeroplane which had been built on the roof. Adnan used to joke that when the house was being built his elder brother had failed in his attempt to join the air force, so he insisted on the plane as consolation. Whatever the reason, the model proved to be a problem in times of national emergencies, because the authorities feared that it might draw the attention of enemy bombers. Consequently, whenever there was regional tension they received a request from the army to disguise it or cover it up.

Another couple we became friendly with were Iraqi. The husband was an engineer in the army and had been in primary school with Zane. In true Baghdad style, when they bumped into each other one day soon after we arrived they recognised each other immediately. His wife was a teacher and we frequently shared evenings out together. On the first occasion, we went to the cinema and just as the main film started I was astonished to find her opening her large handbag and taking out foil-wrapped packs of food which she passed along to us. She had brought huge meat and salad sandwiches, pickles and other accompaniments, a full scale meal if they had been laid out on a table. It was quite difficult to unwrap and eat in them in the dark without completely ruining my clothes – delicious, though. The film we went to see wasn't a comedy, but every so often as we watched it I had to stop myself giggling because the smell of her deliciously spicy sandwiches hung over us in a fragrant cloud until we left the cinema.

Quite soon after we became friendly with them our wedding anniversary came around so we had arranged to go out with them to celebrate. Layla found this a very strange excuse for an outing and kept telling anyone who would listen that people did not celebrate wedding anniversaries in Iraq, it was 'Ebb'.

'Ebb' was one of the words which dominated every Iraqi's life, particularly if they were female. I have never had its meaning clearly explained to me, but I understood it to mean doing something which was socially unacceptable, something which would bring embarrassment or even ridicule on your family. Children were rarely told that they were being naughty but from their earliest days they were regularly reined in from enjoyable activities by the word Ebb. Although Zane pretended to ignore her he was becoming increasingly wound up – the ever present conflict between his family's expectations and mine were once again simmering under the surface.

Summer had not yet been put to bed and I knew she would probably still be awake when we came home that night. She was very excited, sensing that something unusual was going on, and kept jumping all over the settees. Mum was fanatical about treating the furniture with respect, but as fast as I lifted her down and told her she was being naughty she wriggled away from me and climbed back up again. I was just pulling her off once more when Zane blew his top. He grabbed her and gave her a light smack on the legs. This was so out of character for him and so unlike what she had come to expect from her devoted Daddy that she let out a yell, followed by a yell from me as I told him off for daring to smack my beloved daughter. His response was so unexpected that I stood rooted to the spot for a moment as he turned around and hit me too. Then I went berserk; my parents weren't into corporal punishment and in fact I cannot remember ever being hit in my life before. I rushed out of the room to the kitchen where I grabbed one of Mum's large cooking knives and ran back to the family room where I found my sisters in law giving my husband a good telling off. I rushed towards him, but luckily they saw the knife and left that job to grab my arms, pushing me back as I leapt about trying to get at him from over their heads. Just at that moment the door- bell rang to announce the arrival of our friends.

Incredibly, Zane still wanted to go out, but as I hadn't finished yelling at him someone went to tell them that I had been taken ill and would have to postpone. When the hubbub eventually died down, I found that I had earned a lot of respect from my sisters in law for my temper tantrum. 'You don't put up with anything, you're just like us' Sajida told me admiringly. I later received a very penitent apology from my dear husband, following which we went upstairs to celebrate our anniversary on our own. It didn't turn out to be such a disaster after all.

The other couple who befriended us in those early days were a South African couple whom Zane had met through work. They were quite a bit older than us but very sociable. We usually went out somewhere with them but on one occasion we made the mistake of inviting them to spend an evening with us at home. As good Moslems Zane's parents didn't drink, of course, so I wouldn't have dreamed of serving alcohol in their house. Nevertheless, as I would be offering them cold drinks, I didn't think there was any reason not to serve the usual nibbles which accompany alcohol, so I laid out plates of crisps, nuts and dips on the sitting room tables. When our visitors arrived I was very annoyed to note, as I ushered them into the sitting room, that these had been removed. After we had chatted for a few moments, on my way to the kitchen to fetch drinks, I asked Layla what had happened to my appetisers. 'I took them away, they're not children, you'd think it was a birthday party – Ebb'.

I gave up and returned to the sitting room with the drinks, which looked rather mean and lonely all on their own. We continued our chat, only to be interrupted by my mother in law passing through, ostensibly towards the kitchen, but having a good look at the foreigners on the way. A bit later, Layla also made her way to the kitchen, making no attempt to come near enough to be introduced but also giving our visitors the once over. After that there was a small but steady stream of people passing through the room, our kitchen must have been the most popular in the country that night. Even Oom Sami came over for a look. She was in the advanced stages of a pregnancy that had left her feeling unwell for the past few days, but she sailed through the dining room, stomach pushing out to the front and eyes fixed firmly to the right like a sergeant on parade. Not surprisingly, the visitors didn't stay very late: I believe they left before the coffee and cake which I had planned to serve later in the evening, and I never made the mistake of inviting foreign visitors home again, apart from Selwa.

These evenings out didn't prevent me from feeling increasingly home-sick, though, and I was saving every spare penny so that we could go home for a visit in the summer. Selwa's mother used to send her parcels of the *Daily Mirror* which she passed on to me after she had read them. I read voraciously the so-called news stories and articles which sometimes surprised me by the raciness of their content. Perhaps I was adopting the prudity of my in laws, but I didn't think so. My younger brother, who was the most reliable letter-writer in my family, had told me about a band called the Beetles and how he wore a suit like theirs and was growing his hair so he could copy their hair styles. It felt as though Britain had turned into a different country in the short time I had been away and I longed to go back. Although I had grown fond of my in-laws, their intensity and constant nit-picking exhausted me. I longed for the cheerful, teasing humour of my family which had so annoyed me when I lived at home.

I began planning a trip home in the summer, Zane didn't want to go at that time because he was so involved in his job, which he enjoyed immensely. If he took time off there would be no holiday pay, which was obviously an important factor, but the truth was that he was already showing signs of the workaholic he was to become. But there always seemed to be some extra household expense which we had to chip in for and that summer it was the windows. Most Iraqi houses had fly screens and ornamental bars on their windows. These were also believed to act as a deterrent to burglars, not that burglary occurred very often then, quite the opposite. Apart from that, we had our own unique burglar alarm system, which consisted of Dad. He had this theory that all thieves are essentially cowards who will always prefer to steal when there is no risk of being caught. To deter any would be burglars he would get up several times every night and walk around the outside of the house, coughing loudly to let anyone who might be lurking know that he was on the alert. Although the family laughed at his self-imposed guard duty it was probably as effective a deterrent as was needed in those innocent days.

Anyway, when my in-laws built their house they ran out of money before the window screens and bars were installed. All of a sudden this became a major issue for them, just around the time I announced that I was going home for the summer. You could hardly open a window without Layla wailing that we were going to be burgled, while any fly that ventured into the kitchen caused such violent lunges with the fly swatter, usually accompanied by distraught laments over our lack of fly screens, that I was surprised that any insect had the temerity to enter. The nearer my proposed trip to England came, the more the moans increased and they were now accompanied by pointed remarks about Zane's high salary, followed by tales of how other sons looked after their mothers. This campaign, added to the outright hostility which now existed between Zane and Omar, made home life unbearable for me. It was all right for Zane; he was away from home most of the time and in the evening he was often too exhausted to do much more than fall into bed early. I wished that he would make more effort to fit in with what the family wanted for my sake, but he was just as uncompromising as they were. In the end I couldn't stand it any longer, and exploded one afternoon: 'For God's sake, have the bloody windows done, and let's all have some peace', I told him. It took all of my savings, of course, so my visit home had to be put off until next year and I faced up to the fact that I was in for a long, hot summer.

# Chapter Five

Oom Sami's mother-in-law arrived to look after the children until the new baby came. I could never work out the dynamics of that family. They were obviously fairly well off, yet their house was furnished with the barest essentials, and Oom Sami never seemed to have any money. When my mother in law went shopping in town, for example to buy bedding or fabrics for nightclothes for all the family, she always bought enough for their family too. Oom Sami never seemed to be able to repay her and Mum always had to wait until the husband finally gave in to her requests for money and paid up. When she eventually went into labour it was my mother in law who took her to hospital – to the large government maintained 'Republican Hospital' which most comfortably off people avoided if they could. The hospital was well staffed with highly trained doctors and nurses but its services were under pressure because of the immigration into the capital from the countryside, so anyone who could afford to tended to use one of the privately owned and operated hospitals.

Oom Sami was a tiny little woman, yet every time she gave birth the baby was larger than the one before. She was always boasting how Zaid had weighed in at over 10 pounds, in comparison to Summer's rather puny 7 pounds. Not surprisingly, her babies took rather a long time and a lot of effort to produce, so no-one at home was particularly surprised that my mother in law was away until late at night. When she finally returned her face was sombre – the baby had died during the labour, and Oom Sami must stay in hospital for a few days because she was very poorly. She had been warned by the nurses at the hospital that this must be her last labour as another confinement would probably kill her.

By this time the summer was well and truly upon us. Few houses had air conditioning yet but there was an ingenious device known as an air cooler which was in widespread use. It was basically a fan belt around a central drum housed in a large aluminium container. The walls of this container were louvred and lined with some sort of coarse straw-like material which was kept moist by a hose which fed water into it. As the drum rotated it sucked in air which was then cooled by the water and fed into the adjacent room through a duct. My in laws, like most families, only had air coolers in the reception rooms as they slept on the roof throughout the summer. Bedding was taken up to the roof and laid on the metal bedsteads every evening after the tiles had been hosed down, then removed again in the morning as soon as the sun came up. The air would become deliciously cool at night and even after air conditioning became widespread, most people preferred to sleep on the roof. I always hated it – I would look up at the palm fronds overhanging the roof and imagine all sorts of creepy crawlies running down them and finding their way onto the bed. To make matters worse, when I did finally manage to fall asleep it seemed that hardly any time at all had passed before I was being woken again by the tiny little flies that appeared as soon as the sun came up, forcing the family to gather up their bedding and retreat downstairs, where they would soon be fast asleep again. Sadly, I was never able to develop their apparent ability to drop off to sleep at any time, so the flies would mean the end of sleep for me for the rest of that day.

My dislike for al fresco sleeping arrangements was also increased by the layout of the house. It had two roof terraces, the first leading out from the first floor landing whilst the second was reached by a staircase running up from the first flat roof. The family all slept on the cooler, higher roof, which was also the smaller of the two, telling us rather magnanimously that they were leaving the larger, lower roof to us. Of course, this meant that anyone going to bed late or returning into the house for any reason had to make their way past us. Not only that, anyone could look down on us from the higher roof as we slept, or didn't sleep as the case may be. I found it very hard to relax and fall asleep under these conditions not to mention the effect it had on our marital relations. If the night was not too hot, I would wait until everyone was asleep and the air had cooled down and then return to our bedroom, but the air which was so delightfully cool up on the roof would still be uncomfortably warm indoors, even with all the windows open. My in laws thought I was mad, but they could never understand my need for privacy. Soon after we arrived in Baghdad, Layla asked me why we always slept with our bedroom door closed. 'You married women are shameless, what do you get up to in your bedroom every night?' The wicked grin which accompanied this question left me in no doubt as to what she thought I was up to. Actually, as often as not I would be reading a book late into the night, a life-long habit, whilst Zane and Summer slept peacefully beside me. However, I didn't feel this was any of her business so I left her to enjoy her obviously prurient imaginings.

After lunch most people took a siesta; thin mattresses would be laid out in the reception rooms so that the whole family could make the most of the air coolers. My in laws urged me to join them but I was simply not comfortable sleeping in the same room with them, it felt weird. I would sit up in our bedroom, dripping with sweat and longing for the day to be over. I was losing a lot of weight, had lost my appetite and my clothes were hanging off me. I came to love Iraqi food, but that summer the smell of the clarified butter, liberally used for cooking, turned my stomach as did the water melon rinds which filled the rubbish bins after every meal. My mother in law tried everything to get me to eat. She bought tinned and processed foreign cheese at great expense and locked it in the cupboard so no-one could eat it but me. I found it revolting and insisted that everyone else should share it with me, to her intense annoyance. Every time she returned from the market she would offer me the best grapes or peaches, whatever had just come into season, to tempt my appetite. 'Are you missing Momma and your sisters? Come on, eat, eat,' and there would be a new canned delicacy which she hoped would do the trick.

Zane was also worried about me and so we began sleeping on the floor in the air-cooled lounge at night where I was at least able to get a good night's sleep. Once I had got used to that, I began sitting downstairs in the afternoon, reading whilst my in laws slept. I was not yet able to lie down on one of the mattresses, but no-one really slept very soundly in the afternoon anyway because of the different time tables they followed. Zane's parents were always up in time for the dawn prayers and he left for work very early himself. His father walked into the centre of Karrada virtually every morning where he met his friends in the coffee house for a chat. He used to return, have a very early lunch and then have his afternoon nap. By the time the rest of the family were settling into their siesta he was waking up and asking for tea. Sometimes he would switch off the air coolers to save electricity and walk around the house calling out: 'Wake up, wake up, if sleep was going to do you any good, it would have helped those people lying in their graves'. I often thought that there was quite a lot of truth in this observation, but its underlying wisdom was completely lost on his sleepy family, especially those who had just made the hot and dusty trip back from the city.

My father in law was a sweet old man; his father had been the original owner of most of the land in the area and when he sold it off to a developer, sadly too early to become rich from it, he had paid for the local mosque to be built. Partly because of this, but also because he was pious and honourable, he was very well respected in the area. He never missed Friday prayers at the mosque in addition to faithfully praying at home five times a day, unlike most of his children, who showed little sign of observing the requirements of religion in those days. He was a born story-teller, keeping the oral tradition alive with tales of his boyhood which dated back to the time of the Ottoman Empire. He would sit cross-legged by the primus which was keeping the tea pot warm and recall long past events, like the time his mother had rushed into the house calling out that an 'iron horse' had just passed by; it turned out that she had just seen her first bicycle. He had married my mother in law when he was aged around 19 and she was about 13 and I believed him when he said that he had never looked at another woman since then. She once told me how she had been prepared for her wedding day. The traditional method used by women to remove unwanted hair was threading. This was a tricky business usually carried out by professionals at home, rather like using a mobile hairdresser, and involved plucking out every individual hair between two twisted cotton threads. The practitioner would hold one end of the heavy threads in her mouth, then arrange them over her fingers rather like the threads in a game of cats' cradle, and she would be off, ignoring the squeals of pain as she plucked away. Anyway, the day before her wedding, this young girl had her eyebrows plucked to a fine line, then all the down on her face was removed, using the 'two thread' method. After that all her body hair, including pubic and under arm hair, was also removed. She then had a decorative dark blue line tattooed just under her chin. It extended down her throat and chest, ending between her breasts. She also had some small diamond shaped tattoos applied to the back of her hands, which were then decorated with henna, as was her hair. Her nose was pierced and very large, heavy earrings were put into her already pierced ears. She was then taken into the bedroom to await her new husband, a virtual stranger. She told me that her most vivid memory of her wedding night was that wherever he touched her, it hurt.

After their marriage they lived with his parents and three sisters and she was soon doing most of the household chores for the whole family. They shortened her name, Zahara, to

Izhara, signifying her child-like status within the family and this name was still used by her husband and children whenever she had annoyed them. Never to her face, though: she was the driving force and unacknowledged head of the family. She had 11 living children, and although she was herself illiterate she made sure that they all became graduates, apart from her two elder daughters who were born before female emancipation had begun to seem a possibility.

Obviously, her life had not been easy, as her husband was the first to admit. Once as we sat drinking tea with them, he began telling Zane and Emir of their life together and the sexual demands he made upon her when they were younger. According to him, they had sex every night several times, every afternoon when they took a siesta, and after their morning and evening prayers. 'I never gave her any peace, I always kept her busy', he boasted to the accompaniment of their admiring chuckles. His placid and easy going nature complemented her fiery and ambitious one; they made a good team and they had a very successful marriage. He didn't mind that their house was known as 'Oom Omar's house' instead of his, he knew that everyone knew who he was. As he grew older he became a bit forgetful and one day, feeling too tired to walk home from the coffee house, he took a taxi. He became confused about where his house was, so told the driver to pull over so that he could ask directions from some boys playing in the street. He stuck his head out of the window and called 'Where is the house of Haji Toma?'

'Uncle, why are you asking us, you are Haji Toma' was their surprised reply.

The summer dragged on, seemingly never-ending, and the arrests continued. Emir, outspoken and unwise as ever, got into an argument with some Baathists. Soon after that a group of them cornered him in a quiet street one night and it was a miracle that he managed to escape without a beating, or worse. One of his attackers was Tariq Aziz, who became Saddam's foreign minister and later managed to convince the international community that he was the urbane and acceptable face of Saddam's Baathist government.

We were sound asleep in the sitting room when the doorbell rang. As we struggled awake, two soldiers with rifles slung over their shoulders came into the room followed by my mother in law, who was protesting as she went: 'Why are you going in there? Get out, you can see he's not here.' She ushered them out of the room as we jumped up, threw our dressing gowns over our night clothes and followed them back to the family room. A short young man with a turn in his eye and a very smart suit was waiting there. He was a local boy so my mother in law knew exactly who he was. 'Well, Aunty, when do you expect Dr Emir to come home?' He was amazingly polite and pleasant. 'I have no idea, why are you disturbing us at this time of night? Come back in the morning.' She walked him to the door, turning to indicate to the soldiers that she expected them to follow, which they did, then closed it firmly behind them. We watched from the window as they walked down the path and out of the gate, then controlled pandemonium broke out. The girls had all been huddled together in the back lobby listening and someone ran upstairs to tell Emir. Sajida got on the phone to a friend whose father was in the police force, asking him to 'put a word in' for Emir while Nadia ran up to the roof to see whether the callers had really gone. They hadn't – they had stationed themselves near a car parked a few houses down and there was also a jeep parked up the street in the opposite direction. Emir could have tried climbing over the high wall at the rear of the property and escaping across the garden of one of the adjoining houses – he'd done this before, hiding under the bed of a Turkish neighbour until his persecutors got tired of waiting and went away. But that was under a previous regime. The people he was dealing with now were much more determined, and would have soldiers waiting for him at every point of exit. He was amazingly calm, returning briskly to his bedroom while the silent but feverish activity went on all around him.

They came back again in about fifteen minutes, still polite, asking when he was expected to return. Mum fobbed them off again; it was a cat and mouse game with no likelihood of the mouse escaping. I don't know how long the politeness would have continued because after their second visit Emir came downstairs. He had changed into an old shirt and trousers and as he entered the room he took off his watch and handed it to Zane for safe-keeping. 'Go back upstairs, they don't know you're here, maybe they'll go away'. He knew better, and sure enough the doorbell rang again almost immediately. I think he knew that if he didn't go with them soon, they would force their way back into the house and a scuffle would break out in which someone would inevitably get hurt. The family were all amazingly strong. Although they were white faced and solemn, I didn't see anyone cry until the next morning, when I noticed tears rolling down my mother in law's face as she poured the morning tea. They could yell and scream at each other every day of the week, but when one of them was in trouble they would all rally round and pull together to solve the problem.

Later that day I went into Emir's bedroom to dust the furniture. He was a very heavy smoker, like Zane, and there were always boxes of matches and half empty packets of cigarettes strewn around his room. His large ash-trays were overflowing as usual and as I moved to empty them into the metal waste paper bin I realised why he had remained upstairs so long the previous evening. He had been burning papers; they probably held information about people whose identity he wanted to protect. The soldiers could easily have searched the house but they made no attempt to do so. If they wanted to find out who the associates of a prisoner were, they seemed to prefer to beat or torture the information out of them. They also preferred confessions forced from prisoners by the same methods rather than based on firm evidence easily collectable.

I don't imagine that Emir could have posed a serious threat to the government, but dissent was something they would not tolerate and the way they operated was a constant reminder to everyone of what would happen to dissenters.

The house was solemn and hushed the next day. Mum and Dad alternated between quietly cursing Emir for his stupidity and praying that he would be all right. 'That bugger, he's been nothing but trouble from the day he was born' was his mother's lament. 'Bugger's right, they're probably buggering him right now' replied Dad, shaking his head and wiping tears from his eyes at the same time. There was a constant stream of visitors; they all knew what had happened and all of them came to suggest people they knew who might be able to 'put in a word' or pull some strings. Zane did not go to work, but went to try and find out where his brother was being held via the Baghdad grapevine. They had taken him to the 'People's Centre' which was next to the old ministry of defence. Once he had located him, Zane visited the prison every day, taking him fresh clothes, demanding to know what the charges were and requesting a visit to his brother. After a couple of weeks of this, we received a warning that the prison guards were fed up with his demands, considered him stuck up and big headed and were contemplating arresting him too. Of course, I was terrified and Zane, who had heard the sounds made by prisoners as he waited for news, thought it would be prudent to stay away for a while.

It was late afternoon and several of the neighbours had called round to see if there was any news. We were all sitting around the tea tray, some of the family on the cool tiled floor, when someone came in and said that they had heard that Emir had been moved to the 'Castle of Doom'. Everyone was shocked and silent, tears sliding down their cheeks as we contemplated this news. Anyone who might possibly have been able to help had already been approached. Omar tried to pull strings with influential friends and Saleh, the brother who was Chief of

Police in Basra, had contacted everyone he knew in the police force. If he had really been moved to this prison, which people seldom left alive, then it would need a miracle to get him out and we all knew it.

I don't know whether Emir was sent to the Castle of Doom but he was eventually released after a friend of Omar intervened on his behalf. This friend was a minister in the newly formed government, which needed the support of the army and as a consequence was not exclusively Baathist. There was a condition – that Emir must leave the country immediately and this had been agreed; he was to go to Cairo. Before he was released, he was transferred to the hospital to be patched up and then he was dropped off by a car at the end of the road. He was pale and thin but otherwise looked much as he usually did, except that he walked very stiffly and one of his eyes was very swollen and bloodshot. He sat down and drank a cup of tea with us all then went upstairs to rest in his bedroom. Later, he gave me two bundles of clothes he had brought with him from the prison. He asked me to burn one and put the other through the washing machine. 'Don't let my mother see them' he asked. Always squeamish, I tried not to look as I pulled the clothes apart and sprinkled washing powder liberally onto the blood-stained and discoloured clothes in the machine.

Whilst I was burning the other bundle in the bread oven in the garden, Layla appeared at my side, 'What are you doing? Why are you doing that? Are those clothes unclean?' Never had her puritanical adherence to the hygiene requirements of religion been more unwelcome. I ignored her and carried on with what I was doing and for once she bit her tongue and walked away.

'Unclean' did not mean simply dirty, it meant defiled; a person who was defiled was unacceptable to God and could not pray. Body fluids in particular were unclean, necessitating thorough washing after a visit to the toilet. Menstruating women were unclean and women were also considered unclean for the first six weeks after child birth. It was very important to keep unclean objects separate from food, hence Layla's unhappiness that the clothes were being burned in the bread oven. As soon as they were charred to a cinder she pushed me aside and began cleansing the oven by sprinkling it with water whilst repeating all the names of God, just as she did when she was rinsing newly washed clothes.

There were a host of other things which were considered unclean, among them dogs. My mother in law often put food scraps out on the street for the hungry wild dogs which came down from the river bank in cold weather, but she would never have dreamed of keeping one in the house. Imagine her horror when Zane arrived home one evening with a puppy for Summer. Summer was delighted, but the rest of the family was in uproar, and only calmed down when the poor puppy was consigned to the garden, away from the praying members of the family. Naturally, being a puppy it didn't stay there but kept trying to get into the house in search of company, frequently wee-ing on the patio on the way. It also fouled the garden, until even long-suffering Dad began to get annoyed. The whole thing blew up into a huge row and the puppy was returned from whence it came.

Emir's kidneys were irrevocably damaged by that particular stint in prison and his eye sight was never the same again. As soon as his passport and other travel documents were completed, Omar drove him to the airport and put him on a plane to Cairo. The Egyptian government was giving financial help to Iraqi political exiles at that time, so it was hoped that he would complete his medical studies there. We all breathed a sigh of relief. For the first time in months we had nothing to worry about but the price of tomatoes and the increasingly acrimonious family rows.

# Chapter Six

For the greater part of the day we were a house of women; Sajida and Nadia had finished school for the summer and there was constant bickering over the housework. I don't know why this was really because Sajida usually jumped up and washed all the floors early in the morning without having to be asked. She usually flew through the cleaning, then disappeared into her bedroom, where she would spend the rest of the morning reading magazines, studying the latest styles in hair and fashion. Sometimes an old school friend, May, would call in to see her. May was considered very beautiful because of her fair skin, and had consequently been snapped up by a cousin, who married her when she was about 17. She lived in a huge house at the end of the road which she shared with her parents in law and a married brother in law, each couple occupying one floor of the house. This was quite a traditional arrangement, and it was not unusual for people to build very large houses in the hope that their children would remain with them after they were married. Kruschev, on a visit to Baghdad, once asked how many families were accommodated in one of these large houses. Apparently he was astounded to learn that one family could occupy so much living space. May was a chatty, jolly girl; I found her very easy to get on with and we would sometimes walk into Karrada together to go shopping. Her own parents lived in our street with a couple of her younger, unmarried siblings. There was an elderly maiden aunt who also lived with them, but she was very different from Layla or Shetha. In contrast to them, she made no effort to help around the house, on the contrary everyone seemed to dance attendance on her. Worse than that, she sometimes caused her family acute embarrassment because of the way she behaved. To put it bluntly, she was man-crazy and especially besotted with Emir. They tried to prevent her from coming to our house, but whenever the opportunity presented itself she would slip away and come knocking at our door. If Emir was at home, she would simper and smile, hanging around him like a teenager, whilst he good-naturedly parried her attentions until one of her relations arrived to take her home. If he happened to be out, she would make pointed enquiries as to why his family had still not arranged a marriage for him, leaving them in no doubt that she would be happy to step up to the mark if asked. Mum and Layla would wait for one of her relatives to miss her and come and collect her, apparently unaware of the inappropriate flirting. However, this was mere politeness and as soon as she had been taken away Mum would chuckle and dismiss her with a snorted 'lunatic'. Layla, on the other hand would be outraged and call her something far more impolite and uncomplimentary.

I always tried to do my share of the housework, but they were such perfectionists about everything that my efforts rarely met with approval. The floor tiles had to shine without a smear and there could not be one speck of dust left on the furniture. I found the most difficult job was the long dining table; although it was made of solid wood, it was veneered with shiny formica in a light oak finish for easy cleaning. In fact this made it harder to clean, as it was difficult to get a smear free finish on the hard surface so Layla invariably attacked it again once I had finished. One evening I offered to hose down the roofs before the beds were made up for the night. Summer and I had a wonderful time splashing around in the water as we washed off the dust, then swept the water out through the vents into the down pipes. Later Mum came up, ostensibly to hang out some washing but I knew that really she wanted to inspect my work. She looked around, shifting the bedsteads to check whether any dust lurked beneath their feet, before passing judgment. 'Didn't Mummy teach you how to wash the roof down?' My work had obviously fallen short of requirements once again.

She and Layla were the worst bickerers, mainly because Mum couldn't bear to stay at home for a moment longer than she had to in the daytime. She used to rush to prepare the mid-day meal, which usually needed simmering for at least an hour, then leave it to Layla to watch while she went off to visit one of her friends. This infuriated Layla, who complained that she was doing an unfair share of the housework, particularly as she then had the extra job of cooking the rice. Actually she didn't do that much in the summer when the girls were at home, I think she was just envious of her mother's freedom to come and go as she pleased. Layla seldom went out on her own; I don't know why that was, but it was her choice – she would do anything to avoid even going to the corner shop, sending one of the local children whenever we ran out of something. Even when Mum was at home something always seemed to take her away from the kitchen. She would boil and strain the rice, add piping hot clarified butter then place the saucepan on the small primus until a golden crust formed on the base. My in laws loved this crispy rice, particularly Zane, but she often forgot about it once she had left the kitchen until the smell of scorching food would send her hurtling back. She would fling off the saucepan lid, turn down the primus and put a round of flat bread on top of the rice to absorb the smell of burning. This didn't always work; when it didn't the rice would have an unpleasant, smoky tang which would inevitably be the cause of another argument.

The small primus was actually a camping stove; it was often moved around the house in the summer so that tea could be brewed on it until it was black and strong, just how Iraqis like it. One afternoon after siesta it had been placed in the rear lobby where we were going to have tea. We were all sitting on the cool tiles with the door open, enjoying the delightfully cool breeze which blew out from the family room. Mum mentioned that she was going off somewhere or other after she had showered and an argument broke out. Sajida joined in and it soon became a free for all, with everyone accusing Mum of not pulling her weight. I thought that this was rather mean of them as she still carried all the shopping from town and rose at dawn every morning to make bread for breakfast even though she must have been at least 60 by then. She didn't need anyone to defend her, though. Infuriated, yelling that they could make their own bloody tea from now on, she picked up the burning primus, tea pot and all, and hurled it into the garden where it flared up and burned brightly for a few minutes until all the kerosene was used up. Mum went out as planned that evening, leaving the primus stove in the spot where it had landed in the garden. The next morning at breakfast, it was back in its usual place under a shady tree, with only the scorched patch of grass on the lawn to remind us where it had been the day before.

One of the magazines Sajida bought regularly was the German produced *Burda*. It not only showed the latest fashions but contained paper patterns of the clothes featured in its pages. Layla only had a few years schooling so the instructions were beyond her, but Sajida helped her to cut out the patterns so that she could use them for her dress making. It was a convenient and cheap way of making every-day clothes so I began trying my hand at making clothes for myself. It helped to pass the time on long summer days and the skill was to come in very useful in days of austerity when there was little to buy in the shops. For smarter clothes everyone went to dressmakers. They could produce almost any style you wanted if you showed them a picture of it, with varying degrees of success, of course. The dressmaker used by my in laws was a Turkish girl called Zahara. She had a real flair and was very good at advising on the best material for a particular style; she also told me that I had the longest arms of any of her customers, I was never sure whether to be proud of this distinction or not.

Nadia and Zakiya also spent a lot of time in the bedroom with Sajida. They would sit on either side of her, looking like a couple of book ends as they discussed the latest fashions, then switch on the iron so that they could straighten their long hair on the ironing board. Whilst they were doing this, they would be listening to pop music on the radio, jigging around and threatening to inflict serious burns on themselves as they scorched their hair. Often, if Layla wasn't about, they would go on to practice the latest dance steps, trying to keep one eye on the door because chaos would ensue if she caught them. She would rush into the room and lay into them with whatever was to hand, threatening them with hell-fire and damnation and denouncing Sajida for letting them get away with it. 'You trollops, have you no shame?' She would yell at their retreating backs as the girls ran for cover. If Dad was at home Nadia would run to him first for protection and he always provided it. 'Come on, come on, leave her alone, she's only a child'. He would try to calm the situation, which often ended with Nadia cuddling up to him on the chaise longue in his bedroom while he reasoned with her quietly.

This infuriated Layla even more. She considered Nadia far too old to be cuddled by her father and was never backward in saying so. I used to feel sorry for Nadia sometimes. As the youngest child in the family it seemed that everyone was always on her case, criticising her behaviour, her clothes, the way she did her hair. For some reason, Emir was her worst critic; he often shook his head at her behaviour, predicting that she would bring shame on the family. I thought this rather ironic considering some of the people he must run around with. Anyway, she didn't need anyone else to fight her corner and always gave as good as she got. This fighting spirit stood her in good stead in later years. She was bright and hard- working and eventually gained a place in medical school, but whilst she was working as a junior doctor she was approached by local Baath party officials and ordered to tamper with the marks of students who refused to join the party. This was totally unacceptable to Nadia, so as soon as the opportunity presented itself she enrolled on a post grad course which enabled her to leave the country, eventually becoming a paediatrician. After working for several years in the Gulf States, she met and married an Iraqi engineer and they later moved to America with their two children. In the States Nadia managed to combine a full time career and raising a family with charity work, in particular helping young refugees from war torn countries. Her efforts were recognised by the US Congress who offered her an award for her efforts, but she declined it, saying that she did what she could to help people, not because she wanted any reward.

To get back to her teenage years, though, her feistiness contributed to a home life which was lively, spirited and often downright annoying. Although I found that first summer interesting and even educational, I still welcomed the arrival of September.

The weather began to cool off, schools and colleges re-opened and everything returned to normal. Zane's work at the airport was coming to an end and he was looking around for another job. He complained constantly that neither of his two eldest brothers seemed keen to 'put a word in for him', so I knew this would be the cause of more argument in days to come. I tried to persuade him to stop relying on his brothers and stand on his own two feet, but part of me knew that this was just the way the system worked in Baghdad. Even if that hadn't been the case, I didn't expect much help from his two eldest brothers because they always seemed determined to undermine us and everyone thought it was something to do with me. It was clear to me by then that the family disliked Alice, although they became quite fond of her in later years, so I think this dislike stemmed from the time she lived with them. Basra used to be very cosmopolitan, employing many foreign workers in the port, so Alice did not experience the total immersion into Iraqi culture which I had. When she moved in with the family she continued to live much as she had in Basra, unaware of the offence this sometimes caused. Apparently she brought home bacon and pork sausages and went shopping for treats for her children which were not offered to Nadia, who was then quite young. Nor was Nadia invited when she took her children out on excursions, although she would have loved to go. I don't think it was Alice's fault, Omar ought to have warned her, but he was so used to being deferred to in the family that it probably did not occur to him that anyone would question what he did. Anyway, the fact that I was living and for all intents and purposes getting on with their family obviously annoyed the brothers intensely, so they never missed an opportunity to make things hard for me. I suspect the family whipped up this irritation by singing my praises to them, not out of genuine affection but rather with the aim of underlining what they saw as their short-comings as dutiful sons.

One afternoon I was doing something in the kitchen while Omar was visiting. I must have been miles away when Nadia came into the kitchen and, seeing my absorbed face, put her arm round me and said 'Don't take any notice'.

'Don't take any notice of what?'

'Of what he said, none of us believe it'. It took me a while to find out what she was talking about, which was essentially that he couldn't understand why everyone made such a fuss about me when I was a nobody whom Zane had picked up on the streets.

Stunned, I considered my options. I could rush in and have it out with him, but why should I have to justify myself to him? I opted for dignity and although I stopped avoiding him from that afternoon, I didn't speak to him for several years either. I would sail across the room with my nose in the air, looking straight through him. This stony silence discomfited him much more than any row would have done, until in the end he complained to Zane that I would speak to the angel Gabriel before I would speak to him. That was exactly how I felt. I'm not sure why the second brother disliked me, but he was very close to Omar and I think merely followed his lead. We saw very little of him and his family in those days anyway because of course they lived in Basra, but he seemed a kind man and was wonderful with children. He had married the only daughter of a very rich man, but unfortunately the marriage was not a happy one and my in-laws blamed her for this. When they visited Baghdad, they always stayed at her family's house, which was not the way with traditional Iraqi families. I'm sure it was more convenient for them and their three children to stay there because their house was much larger and they also had live in servants, but my in-laws interpreted this as a sign that he was hen-pecked.

Saleh had inherited his father's gift for telling stories and as the chief of police he had many interesting tales to tell. He arrived one day to tell us how he had sent men all over the south searching for a young couple who had run away to marry without the permission of their families. Unfortunately, the girl's family found them first and the girl had been killed, much to his regret. This was the first time I had heard of honour killings, which were comparatively unusual in Iraq then, at least in the cities. Iraqis had their own way of managing unruly daughters, often depending on their class position. The daughter of one of our neighbours was rumoured to have had an affair with a visiting plumber, so her family contrived a marriage with a man from a small town a few miles outside of Baghdad. He was not her social equal and rumour had it that he treated her quite badly, sometimes even knocking her about. The marriage became impossible and she went to her family to ask if she and her two children could return to live with them. Their answer was that she could go back to live with her parents but not her children. It was the Iraqi version of 'you've made your bed and now you must lie in it' and lay in it she was forced to do.

There were other options. There was the gynaecologist who was well known for carrying out abortions and reconstructing hymens on unmarried girls. She was frequently quoted as saying that she considered herself to be carrying out a useful social function by sparing families from shame, and who could argue with her? She came from a well- known Karrada family but sadly both she and her brother were later murdered by the Baathists. Her brother came to visit us in England soon after Summer was born, leaving her with a present of half a crown tucked into her fist. I thought this an unusual gift from an Iraqi; it was more like something my grand-dad might do. Perhaps it was an indication of the family's ability to deviate from the mainstream and adopt other ways. Either that or he was tight.

That autumn, I was quite surprised to find I was pregnant again because I had somewhat naively imagined that I had become infertile after the haemorrhage in Turkey. We were delighted by this unexpected news, as were all my in-laws. Zane was confident the baby would be a boy; most Iraqis expect and want a boy when there is to be a new addition to the family. Paradoxically when a girl arrives they seem to fall in love with her immediately, showering her with love and attention, and Zane was no exception. He worshipped Summer, but still he wanted a son. The only problem was that we would have to postpone our plans to find a home of our own. Zane had at last agreed that it was time for us to move out, but his new job was too far away for him to come home every evening and now that I was pregnant he was reluctant to leave me alone at night. The political situation was also very uncertain: a group of army officers threw the Baathists out of government in a military coup that left everyone feeling uneasy, as some of them were the same officers who had collaborated with the Baathists. There were many arrests and details were published of atrocities carried out by the previous government. Somehow this did little to reassure everyone that more settled times were on their way.

Saleh told us that the police in Basra had been inundated with phone calls from Baathist party members requesting that their weapons be collected by police officers. Like all bullies, they caved in once they were deprived of their back-up; apparently some of the police officers were none too gentle when they went to collect the weapons, but Saleh did not approve of such unprofessionalism, wisely realising that it would simply create grudges which might open the door to future reprisals. Amidst all this, Emir arrived home unannounced; if he thought he would receive a hero's welcome he was wrong. Everyone in the family was furious, they had thought he would have the sense to knuckle down and graduate at last but it was obvious that he had been feted in Cairo as a political dissident and had done little, if any, work. He even told us that he had met President Nasser, but we felt that he added this little detail not only to glamorise himself but also to justify how busy he had been. Who knows, perhaps he did. Omar declared to his parents that he washed his hands of him and was not to be contacted if he got into any more trouble. Zane and Layla immediately jumped to his defence, but to be honest, who could blame Omar?

# Chapter Seven

Emir took to bringing a Palestinian medical student home every evening so they could study together. The family did not consider this a good sign as it was hard to understand how a Palestinian could be non- political. There was a small Palestinian community in Baghdad, many of whom lived in a specially built apartment complex, probably so the government could keep tabs on them. This particular boy, Issam, was extremely nice, unfailingly polite and he turned out to be very helpful to me.

Emir suggested a good gynaecologist and I used to visit her once a month for a check- up. My in laws thought this an outrageous waste of money – doctors were for when you were ill, not pregnant. Mum kept telling me how she had borne 11 live children without any help from the medical profession. Nadia had been born in hospital but only because Omar, who was an adult by then, insisted. Apparently the nurses had assumed he was the father as she looked so young. In fact, the doctor's fee was ridiculously cheap and I couldn't understand what the fuss was about. Anyway, this pregnancy seemed to go quite smoothly and I did not have the dreadful morning sickness I had experienced with Summer so I took this as a sign that I probably was carrying a boy this time. One day I overheard a mother calling her child in the street and liked the name so much that I decided if my baby was a boy he would have the same name – Ali. When I told Mum she was overjoyed – I had unwittingly picked upon a name highly favoured by Iraqi shia Moslems. When my son was born he was duly named Ali, making his full formal name Ali Zane Toma. I had no way of knowing then that this combination of names made him instantly identifiable as a shia Moslem. This was pointed out to me on occasion as he was growing up but I don't think it ever caused him any problems.

Some women, apparently distant relatives of Mum, arrived for a mysterious visit. I had never seen them before so I went in to say hello, but for once they didn't seem very interested in me and I had the distinct impression that she wanted to talk to them alone. I left the room, but it soon became clear what all the secrecy was about when Layla told me that they were trying to arrange a marriage with Sajida. The boy in question had recently qualified as a quantity surveyor and was looking for a wife. If the wedding came off, Sajida would be only the second out of Mum's 11 children to have an arranged marriage. As it happened she would also be the last. The boy's family were local land owners who still worked their extensive orchards, so they were quite well off, were well known to my in-laws and had a good reputation locally. This made the boy an ideal match and the family were disposed to accept but before anything concrete could be agreed upon the couple had to meet.

I probably remember that first meeting almost as well as Sajida because it seemed such an odd way to get to know a prospective husband. He came alone to the house one evening and sat in the family room where he was served first a cold drink and then tea and cake. He was very tall and thin, his freshly trimmed hair unfashionably slicked back with grease and he had a moustache. He seemed to be perfectly relaxed and at ease as he sat chatting to us women. Summer was called upon to do the cute things she had learned to do, singing nursery rhymes and so on and he seemed to pay much more attention to her than he did to Sajida, who hardly spoke. He left after an hour or so, and everybody agreed that he seemed a good lad except for Sajida, who once again hardly said anything.

After that there was quite a flurry of visits back and forth; a group of the prospective bridegroom's male relatives arrived for a visit with my father in law and then the women came again.

I had heard a lot about how girls had the right to refuse a prospective suitor, so when Sajida finally blurted out her feelings over breakfast I was a bit surprised at the reaction she got from Layla. 'I'm not sure about that boy, he's too old-fashioned. I don't like the way he dresses and I don't want him.'

'What do you mean, you don't like the way he dresses, he was wearing a jacket and tie.'

'But I didn't like his jacket, it was tasteless and had silver thread running through it. His clothes are old fashioned and his behaviour is old fashioned and I don't want him.'

Layla got into her stride: 'Who do you think you are, do you think you're better than him? He's a university graduate and you only went to teacher training college. What makes you think you'll find anyone better than him? Who else do you think would want to marry you?'

I'm sure a lot of people would have liked to marry Sajida with her thickly lashed hazel eyes and her naturally highlighted chestnut hair, perhaps someone who looked more like the trendy Lebanese and Egyptian celebrities she read about in her magazines. 'Anyway, once you're married you can make him dress however you like.' Her confidence in the power of family members to order the world as they wanted it to be was unshakable. For their part, they were obviously delighted with the match and the idea that anyone would fail to toe their line simply did not occur to their naturally assertive personalities. That was the only time I heard the bride herself express a disinclination for the marriage. As it turned out the family knew a thing or two, because after the wedding it soon became apparent that they were well suited and as far as I could tell their marriage appeared to be happy. Before it took place, however, there were agreements to be reached and ceremonies to be carried out.

All the brothers were consulted and no-one raised any objections. Omar did stipulate that the couple must live in a house of their own. 'We don't want any hassle over arguments

with in-laws about doing the cleaning or any of that nonsense.'
Everyone agreed but I could have cried at the irony of it all.
There were negotiations over what gifts would be offered to the
bride, and how much the dowries would be. There are two
dowries, the pre-nuptual one which stipulates exactly what will
be provided for the couple's new home, right down to the
furniture, and a contingency dowry which consists of a written
agreement that a specified amount of money will be paid by the
bridegroom to his wife in the event of a divorce. This agreement
is legally binding and written into the marriage contract, which
is signed at the engagement party. The amount varies according
to the means of the family but the higher the amount which is
agreed for the contingency dowry, the more prestige it attaches
to the bride. It seemed to me that the prestige aspect of the
agreement far outweighed considerations of future financial
security for the bride, since divorce was unlikely to be on the
cards and most marriages were for life.

I don't remember the amount agreed upon for Sajida's dowry
but I think it was quite high, unlike my own. We were married
in the mosque at Woking, which I believe was the only one in
Britain at the time. My father was nonplussed when the
Pakistani gentleman who carried out the ceremony turned to
him and asked what dowry had been fixed on. He had no idea
what he was talking about, no-one had mentioned it to me and
Zane had not given it a thought. In the end he suggested the
dowry should be fixed at £1, which apparently was the amount
agreed between Omar and Alice, but the kindly official took my
father aside and advised him to make sure it was enough for
my plane ticket home from Baghdad. That was how my dowry
came to be fixed at £100.

Preparations for Sajida's wedding took up a great deal of time
that winter. Her new in-laws had brought her several lengths of
very beautiful cloth which was to be made into cocktail dresses
for the engagement ceremony, necessitating constant visits to
Zahara the dressmaker. They also gave her a complete set of

matching gold and diamond jewellery, necklace, earrings, rings and a bracelet in addition to a wedding ring which she would wear on her right hand until the marriage was consummated – I often wondered at exactly what point the ring would be changed to the other hand. My in-laws' contribution was the more personal items such as underwear, nightwear and the bedding for their new home. Sajida's father in law had provided a house for them just a few streets away, situated roughly half way between their house and ours. It was one of a pair owned by their family, situated right opposite the spot where Saddam would later build a bridge to link the area with the oil refinery at Dorra, close to where Selwa lived.

The second house was to be occupied by Sajida's brother in law who was at that time studying abroad but was soon to return with his Belgian wife. Sajida and Mum made several visits to the furniture makers, finally agreeing upon a complete set of furniture for each of the rooms, again paid for by her in laws. The engagement ceremony took place and I was surprised to find that the men left once the wedding contract was signed, leaving only the women to receive the invited guests. The only man who stayed was the bridegroom, Mohamed, who sat by the side of his new wife for the rest of the afternoon valiantly trying to get to know her under the close watch of the tea-drinking women. Every so often, Sajida would get up and go and change into a different cocktail dress then parade round the room. The guests would then express their admiration by the 'hel-hula' sounds which accompany every celebration and which are so very hard for a foreigner to reproduce. It was mind-bogglingly boring, although the tedium was temporarily alleviated when one of the children accidentally knocked over one of the huge ornamental candles flanking the bridal couple, threatening to set the house on fire.

Although this was the engagement party, the contract had been signed and so the couple were now legally married and free to go out on dates together. This seemed very odd to me, but Saleh's wife explained that good families rarely allowed engaged couples to go out together before this as 'kisses and cuddles might take place' which could cast doubt upon the bride's chastity. Now they were free to do as they liked – within reason – although they weren't expected to sleep together until after the wedding party, when they would leave for their honeymoon. It was at this party that the wedding dinner would be served; both men and women, mainly relatives, would attend this event. The date for it was to be fixed once the furniture order was completed and the house was ready for occupation, probably in the summer.

The other thing I remember about that winter is that it was particularly cold – cold enough for snow, which hadn't been seen in the capital for many years. My baby was expected in April and that fact combined with the extreme cold made the spring particularly welcome that year. Omar and Saleh successfully tendered for a contract to build a pumping station to improve the water supply of a little town called Oom Kuser, near to the Kuwaiti border. Since neither of them had ventured into the sphere of contracting before they persuaded Zane to manage it for them. I had severe reservations about his working for his brothers, I just could not see it working out, but it was a very big responsibility for a young engineer and he was keen to take it on. The other downside was that Basrah, was much further away than he had worked before, which obviously meant that he would be away from home even more. There was now a small rocking crib for the baby lined up next to Summer's cot, which she seldom used as I usually gave in and allowed her to sleep with me on those nights when Zane didn't come home. Layla was planning that she would move downstairs and sleep in Sajida's bed after the wedding, but I was planning that we wouldn't be there by then.

I had been experiencing the usual Braxton Hicks pains, so when they worsened on one of the rare occasions when Zane was at home it seemed perfect timing. We set off for the hospital accompanied for some reason by both my parents in law; there was quite a carnival atmosphere about the trip and I left them all excitedly sitting in the waiting room whilst I went off to be examined by the mid-wife. She confirmed that I was in the early stages of labour but advised me to go home and wait as she didn't think the baby would be born that night. 'You'll be paying an extra night's hospital fees for nothing' was her advice. Deflated, we all went home. I went to sleep and woke up the next morning to find that the mid-wife had been right – all symptoms of labour had disappeared. Zane returned to work fully expecting to be recalled during the course of the day but it seemed that the pains had been a false alarm.

Then a few days later my waters broke. I told Mum, who said that labour would soon start now and since this particular sequence of events had not happened when Summer was born I took her word for it. Day after day I waited, but nothing further happened and I was once again well over my due date. This went on for three weeks until one night I felt particularly uncomfortable. I could not sleep and kept going to and from the bathroom until eventually there was a knock on my bedroom door. It was Emir, who had heard my to-ing and fro-ing and had come to see what was going on. He was horrified when I told him that my waters had broken three weeks ago and went to consult with Issam. They both agreed that I should have gone to hospital straight away and Emir undertook to take me to the gynaecologist the next day. She too was horrified when she heard. She jumped up from her desk, instructed Emir to take me to the hospital immediately and said she would meet us there as soon as she had phoned them and made a few arrangements.

Once we arrived at the private hospital I had chosen, Emir left me in the capable hands of the midwives and went off to try and contact Zane. What a difference from my earlier visit. The doctor arrived and explained that there was now a very high risk of infection, so she would have to induce labour immediately. Drips were attached to my arm and once again I found myself forced to lie flat on my back whilst I awaited the birth of a baby. I was all alone, the nurses spoke very little English and I was so grateful to that doctor for staying with me. Mum turned up and ordered her to leave me alone: 'What are you doing to her? Take out those needles, you're going to kill that baby.'

'Aunty, this is not your business; you go home and leave me to do my job and if God wills you'll have another grandchild in the morning.'

Off she went, shaking her head and muttering that 'babies came when they were ready and not before'. Thankfully the doctor was right and early the next morning after checking the sex of my newly delivered baby she was able to say to me with great satisfaction 'Ali's here'. Her fee for abandoning all her professional obligations for the day and staying with me throughout the night until the baby was delivered was ridiculously low. I continued to use her services occasionally over the years until it became apparent that her private clinic had deteriorated into a quick abortion centre and I looked for another gynaecologist. I heard that she had become an alcoholic, which probably explained her need for a constant source of extra income, considering the price of alcohol in Baghdad. Despite this, I was always profoundly grateful to her for probably saving the life of my only son, possibly my own as well. As for Ali, he was perfectly healthy although three weeks without the protection of the amniotic fluid had left him looking as blue and scrawny as a newly-hatched bird. It was a very busy night at the hospital and all the rooms were full, so I had to spend the first day in the doctor's room. When a young doctor came in for his coffee break, he was surprised to find me laughing at my son's comical appearance rather than cooing over him in the time honoured way.

School broke up a few weeks after Ali was born. Saleh's wife and children were going to spend the entire summer in Baghdad with her parents because he was going to the UK on a police training course, so when he offered us the use of his house in Basrah for the summer, I was delighted and accepted immediately, but my in-laws were disappointed that I would miss the wedding party. Privately I thought that if it was anything like the engagement party it wouldn't be a great loss. There were regular internal flights to Basra and Mosul in those days and people used them if they could possibly afford to as the inter-city roads were often highly dangerous. Although the road to Basra was called a highway, there were regular pot-holes and the majority of cars on it were long distance taxis whose drivers kept to the maximum speed of 100 kilometres an hour all the way, not even slowing down for approaching farmers who were trying to lead their flocks across the highway.

Zane regularly passed road accidents on his journeys to and from work and on more than one occasion was first at the scene and had to ferry injured people to the nearest hospital. When Ali was older he loved to accompany his dad to work in school holidays, and was with him once when they came upon a family of three who had all been injured in a crash. Zane piled them into the back of the car and drove them to the nearest town where he deposited them at the hospital. Blood from their injuries seeped into the fabric of the back seat of our car and by the time Ali came home his face was green and he was feeling queasy. Despite my best efforts, the blood stains never came out, although they did fade with time.

Anyway, we were travelling by plane – my first plane journey – so I was almost as excited as Summer that morning as we set off for the airport to catch the plane to meet her beloved Daddy. I felt as though I was going on holiday with my children for the very first time and of course I couldn't wait to be with Zane. The terrain changed as soon as the plane left Baghdad; the land was still flat but it looked yellow and dusty with a scattering of small towns and hamlets which were never too far from the road. The climate was very different too and this was apparent as soon as I stepped off the plane. I had thought Baghdad was hot but Basra was hot with a humidity which sapped your energy and ruined your hair-do within minutes of going outside. Thankfully, Saleh's house was fully air-conditioned so the children were quite comfortable indoors. There was little for me to do around the house because they had a manservant, Abdulla, who did all of the housework and normally all of the cooking. However, I decided this was an ideal time for me to practise the Iraqi cooking skills I had absorbed from watching Mum and Layla. Abdulla seemed quite put out about this and would mutter and shake his head over my attempts, particularly at cooking rice, but apart from giving me something to do I knew I would have to begin cooking for my family once we had our own home so I thought I might as well make a start.

I was also still breast feeding Ali, not very successfully. Every time I had a child I was determined it would be breast fed, but something always went wrong. Summer, who had been born hungry and had latched herself onto my breast almost as soon as she was cleaned up by the midwife, had given me such sore, bleeding nipples that my GP had advised me to give up after a few weeks. I had tried to avoid this happening again by rubbing them with cream throughout my pregnancy, but feeding was still agony. I stiffened and winced every time Ali wanted to feed, which probably explained why he was fretful and cried a lot, so I was already supplementing his feeds with bottles. The result was that I never knew when I would have milk on offer; sometimes I would be leaking milk all over my clothes and at other times I would need a bottle when I hadn't prepared one. Because of this, I tended to stay inside with the children for most of the day, just waiting for Zane to come home. I didn't know anyone in Basra anyway and the climate made taking the children for walks was an unpleasant chore in the summer. Apart from a few trips to the stores in town or a walk along the corniche in the evening we did very little and I was surprised to find myself marking time until we could return to Baghdad again.

Sajida and Mohamed were coming to Basra for their honeymoon; I couldn't think why but it was a popular honeymoon destination in those days. Layla had phoned and instructed me to look after her 'as her big sister' – Sajida was in fact a year or so older than me. I understood that there was something I was supposed to do in this role but I hadn't a clue what it was. We went to meet them at the airport and accompanied them to their hotel where we had a drink with them in the bar. I had the feeling that Sajida would have liked us to stay longer but it didn't seem appropriate. Zane was obviously embarrassed and couldn't wait to go so we made our excuses and left them to it. The next afternoon Sajida phoned, 'Can you come and see me – just you – Mohamed is going out for a walk'. Zane dropped me off at the hotel, where Sajida was waiting in her room. She told me more about the wedding night than I really wanted to know, how painful sex had been and how Mohamed had put his hand over her mouth to stifle her cries of pain. 'Mum said that his family are old-fashioned, so I'd better put a cloth on the bed to show them when we get back. There was lots of white blood'. I tried to suggest as tactfully as I could that this might be semen, but she was adamant that it was 'white blood'. Throughout all of this I was totally unaware that my role as 'big sister' was to certify her virginity by asking to see the piece of cloth. It was not until years later while watching a TV programme on North Africa, where the practice of producing the piece of cloth for the in-laws is apparently still followed, that the penny dropped.

The 'cloth test' struck me as highly unscientific and probably open to abuse by dissatisfied husbands, and I wondered what happened to girls who didn't pass the test. I already knew that divorce was frowned upon, and rarely an option among Iraqi families. My in-laws had persuaded Omar to enter into an arranged marriage when he was younger, but immediately after the wedding night he rejected her on the grounds that his new bride wasn't a virgin. The family were terribly disappointed, since they had arranged the match. The girl was from a good family and they didn't want to embarrass them, so the bride continued to live with her new in-laws for a few months, while Omar enrolled on a course in Britain and left. Layla told me that she was a sweet girl who got on well with everyone, and they were all very upset when Omar sent news that he had divorced her while he was away. When he eventually returned to Iraq he was accompanied by Alice, setting the precedent for marrying abroad that his brothers enthusiastically followed.

The other event which sticks in my memory about our summer in Basra is that Omar, visiting the city on business, came to stay at Saleh's house. He just turned up one afternoon, no doubt anticipating that my position as de facto lady of the house would ensure that I made him welcome, but I didn't. I simply carried on as I usually did, playing with my children and ignoring his presence. He went into the bathroom, emerging later showered, shaved and wearing fresh clothes and left the house. He did not return and I believe he went to a hotel that night. Looking back, I suppose it was appalling behaviour on my part, particularly as he was now my husband's boss as well as his brother and it probably didn't help their troubled relationship, but he had insulted me and until he retracted I was determined to continue to treat him with the contempt I felt he deserved.

The summer came to an end, Saleh's wife returned to her home and I left for Baghdad the next day to be welcomed by a very enthusiastic family. They had missed the children terribly and their absence, coinciding as it did with Sajida leaving home, had made the summer a lonely one for them. They had something to look forward to, though, because Zane's younger brother, Hatim, who had been studying in Scotland, had written to say that he had qualified and would be returning home soon. The next day Sajida called in after school for lunch just as she did before she was married. Half way through the meal she jumped up and rushed out of the room looking rather green. It turned out she was already pregnant, so I was obviously right about the 'white blood'.

I had already met Hatim in Britain when he came to stay with us during the Easter holidays. While he was there, a young friend of Zane turned up on our doorstep and offered to take us all on a day trip to Brighton. He drove us there in his brother's car, but his driving was so erratic and he drove so fast that we were all afraid he was going to kill us. I was particularly frightened for Summer, who was just a tiny baby at the time, but the more I told him to slow down the faster he seemed to go, tooting his horn as he went to show his irritation at my lack of appreciation. In the end, Zane ordered him to stop the car and Hatim took the wheel, but his driving turned out to be only slightly better; he seldom kept to the speed limit, weaving between cars and whizzing round corners without slowing down. He drove that car as if it were a fighter plane escaping from an enemy. The exhibition ended when he sped through a narrow gap between 2 cars, scraping all along the side of one of them in the process. Instead of slowing down he put his foot down and tried to escape. By the time we had persuaded him to stop we were quite a way down the road, so it was an easy matter for the original driver to swap places with him before the irate owner of the damaged car caught up with us. Unfortunately, he spotted the change-over straight away and an argument developed. It took the combined talents of all three boys to persuade him that he was mistaken, but they managed to convince him, insurance details were exchanged and we went on our way. 'Why did you lie about Hatim driving?' I was such an innocent.

'He hasn't got a British licence or insurance'. As it happened, neither had our original driver: I found out later that day that he wasn't only using his brother's car but also his documents. He was so fed up with my complaints about what he considered to be his driving skills that he went off on his own for the day, leaving the rest of us free to have a really lovely time. He must have driven us home again that evening although I can't remember the return journey, so I suppose he must have calmed down by then.

Hatim was a rather intense young man, handsome and smartly dressed with trendy long hair but very stiff and self-conscious. The first time he visited us in Britain I was busy reading up on the history of Arab civilisation. It seemed to be a sensible preparation under the circumstances and Zane encouraged me to learn as much as possible about his heritage. Not Hatim, though, he told me that I was wasting my time and would do better to learn about housework and looking after a family.

Anyway, he duly arrived back in Baghdad and settled into his job of servicing planes at the airport. I suppose he must have shared Emir's bedroom, I really can't remember, all I'm certain of is that he was very fond of Ali and spent a lot of time playing with him and sometimes even bathing him. This was just as well because Omar was making it very difficult for Zane to come home regularly, there always seemed to be a reason why he had to stay in Basra. We had ordered a rather expensive set of solid teak bedroom furniture in preparation for when we would have a home of our own; Zane bought a Persian carpet to complete the décor and once everything was in place the whole family came upstairs to admire the room. Summer was excitedly jumping up and down on the bed, threatening to take off at any moment in the opposite direction to my spirits, which did a nose dive as Dad patted the wood and said 'Good, good, that's it, you'll never leave us now'.

Apart from Hatim being there, life went on pretty much as before. Ali turned into a handsome little boy, very sweet natured, friendly and curious, with his fore-finger always pointing towards some newly discovered curiosity. There was no let-up in family rows, Hatim took up where Zane had left off in that department, but he had a mean streak and could be much more hurtful than Zane ever would. Zane was now away so much that Oom Fatin took to commenting that he must have another wife in Basra; she was only half joking and I suppose it says a lot about our relationship that I never had any worries in that respect. But I was fed up with the life we were living and told him that his next job must be near home; I was determined that we would have a home of our own by then. I was also hoping to pay a visit to my family in England the following summer because my younger sister was getting married and wanted Summer as a bridesmaid. Long before this, we unexpectedly received news of another wedding in the family, triggering yet another family row.

Mum was always desperate for news from her boys abroad and she always encouraged prompt delivery of the mail by giving the postman a quarter of a dinar whenever a letter was delivered to the house. One of her sons, Samir, lived in Denmark so when an envelope with a Danish post mark arrived she didn't hesitate to open it even though it was addressed to Zane. She handed the letter to Nadia to read aloud, while she began to leaf through the photos which had been tucked inside the pages. They were unmistakably wedding photos, showing groups of people surrounding her son and a woman who was quite a bit taller than him. All hell broke loose as Nadia read aloud from the letter, announcing his marriage to a German girl and describing the lavish wedding reception which had apparently only needed the presence of his family to make perfect. The photos were passed from hand to hand while a flurry of critical comments and rhetorical questions burst out from all sides: 'She's too old, she's ugly, she's too tall for a girl, what's wrong with Iraqi girls?' I couldn't believe the fuss they made – this particular brother had lived abroad for years and was well into his thirties, so he was hardly going to take a child bride. In addition to this he was the least attractive of all the family, owing to a childhood accident which had left his face disfigured, so they were quite well matched in the looks department. Zane arrived home in the midst of all the lamentations and was called upon to agree that the marriage was a calamity. Naturally he did not, probably partly because he felt that it was insulting to both of us to make such a fuss over marriage to a foreigner. He took the letter to read for himself, stiffening immediately as he read the salutation.

'Who opened this?' In one second the argument veered from whether or not Samir should have married this girl to how anyone could have the audacity to open his mail. Everyone joined in, enthusiastically confirming Mum's right to know about everything that entered her home. Samir was forgotten and Zane was once again in the wrong with his family for his high handed foreign ways. Sajida's friend May popped in for a visit and joined the fray, admiring the undeniably pretty wedding dress while trying tactfully to avoid commenting on the bride's looks. Even Nadia was fuming and chose that moment to announce that, since her brothers all chose to ignore their countrywomen and marry abroad, she intended to do the same and planned to marry an Englishman at the earliest opportunity. Smaller groups were forming by that time as her mother and sister turned on her and everyone began to zoom in on their favourite argument. Emir, arrived home just in time to hear Nadia's announcement which apparently confirmed what he had long feared – that Nadia was out of control and needed to be cracked down upon. 'Stop her going out in the car with Sami, she's getting too old, she's going to bring shame on us' was his advice as he waded through the outlying skirmishes of squabbling family members, doubtless on his way upstairs to work on one of his schemes to bring equality and democracy to the nation.

I gave up, took the photos and went out to the garden to have a closer look at the photos of Samir's wedding. He was a sweet guy, laid back and non-judgemental, tending to accept people for what they are, unlike the rest of the family. He had helped Zane financially whilst he was estranged from them after failing his exams, rallying round without hesitation, never wondering who was in the right. I felt he had just the right personality to make a good husband.

Soon after that, Zane bought a car, an old fashioned black and white Morris. It was one of several which were being sold off by the municipality of Basra. They were only available to government employees so he asked Saleh to make the purchase for him. Although he paid only 350 dinars for the rather quaint and out-moded vehicle it ran like a dream, probably because it had been expertly cared for by police mechanics. The plan was that he would leave it in Baghdad so that Hatim could chauffeur us around, particularly Mum who still carried all the shopping, including heavy fruit and vegetables, from town. She rarely took a taxi, begrudging the extra quarter of a dinar this would add to her shopping bill. Unfortunately, she usually did the shopping either in the morning when he was at work or in the early afternoon when he would be taking an afternoon nap, and she stubbornly refused to deviate from her normal routine. Hatim liked to take a drive around town in the evening and often asked me and the children to go with him. Sometimes Nadia would come with us, but usually the family had other plans at that time of day so often it was just us. Inevitably, the moans started, often fuelled by digs from Oom Fatin. 'I see he's bought a car for his wife to ride around in, that's OK, his brother can be her chauffeur'. 'It's all right for you to walk to town, Aunty, so long as his wife has her driver' were just some of the comments I couldn't help but overhear since the speakers made no effort to be discreet.

I began to decline the invitations to go for a drive; the weather was getting too hot to make them enjoyable anyway since there was no air conditioning in the car and after a few of these trips I found them as pointless and boring as the children obviously did. Unfortunately, Hatim was offended by my refusals, since he was trying to be kind and make life more pleasant for his brother's family. Soon after that, Sajida gave birth to a baby girl which Layla was going to look after when she returned to school in the autumn. Having more or less brought up her younger brothers and sisters single-handed, she now looked forward to her role as surrogate grandmother, confiding to Shetha in her loud voice that a brother's children can never be as dear as those of a sister. One afternoon when her baby was about two weeks old, Sajida phoned me to say that she felt really down and would like me to go round to see her. Hatim had come home late that day and had not yet gone upstairs for his nap, so I asked him if he would mind dropping us off at her house, which was about five minutes away by car. 'No, I'm tired, I'm not going out now', he replied curtly. In fact I didn't mind as dusk was already falling so the walk to Sajida's house would be pleasantly cool. I gathered some things together for the children, put Ali in his push chair and off we went. We were half way up the road when I heard someone calling my name. I turned to see that it was Hatim, shouting and waving his arms at me. As I stood there trying to understand what he was saying, Emir appeared at his side, gesturing to me to continue on my way, which I did and they both went back into the house.

I didn't give another thought to the incident and spent a pleasant evening with Sajida, glad to be able to help her through her 'baby blues'. When we got home, neither Emir nor Hatim were there, but Nadia told me that Hatim had been furious that I had gone out alone and threatened to 'teach me a lesson' whatever that meant. No-one else said anything more, but it was obvious to me that the car was rapidly turning into just another source of conflict in the family. If I refused a lift I caused offence, if I asked for a lift I confirmed the idea that Zane had only only bought it for my convenience, reducing Hatim to the status of my chauffeur. Since it was impractical for me to drive myself with two such young children and no car seats, there was only one solution. I never mentioned what had happened toZane, I simply asked him to take the car back to Basra, saying that I would prefer him to use it so that he could come home more often. Shortly after that, someone offered to buy it for 700 dinars, a good profit which would be a welcome addition to our 'setting up home' fund.

Unfortunately, the sale had to be made through Saleh, as the official owner of the car. He negotiated the deal and accepted the money on behalf of Zane. By then I thought that there was nothing that the brothers wouldn't do to upset me but I was still astounded to hear that Saleh and Omar refused to hand over the money to Zane. 'You always say you want to help your family, so we're giving it to them' was their reasoning. We never got the money: I don't know whether it ever reached my in-laws, and if it did they never mentioned it or thanked us for it. In those days I would have been too embarrassed to even mention financial matters, let alone ask for what was rightfully ours.

Although Zane never suspected that the car caused such bad feeling, Hatim could not believe that I had not told him about the whole saga. He thought that I used the affair to cause bad feeling between the two of them. Outwardly we continued to be on good terms, but it was obvious he had begun to resent me from occasional snide remarks and sometimes even spiteful little acts. When Selwa brought her gifts of old newspapers I would find them ripped in quarters then replaced in the same tidy pile, unreadable.

Around this time Emir failed what were to have been his final exams and was promptly sent to Coventry by the entire family except myself and Zane. Everyone was furious with him and Mum and the girls refused to do his washing or serve him any food. He still worked in the hospital every morning and when he came home he would creep into the kitchen and clumsily try to serve himself from the saucepans being kept warm on the primus. When I caught him I would always fetch plates and dish up a meal properly, placing the food on one of the traditional round trays so that he could take it up to his room, but he was so ashamed that he tried to sneak into the house without anyone knowing, so I didn't always know when he was there. He also tried to wash his own clothes, but after I found him standing in his underwear, trying to work out the intricacies of the electric wringer attached to the top of the washing machine, threatening to electrocute himself in the process, he agreed to delegate his laundry to me.

This situation didn't last long, however: he was soon forgiven and the anger of the family turned back to the real cause of all their misfortunes – the government. It was not always the same government, as these came and went with monotonous regularity. They were all basically military governments made up of people with an assortment of political beliefs. Most of them could roughly be described as coalitions, usually including some tenuous links with the Baathists, and they always ended in tears. It seemed almost obligatory for the outgoing president to die in a mysterious helicopter crash at that time, like General Aref, a plump career soldier who tried to hold the country together for a while until a fateful helicopter ride when he 'went up as fatty lamb and came down as charcoal' to quote a popular rhyming jingle of the time. The helicopter crash was later a favourite of Saddam Hussein when he wished to eliminate people who became so powerful that he considered them a threat. Most notable of these was his cousin and brother in law.

The Kurdish inhabitants of the northern part of Iraq were launching guerrilla attacks against the army again, a pastime they periodically indulged in. Mohamed, who had completed his national service before he and Sajida were married, was recalled to go and fight in the mountains, leaving her understandably anxious. Whenever a letter from Mohamed arrived she would read it over and over again, poring over the pages until Layla would lose patience and yell 'Aren't you embarrassed, behaving as if you can't do without a man?' or some other remark which could only come from a middle-aged spinster. The Kurds wanted freedom to form a separate state, complaining of lack of opportunity and limitations on their right to practise their traditional culture and customs. My view was that they had about as much freedom, or more accurately as little freedom, as any other Iraqi. As for opportunity, high ranking Kurds were to be found in most walks of life, as were people from the other ethnic groups which made up the population. Education was universally recognised as the means of social mobility and while it was true that children living in remote Kurdish villages were unlikely to have local access to secondary education, it was equally true for people who grew up in remote Christian or Arab villages. The Kurds are a proud mountain people with a rich culture and, although many ethnic jokes were made about them, they were admired by most Iraqis for being hard-working and determined. They were also in the fortunate position of living in terrain which made it easier to hide from their enemies than people living in the lowlands of the south. However, I disliked the way Kurdish tribal leaders periodically switched allegiance, for example from Iran to the Soviets, depending on which state the Iraqi government was on bad terms with. It seemed as though they were the cause of much of the instability in Iraq during those troubled years, but the Kurdish inhabitants of northern Iraq paid a terrible price for it, particularly under Saddam Hussein, perhaps the most successful, if notorious social climber in the country.

# Chapter Eight

That summer we invested in an air cooler for our bedroom. I was looking forward to being able to sleep soundly on hot summer nights, but my enjoyment was rather spoiled by moans from Mum and Dad about the increased electricity and water charges which they expected to be something on the scale of the cost of lighting up London, to hear them talk. On top of that, as the nights grew warmer, Emir took to sleeping on a mattress outside our bedroom door so that he could enjoy the cool draught which blew under it onto the landing. He still kept very irregular hours so we never knew whether he was out there or not, which was rather inhibiting, and if I needed to go to the bathroom during the night I had to step over him.

Despite this, sometime during that summer I became pregnant again. It was not planned: Ali was still in nappies and showing no inclination to come out of them. Home life was difficult and very stressful, I was often lonely at that time and I suffered terrible sickness and headaches throughout the pregnancy. Emir told me about some new miracle pill which could prevent pregnancy so long as it was taken every day and I wondered why on earth he hadn't mentioned it before. I consulted a doctor who pronounced me fit and healthy. After asking a few questions about my home circumstances his diagnosis was that he thought the headaches were the result of my having problems with my mother in law! 'It's not her, it's the rest of the bloody family' I wanted to yell, but of course I didn't. Mentally I included Zane in my resentment. He continued to insist that we lived with his family whilst making little attempt to get on with them, swanning off for days on end and leaving me to suffer in silence the barbed comments which resulted. I had decided early on that I would keep my mouth shut, provided that I was not directly involved myself in the family arguments. They had expectations which arose from their traditional culture and I didn't feel that it was up to me to tell them they were wrong. That summer passed in a haze of tiredness and nausea. Zane's youngest brother, a student in Manchester, came home for a visit and told me he didn't know how I coped with the lack of privacy. In rare moments of clarity I wondered how my own husband could be so lacking in insight, but of course he was seldom at home. Oom Sami was also pregnant, much to everyone's horror. Mum would shake her head and predict doom and gloom, and curse the ways of men, but it seemed the pregnancy was all Oom Sami's idea. 'Children bind a man to his wife, you have to keep giving him children' she encouraged me when hearing of my pregnancy. The idea of her remote and taciturn husband being bound to anything but his business seemed unlikely to me, but of course he may have been totally different at home.

Whilst I was pregnant, Mum and Dad made the pilgrimage to Mecca. I was surprised to learn that among the things they bought for the journey were two shrouds: apparently everyone who goes takes one in the hope that they will die in that holiest of places. The other thing I found odd was that Dad came home with a large money belt to ensure that he would be safe from pick pockets whilst he was at that holiest of places. They set off excitedly to make the long journey by bus, leaving Layla and me to prepare the house for the celebrations which would take place when they returned. Neither of them had been out of the country before and they were overjoyed to be making the pilgrimage. When they came back, Mum was full of stories about what they had seen and experienced while Dad sat quietly and let her do most of the talking, as usual. She had lots to say about the extreme fundamentalist ways of the Saudi Arabians and couldn't get over the fact that even little girls had their heads and faces completely covered. Among the things they brought back was a box of matches with the trademark 'Zara matches'. I thought this a lovely name and asked Mum whether it was for a boy or girl. I was a bit disappointed to hear that it was a girl's name as I was hoping for a boy. I wanted a companion for Ali and I also wanted Summer to remain the pampered little darling that she had always been, but I decided there and then that my baby would be named Zara if it turned out to be a girl. Although Mum agreed with me that a boy would be better, for rather different reasons than my own, she was delighted with my choice of name as I had once again inadvertently chosen a name which was dear to the hearts of the shia.

Zane had more or less completed the pumping station, in record time, and was thinking of where he would work next. In recognition of his efficient and speedy completion of the project, Omar made him a proposition. There were some second hand cars in Germany which were due to be exported overseas. Through contacts he had there he would arrange for Zane to have one for a nominal fee. He could then drive it to Iraq and we would have a cheap and good quality car for very little money. The whole thing could be completed in three or four weeks. I would have preferred a more conventional bonus, but characteristically Zane jumped at the chance, just because it was his brother's idea. I was beginning to wonder whether he actually preferred the freedom of bachelor life. Although he always appeared delighted to return to me and the children and was a very devoted and affectionate father, he nevertheless seemed to jump at any opportunity to leave again. This time I put my foot down: I wasn't going to be left behind with the children for that length of time, I'd had enough. 'We'll go to my family then you can go to Germany, collect the car and come back for us' I insisted.

'How can you travel all that way when you're six months pregnant?'

'How can I stay here on my own when I'm six months pregnant?'

'You're not alone, you're with my family' and so it went round and round, but I was adamant, if Zane went to Europe I was going with him. In fact, I was going anyway, I decided. I had been away too long.

And so it was arranged – we would fly to Britain together, then I would stay at my parents' house with the children while Zane went to Germany to collect the car. Everyone thought we were mad, especially my in-laws, who were probably afraid we would not come back. Omar agreed with them; he told Zane not to listen to me because the trip would only be worthwhile if he went alone and returned quickly, but he had set his heart on the car and I had set my heart on going home, so that was that. We booked seats on Czechoslovakian airways as it was very cheap. The downside was that we would have to zig-zag across Europe from airport to airport in order to make the saving, more than doubling the length of the journey.

A few days before we were due to leave I was checking through our papers. Our passports were in order, both children included in Zane's passport as required for Iraqi children. Our tickets were all present and correct, so I started reading through some leaflets which Zane had brought home. 'What's this about an exit visa? Oh, looks like I'll need one as a foreign national.' Zane, did what he had an increasing tendency to do whenever he was wrong footed – rant. 'Nonsense, of course you don't need one, that's for foreigners'.

'But I am a foreigner'.

'No, you're the wife of an Iraqi, you have a residence permit, I'm telling you – you don't need one.' That was the end of that, since he would have to apply for it on my behalf.

The day came when we were scheduled to leave, the children woke early, excited and happy and Emir had borrowed a friend's car so that he could drive us to the airport. We checked in then went towards the passport control desk, which I remember as quite small and informal. The officer on duty was young, friendly and cheerful, joking with the children as he inspected our papers; when he glanced up at me I knew straight away from his expression what was coming. 'You and the children may go through, but Madam will have to stay as she has no exit visa'.

'But she's my wife, she's leaving with me, surely she doesn't need one?'

'Unless she has an exit visa, she can't leave the country: she can't travel, sir', he cut off Zane's protests in mid-flow. His expression was full of sympathy, but he was adamant. Rules were rules and he had doubtless had plenty of experience of the Iraqi tendency to think that they applied to everyone but themselves. I tried to restrain my tears as I explained to my children that they were not after all going to visit their other grandparents today, but they streamed freely down my face all the way home as I sat next to my sheepish and silent husband.

When we arrived the family came rushing out, naturally bursting with curiosity as to why we had returned. Layla declared that it was God's way of telling us not to go, demanding to know what I had to cry about. Mum just shook her head, 'My boys always think they know better, they never listen to anyone'. I couldn't have agreed more. Characteristically, Emir immediately set about finding a solution to the problem. 'Come on, I've taken the day off anyway. Let's go and get this sorted out.' Frankly, I was glad to see the back of Zane at that moment; the disappointment was so great I felt all my inner resources had deserted me – I just wanted to sleep. Leaving the children with Mum I went upstairs and did just that. By the end of that day, my exit visa had been issued and our flights rescheduled. I had one more week to wait then I would be home again.

The plane which took us to London was a small twin-engined job, crowded with Czechs going home on leave. We had to make about five stops on the way, but I can only remember two – Istanbul and Prague. Once we were safely under way, our fellow passengers began to take refreshments out of their bags, sandwiches and flasks of coffee, fruit and cakes. It was like a picnic, with everyone offering food around. Since they didn't speak English, they used hand gestures to invite us to join in and help ourselves. This camaraderie was quite unexpected, since workers from Soviet bloc countries were strictly forbidden to consort with Iraqis or other foreigners. Consequently they had the reputation of being stuck- up and unfriendly, so it was nice to discover that they were such generous and charming people. At some stage in the journey two smiling elderly ladies also introduced my children to cherries, which were one of the few fruits not available in Baghdad at that time.

We had to spend quite a lot of time at each airport along the way, varying from between two and five hours, so it was a gruelling journey to undertake with two young children. Although I felt exhausted and nauseous for much of the day I was spared the embarrassment of actually throwing up. I even managed to enjoy parts of the journey, since this was my first experience of international airports and there were plenty of interesting people to watch whilst we waited. I remember a hippy type being accosted by police in Istanbul. After a brief conversation, he was frog-marched off, struggling and kicking and shouting 'but I've got a ticket' as he went.

The airports of the communist countries were bare and squalid and operated by unsmiling officials. The doors to the ladies toilets were guarded by overall-clad individuals who were presumably female but might not have been. They handed out toilet paper at the door, only one sheet for each passenger. The paper was of the hard, crackly kind I remember from my childhood and I pitied the passenger who developed a stomach ailment along the way.

At last we arrived in Prague, only to find that delays we had experienced along the way had caused us to miss our connection. There were several other passengers scheduled to go on to London, so we all waited together whilst the airline staff tried to get us on another flight. After several hours it became obvious that they were not going to be successful; we were all getting restive and irritated and my children were fed up with running up and down the airport lounge, tripping up other passengers and generally causing mayhem. By this time we were relieved to be told that we were booked onto a flight for the following morning; we would be taken to a hotel for the night, compliments of the airline. Zane and I were quite excited at the idea of seeing something of Prague, and the bus seemed to be driving through quite a large slice of it. He was particularly impressed by the large number of very pretty girls to be seen on the streets, many of them blonde and blue-eyed – the preferred Arab type. Eventually we left the city behind and arrived at a large, isolated building set in pleasant gardens. We all disembarked from the bus and were taken straight through to a dining room where a meal was waiting for us. As soon as we had finished eating, we were ushered upstairs and shown to our rooms, which were adequate though they didn't boast ensuite bathrooms or extra beds for the children. They were exhausted by this time, so I quickly began to unpack a few things for the night. Zane was looking out of the window, breathing in the cool evening air which was so welcome after the Baghdad summer. 'The waiters are rushing off home already – they must have worked overtime to wait for us'. Summer was already half asleep on one of the twin beds, but Ali had soiled his nappy and needed attention. I gathered up a few toiletries, picked him up and headed for the door, but no matter how much I pulled on the door knob it refused to open. Zane came over to help and we tugged at the door in turn, but with no success; our door was locked. Furious, we began calling out and banging on the door but no-one came and we were forced to face the fact that the hotel staff had locked us into our room so that they could all go home for the night.

Presumably they didn't want us to go out and wander around as we had no visas for Czechoslovakia, but it would have been nice to have been given a chance to use the bathrooms first. We were furious, but turned our attention to trying to clean up Ali and get him ready for bed without any water. After that there was nothing else to do but go to sleep, so we curled up on the twin beds, each of us cuddling up with a child, and tried to get some rest. It was easy for Zane, he could sleep anywhere at the best of times and he wasn't pregnant. It was now several hours since I had last visited the awful toilets at the airport and I really needed to pee. If there had been an empty bottle in the room I'm certain I would have tried to use it, but there was nothing I could possibly utilise, so I lay down and tried to ignore my bursting bladder. I expected to be awake all night, but surprisingly I fell into a deep sleep almost immediately and didn't stir until a noise in the corridor woke us all.

Neither of us moved quickly enough to catch the person who unlocked the door, but once we realised we had been freed I rushed out into the corridor to find the toilet. I can't remember what the bathroom was like or whether we were able to wash, but I do remember having quite an appetising breakfast with our fellow captives, all of them irate and trying to find someone among the staff who could understand our complaints. If any of the staff did understand English they wisely kept it to themselves, however. Whilst we ate our breakfasts the same driver who had brought us there the previous evening appeared in the doorway. He waited for us to finish, then indicated that we should follow him outside to where the bus was waiting. It was noticeable that everyone boarded the bus with rather less enthusiasm than we had the evening before. The driver put it into gear and off we went, all fervently hoping that we were headed for the airport. We were, and we arrived there with plenty of time to catch the plane for Heathrow, which took us to London without further incident.

It was wonderful to be home again, everyone was so excited to see us all, but I think my mother was shocked to see me looking so thin and ill. The children were quite at ease with their aunties and uncles and began teaching them some Arabic words almost immediately. My brothers still remember how to say 'Make us a cup of tea' or 'You do the washing up' in Arabic. Nevertheless, life in Britain was very different from what Summer and Ali were used to in Baghdad and they treated it as an adventure, entering into it enthusiastically. Whenever my mother went to the shops she would ask them what they would like for lunch. 'Luncheon meat and chips' was invariably their excited answer – they had both become addicted to it. I was fascinated to watch them adapt their accents to fit in with everyone else; in Baghdad they tended to speak English with an Iraqi accent but they didn't do that in England. Instead they imitated the speech of the children they played with in my mother's cul-de-sac, sometimes surprising and even shocking me, like on the occasion when Summer went round the house reciting 'Oops, ah, I've lost my bra, I've left my knickers in my boyfriend's car'. Ali always had the knack of getting on with people of all ages and he quickly made friends with the milkman, whom he called 'Mr Muscles'. He really thought he pulled his milk float along by brute strength, not realising that it was motorised, and the milkman happily went along with the deception. Every morning he would ring the doorbell, then bend up his arm and flex his muscles while he delivered the milk. After that he would make a great show of summoning all his strength before lifting up the pulley and guiding his float away.

Zane began making preparations to go to Germany almost immediately and left within a few days. My mother took the opportunity to spoil me, taking over the care of the children and insisting that I rest. She took a dim view of the state of their clothes, which always seemed to lose their colour quickly in Baghdad. I had assumed this was because of the heat of the sun but after just one wash in British soap powder the children's clothes returned to their original colours. As my mother proudly displayed them to me I was not entirely sure that she believed that Iraqi soap powder was to blame. I suspected that she felt the fault lay with my haphazard housekeeping arrangements, but that may have been a reaction to three years of living with my other 'mum'. It did make me think about the effort involved in maintaining high standards in Iraq, though. The locally produced soap powder was gritty and grey and very hard on the hands, yet children still went off to school with immaculate white collars while men's white shirts were bright and crisp. It was also very hard on the skin, so I always had sore red hands while we lived at Mum's because they also used it to wash dishes.

Within a week of leaving Zane was back, this time at the wheel of a pale blue Dodge – my namesake. It was huge, like something out of a movie, with bench seats in the front and huge fins at the rear. It caused something of a stir among the neighbours, in fact it caused a stir wherever we went. We immediately began the round of visa applications, much less exciting this time. One day we bumped into a friend of Zane's in London and went for lunch with him. He had not gone home after graduating but had taken a job in Britain instead and seemed to be doing quite well. While we were eating he told us that we were crazy to return to Iraq because things were going to pot there and we were sure to end up returning to Britain sooner or later. How right he was.

Once we had completed our visa applications, Zane set off for Manchester to visit his younger brother before we left, saying he would only be gone a day or two. He returned about ten days later. Whilst he was away he didn't phone and I had no way of contacting him to check that he was all right. My parents made no comment, but I knew they took a dim view of this method of carrying on a marriage, and so did I. For the first time in more than three years Zane and I had the opportunity to spend some time together and he had passed it up in favour of his brother. I felt not only abandoned and betrayed but also embarrassed that he made so little effort to make a good impression on my family. I waited for him to return, trying to carry on as normal but simmering with fury inside. When he

finally returned he brought with him a sapphire eternity ring –
my birthstone – and the explanation that his brother had been
rushed into hospital to have his appendix out. I found it hard
to accept this story, particularly as my parents had now caught
up with my in-laws and had a telephone installed at home. 'You
could have phoned to check that we were all right, I am six
months pregnant'.

'Of course you were all right, I left you with your family, I
didn't abandon you'. I was starting to feel like a parcel, much
easier to leave with someone you trust than carry around; I
knew I was going to have to do something about that, but for
the time being further argument was pointless: he had already
done what he wanted to do.

Despite his reluctance to interfere, my father could not stop
himself from taking me to one side to ask how I was going to
travel so far by car when I was pregnant, particularly with two
young children in tow. 'Why don't you just stay here with us
until after the baby's born, you know you're welcome'. My
mother listened but said nothing and I think it was her silence
which made me refuse. Although I was very tempted to do as
my father suggested, I knew that my mother was being sensible.
With two grown up children still living at home in their four
bedroom semi, the addition of me and two children long term
with a baby on the way would have put a tremendous strain on
everyone, particularly my mother, and she wisely recognised
this.

So once again we packed all our possessions into a car and
set off early in the morning for Baghdad, this time with an
additional child on the back seat. We didn't follow exactly the
same route as before because we were going to stop off in
Denmark to visit Samir and his wife, Astrid, on the way. They
now had a little boy of about Ali's age and we didn't want to
miss the opportunity to see them before going home. In order
to reach Denmark we had to travel through a corner of Eastern
Germany and we also stopped overnight with an old friend of

Zane's in Frankfurt, so we saw much more of Germany too. His friend, whom he had known since secondary school, had a German wife and little boy so they were delighted to see each other and catch up on news of family and friends. His wife was delightful, charming and pretty and a typically efficient German housewife, keeping their tiny flat as clean and tidy as a show home. A few years later this friend returned alone to Baghdad, abandoning his German family and replacing them with an Iraqi wife who was an archaeologist like himself. I was disgusted with him, as were his brother and parents, but he was unmoved and never appeared to show any remorse for abandoning his family.

The morning we left Frankfurt the weather was very cold and gloomy, with thick fog which barely lifted throughout the day. As we drove along the autobahn, visibility was so poor that we were tail-gating with several other cars. Despite the atrocious conditions these cars were maintaining a pretty brisk pace and it seemed safer to do the same in order to keep up with them, as the light afforded by several pairs of headlights was a much more attractive option than crawling along the autobahn on our own in the eerie greyness. The children were bored, so when Summer asked us to stop for a toilet break Zane told her she would have to wait, thinking that it was a ploy to get out of the car. A few minutes later she asked again, 'Daddy, I want to wee, I can't wait'. On edge and trying to focus solely on the road, he ignored her but soon we were being bombarded by an increasingly urgent chorus of 'I want to wee, I want to wee'.

'It's no good, you're going to have to pull over, I think she really needs to go'. Reluctantly, Zane pulled over onto the hard shoulder where Summer did indeed produce an impressively long wee.

When she had finished we got back onto the road but we had barely picked up any speed before a yellow glow appeared in the fog, swaying from side to side as it moved towards us. We strained our eyes to work out what it was: at first it was rather eerie but as it came closer we realised that it was the light from a large torch which was being waved backwards and forwards by a very young-looking policeman as he ran up the road. Breathless and panting, he pulled open the door of the car and gabbled something which we didn't understand, then making a 'slow down' hand gesture, he continued running up the road. We moved forward again slowly as comprehension dawned – there must have been an accident. It was worse than an accident, it was a catastrophe. Through the fog, the glow from several pairs of car headlights ghoulishly revealed about 20 cars which had all piled into one another, most of them very badly smashed up. One of them had been thrown right across the central reservation, and several had spun round so that they were pointing all over the place. A couple had even been thrown halfway onto the roof of the car in front. It was the most horrific accident I have ever seen and the scariest thing was that smack bang in the middle of the carnage were all the cars which had made up our little convoy only minutes before. As Zane pulled the car off the road again we were very relieved to see emergency vehicles already coming up behind us, weaving their way through the vehicles which were now crawling along the carriageway.

As soon as he had killed the engine he reached round over the seat to lift Summer high above his head, then lowered her and proceeded to give her a series of smacking kisses on each cheek. 'Come here my Darling (kiss, kiss) your wee just saved our lives, (kiss, kiss) always tell me when you need to wee' (kiss, kiss). If fate or a guardian angel can be presumed to manifest itself in the form of urine, then I would have to agree with him. It took hours to remove the unfortunate casualties and clear the damaged vehicles from the road, so we hadn't got very far by the time we stopped for the night, but we weren't complaining.

A couple of days later we arrived in Denmark where we were eagerly greeted by Astrid and Samir, who both made us feel very much at home. They lived near the top of a very high block of flats, something I have never done, and there was a baker situated very close to the building who baked the most delicious bread, cakes and pastries. Samir would get up early and go to buy delicious hot bread for breakfast, again something I have never done. I was already feeling shattered and sick again and I remember that Astrid was very kind, pushing me towards the bedroom for a nap whilst the children played and she got on with the cleaning. She and Samir moved to Bahgdad a few years later, where Astrid did not endear herself to anyone, insisting on making biting and critical comments about Iraqi customs to anyone who would listen in the most crude and tactless way. I think she was just one of those people who do not transplant well – she could not be herself outside of her native Europe.

Whilst we were staying with them several of Samir's friends and colleagues invited us round for drinks and meals. We thought this very kind of them, and it was also an indication of how well-liked Samir was. I could not drink alcohol in my very pregnant state and also found it hard to swallow the delicacies the Danes offered us, most of which seemed to be based on raw fish. Nevertheless, these visits turned out to be an ego boost for me, as more than one of the blonde, blue-eyed Danes made it obvious that they found me attractive. One spent some time telling me how he found dark eyes warm and passionate, staring into my own dark eyes all the while. Of course, it may merely be a Danish custom to flirt when out to dinner, or maybe they are attracted to very pregnant women. Whatever the cause, I chose to take all these compliments at face value and felt all the better for them.

The only other experience which I remember from this journey happened in Turkey in the middle of nowhere. We must have miscalculated the distance to the city where we planned to stop for the night because it had grown very late and we had still not arrived. The children were exhausted and really needed a comfortable bed so I started nagging Zane to just stop anywhere, but for mile after mile no hotel appeared. Just when

I was beginning to think we would all have to sleep in the car we passed a small one-storey building tucked into a clearing a little off the road with a large sign indicating that it was a hotel. Slowing down, Zane asked, 'What do you think, shall I go back?'

'Yes, I'm sure it'll be fine; I only hope that there will be someone still awake who can let us in.' When we returned to the spot where we first saw the 'hotel' sign we realised that the arrow which pointed towards the building appeared to have been hand painted by an amateur. Obviously this establishment was not going to give the Ritz any sleepless nights. We drove up the dusty, unpaved track towards the hotel, climbing stiffly out of the car when we reached it. I opened the rear door to get the children ready as Zane banged on the solid wooden door. He had to knock several times before eventually it opened to reveal the large, portly figure of a middle-aged man carrying what looked very like Ali Baba's oil lamp. He lifted it above his shoulders whilst he carried on a brief conversation with Zane, aided on both sides by a lot of hand gestures, then opened the door wider. I took this as a sign that there was a room available and began to get the children out of the car, whilst Zane came to help me with them. The electricity seemed to have been switched off for the night, but with the help of his lamp the man showed us to a square room which had single beds lined up on three sides, whilst a large pot-bellied stove in the corner near the door gave off the most delicious warmth; it was just what we needed.

By then I was so weary that I could have slept on a pavement, so I sank down on one of the beds with my arms round both my children whilst Zane and the hotelier stood at the door, still haggling about terms for the room; I was willing him to agree to anything so that the man would go away. I don't think I could have found the energy to walk out of there that night, so within minutes of seeing money changing hands I had removed the children's outer clothing, then mine and we fell into bed in our underclothes with sighs of relief. The beds were surprisingly soft, with plenty of blankets and the room was so warm that we all fell asleep almost immediately. I had what was probably one of the best night's sleep of that journey and awoke feeling rested and ready for anything. This was just as well because when we awoke we couldn't believe the reality of the cosy place where we had spent the night.

Unenhanced by the soft glow of the oil-lamp the room was revealed as a windowless, filthy hovel with stained and peeling walls and a floor which had not been washed for a very long time. The pillows were soiled and coverless while the sheets were stained and stiff with dirt. The blankets which had been so welcome in the night turned out to be blotched and covered with stains which it was simply better not to look at too closely. On the bright side, the stove was still pumping out warmth, so we each dressed one of the children as quickly as we could in the same clothes they had been wearing the day before. I didn't need Zane saying to me 'Come on, let's get out of here'. As soon as Ali was dressed I picked him up and, taking Summer's hand, opened the door and hurried out, not into a corridor as I had expected but into another square room.

This time it was rough wooden benches which were placed against three of the walls, and they were all more or less occupied. Burly, tough looking men wearing loosely tied turbans were ranged along them, some with one leg tucked casually beneath the other, all with their eyes fixed on us. They didn't look particularly interested in us, nor did they appear uninterested, they simply looked alert. Some of them were drinking from traditional tea glasses, dunking pieces of bread in the sweet black tea as they kept up their surveillance. I say 'surveillance' because several of them were obviously armed, with rifles leaning against the benches and belts full of ammunition strapped across their chests. I stopped in my tracks and let Zane move in front of us, just as our host of the night before entered the room with more tea on a tray. He gestured that we should eat something, pointing towards the glasses of tea on his tray. I had no intention of letting the children eat or drink anything in that place. 'Come on, let's just go'. The man gestured towards the children, obviously indicating that they should eat. 'Just drink some tea, don't offend them' said Zane, taking a glass for himself. His words scared me more than the guns. I wondered what they might do if they were offended. I tried to look grateful and even smile as I took a glass of tea and lifted it to my lips but try as I might I could not swallow any. It didn't matter, accepting the drink was obviously enough to satisfy our host, however, for he nodded his satisfaction as I replaced the glass on the tray. Taking this as a sign that we were free to go, I tugged on Summer's hand and we moved towards the door. Zane gulped down a mouthful of his tea, picked up her up and we walked briskly out of the door where we found that, against all the odds, the car was still parked exactly where we had left it.

We jumped into it and got out of there in record time, only beginning to speculate on the nature of the place where we had spent the night when we were safely on our way. To this day I am convinced that we had stumbled into the haunt of some of the bandits who were widely believed to prey on travellers through Turkey in those days. The positioning of the sparse furniture obviously indicated a 'backs against the wall' mentality; I assumed this was because they lived in fear of the law but of course this may have been wildly inaccurate. Whatever the truth, we were very happy to get out of there with our persons and possessions intact; surprisingly, none of us suffered any ill effects from our night in that filthy room.

We went on to Baghdad without further incident, although our reception at home was noticeably less warm than the first time we turned up on their doorstep. Once again we had arrived more or less penniless, mainly because we had stayed much longer than originally planned. Once again Zane was jobless which annoyed his family a lot because apparently two different contractors, knowing he was looking for work, had tried to contact him with job offers whilst we were away. Worse still, the duty payable on imported cars had been raised to 100% whilst we were away, so it was likely that the car would be impounded. True to character, the family lost no opportunity to remind us that none of this would have happened if Zane had gone alone and returned quickly, and Omar lost no time in agreeing with them, winding them up by bewailing the wonderful job opportunities Zane had apparently missed out on. 'I told him, he wouldn't listen to me, he has to do what his wife wants'. It was useless to remind everyone that we could have bought return plane tickets, gone for a month and still had savings if it weren't for the hare-brained scheme of the car. The point was, we hadn't and we had no-one to blame but ourselves.

To make matters worse, Emir, who had failed two subjects in the end of year exams, had now passed them and was a doctor at last. Of course, this was wonderful news but Omar chose to celebrate by going out and buying him a brand new VW Beetle, just at the time when Zane had to hand our car over to the customs officials. We couldn't help feeling that he had done this out of spite, particularly as he and Emir had never appeared to be close and in fact I don't remember them ever being on speaking terms before that. The next few weeks were a very depressing time; Emir sensed that Zane resented his new car and this put a strain on their relationship, which was a great pity as they had always been such good friends. Fortunately, Emir had to spend two years working as a House Officer outside Baghdad, so the tension didn't progress to any major falling out, but I found the constant heavy hints and moans from the rest of the family very hard to put up with. Hatim was also away on a training course in Britain, so when Zane wasn't out searching for employment he was at home surrounded by moaning women, not least of them me. Eventually he was offered a job working for the ministry of oil. Although the salary would be standard government pay it came with a house and I was very tempted to advise him to take it. However, my conscience forced me to point out that we would not be able to help his family financially if he did, and the truth was that he was reluctant to take the job himself, not least because he loved working in the world of contracting. It allowed him to get out of the office and onto the construction site and also provided the variety which was essential to his restless nature.

I think this restlessness, like the volatility which was evident in several members of his family, arose because there was a creative side to their personalities which could not easily be expressed in their day to day lives. Because the most prestigious professions were medicine and engineering they were all pushed towards the sciences and maths from early childhood. The arts were frowned upon as frivolous pursuits only resorted to by those who couldn't hack more serious subjects and even the law was regarded as a second rate career. Dad had his garden, his living work of art and I know that Zane derived great satisfaction from seeing the completion of an engineering project – he would never have been happy spending all day sitting behind a desk.

Around this time, on one of the rare occasions when Layla wasn't at home, Oom Sami called in for a chat. I offered her a drink and as we sipped our tea the subject of this job offer came up. 'You know, the pay might be less but in the long run it would be better for you. He would be at home every evening, he would work much shorter hours and you would have a home of your own' was her advice. 'But don't tell the rest of the family I said that, they'll think I'm interfering with their daughter in law'. How well she knew them! This was exactly their reaction when I inadvertently let slip what she had said. Mum was incensed and immediately went over to tell her to stop meddling in things which didn't concern her. For several weeks after that neither she nor Layla would speak to Oom Sami, so to my eternal shame, because of my careless tongue she was deprived of her main source of female support and companionship during the last weeks of her pregnancy.

At any rate, Zane didn't take the job and things continued to be difficult at home. Hatim returned to find that he had been awarded a plot of land by the union of aeronautical engineers. This was the first I had heard of the government initiative to help professionals build their own homes by parcelling out land through the unions and I wondered why Zane had not been so lucky. Incredibly, when I mentioned it I found that he had not bothered to register with his union. I couldn't believe that he hadn't even mentioned it to me, particularly as he knew how much I longed for a home of our own, a desire which had intensified in the past few months. Unfortunately, it was too late to do anything about it by then and we never benefited from this admirable government initiative. To make matters worse, there was now something else for the family to moan about, as Hatim needed money to start building and everyone seemed to think it was down to us. There were the usual veiled and not so veiled comments, particularly from Layla. I have no idea where on earth she thought the money would come from – she obviously thought we had money stashed away somewhere.

A few weeks after we arrived, Sofia came over to tell us that her mother was in labour. Apparently her husband had dropped her off at the hospital on his way to his office but, as her mother hadn't arrived in Baghdad to help out yet, she was alone. As usual, Mum was out but as soon as she came home and heard the news she rushed off to the hospital to attend the friend she had ignored for the past few weeks. Just as had happened on the previous occasion, she didn't return until late in the evening and once again her face was solemn as she told us that a little girl had been born after a long and very difficult labour. From her expression I thought that the baby was expected to die again, and it was probably because I was pregnant myself that I found the idea of her all alone in hospital so depressing. Mum also told us that Oom Sami had left home in such a rush that she had not taken everything she needed with her. One of the nurses offered to go to the pharmacy for her but when Mum took Oom Sami's purse out of the bedside locker she was astounded to find that, instead of the expected dinars, it was stuffed with newspaper cut into pieces.

Zane had taken to going to the engineers' club regularly in the evening in the hope of hearing of work, so I went to bed alone that night. The next morning I was awoken very early by the sound of wailing. I rushed downstairs as fast as my lump would allow to find Oom Sami's two daughters in the hallway. They were sobbing broken-heartedly and Layla and Nadia were crying too. It took a few moments before it sank in that their mother had died in the night; even though Mum had told us that she was very poorly it hadn't entered my head that she might actually die. The rest of the morning passed in a blur, but by mid-day the coffin bearing Oom Sami's body was outside her front gate. That was not at all unusual – when someone died they were always buried immediately. The body would be taken straight from the place of death to the nearest hospital where the death certificate would be issued, then driven straight to Nejef to be prepared for burial. Moslems aren't buried in a casket but are placed in the ground covered only by a shroud, so they are transported for burial in a rough wooden coffin – I think they are borrowed from the local Mosque. When everyone had assembled, Dad and Zane went out to accompany the bereaved husband on his journey to Nejef where he would bury his wife. A few relatives and some of the other neighbours went too, but Mum was the only woman – it wasn't customary for younger women to attend burials. The baby was also taken to Nejef to be brought up by her grandmother but I have no idea who took her there, she certainly wasn't brought home that morning.

As we stood in front of our house waiting for the funeral cars to set off there was the sound of wailing and the local cleaning woman came running down the road. As she ran, she hitched up her abaya with one hand and slapped herself on the head with the other in the traditional sign of mourning. She regularly used to help Oom Sami with household chores and laundry and I had often seen them chatting together over the wash tub as they both scrubbed away at the mountain of washing produced by her large brood. When everyone was ready, the car carrying the coffin started up the road, Sami pulled in behind it and followed the remains of his mother as she was taken back to the city of her birth for the last time. The little convoy drove up the street flanked by people standing in silence at every gate as the neighbours waited to pay their last respects. The wake and funeral services would also take place in Nejef, so when the cars turned the corner Oom Sami simply disappeared from our lives without ceremony. Once they were out of sight, her other children went back into the house to begin their life as motherless orphans.

Saleh's wife was also expecting a baby a little after mine was due. She came to stay in Baghdad with her family whilst she waited for it to arrive. This would be her fourth child and she wanted it to be born in a Baghdad hospital because her previous labours had been very long and difficult. She came to visit and it was clear that the death of Oom Sami had upset and frightened her considerably. 'Aren't you scared?' she asked me repeatedly, looking very scared herself. Strangely, I was not: I was very sad about Oom Sami's death, but I found it hard to believe that women still died in childbirth, it was like something out of a historical novel. My due date arrived but once again I had to wait for three weeks before my baby was ready to move. The first labour pains began in the early evening around the time that Zane was thinking about going to the union to meet someone who might have a job for him. When I told him, the news spurred him into a flurry of activity. He rushed upstairs, showered and threw his clothes on then proceeded to go out as planned. I can't say that I wasn't hurt by this apparent lack of feeling, but in my heart I knew that the imminent arrival of an extra mouth to feed placed added pressure on him to find employment. Years later, whilst I was teaching an evening class of English for mature students, one of them wrote an essay describing how her ex-husband had left her alone when she was in labour while he went to the pub. There was great hilarity in the class as she described this as the beginning of the end of her marriage, but somehow I couldn't bring myself to tell them about my own experience.

Anyway, by the time Zane came home that evening I was well into labour and my tiny little second daughter was born a few hours after I arrived at the hospital. She weighed barely five pounds with such shiny black hair and very white skin that she was immediately nick-named Snow White, officially Zara. The next day I waited for visitors, but none came until early evening when Zane arrived. He seemed distracted and left after a very short time, leaving me alone again until the next day when Mum and Layla came to see me. I would have liked to have gone home with them but it was customary to stay in hospital for three days after having a baby, so I had to stay even though I felt perfectly well. Thank goodness there was an English girl working as a nurse at the hospital; she was also married to an Iraqi and she popped in for a chat whenever she could. I think she must have had a hard time because she was living with her in laws in an area where the houses were old and crowded together in narrow streets with hardly any gardens; they must have been hell in hot weather. Despite this she was brisk and uncomplaining and she made me laugh with stories of difficult patients and panicking husbands, helping me forget my enforced isolation. She first came into my room the morning after Zara was born, in response to my bell. I had rung to find out the reason for the blood-curdling screams which must have been heard all over the hospital. 'Oh, a woman's just been taken into the delivery room'.

'But what are they doing to her?' I had mental pictures of babies being torn from the womb without benefit of anaesthetic. 'Nothing, Iraqi women often like to scream when they're in labour. She's been cursing her husband all night too.

I think it makes them feel better.' I obviously had a lot to learn about attention seeking because I certainly wasn't getting much attention from my nearest and dearest.

The English nurse went off duty for a couple of days on the second evening, taking all my English magazines with her, and I was alone again until Zane came to take me home. I always felt the absence of my mother dreadfully when I had a new baby, it was the time when I missed her the most. On this occasion I felt particularly miserable and neglected, especially as he couldn't wait to go out again soon after we arrived home. Layla couldn't wait to fill me in on the details: 'He's gone to our cousin's wake: he died whilst you were in hospital. Zane told us not to tell you because you'd be upset. He's been helping with the funeral arrangements'. Layla was referring to a young cousin who had recently been to the UK for treatment for congenital heart disease. His sister had also died of heart disease a few years before leaving his widowed mother to bring up her little girl. 'But I only saw him once for a few minutes, why would I be upset? I would have felt much better if I had known what was going on'.

'Yes, that's what I said. Why would you be upset? It's not as if you ever worry about anyone but yourself.'

I was astounded, even though it had been impossible not to be aware of the sea change in the attitude of the family towards us since we returned from Britain. Before that they had regularly moaned about Zane, sometimes justifiably, but they had always been careful to exclude me from criticism, at least whilst I was present. It was also very unfair because I had always been extremely mindful of the fact that we were living in their house, respecting their customs and going out of my way to avoid doing anything which might offend them. Not only that, I had helped Layla with her sewing and in lots of other ways and if I'm honest she never did anything for me in return, apart from playing with my children when it suited her. Now, for the first time I was made to feel like an unwelcome outsider. This change manifested itself in various ways. From the beginning, Mum had pronounced that 'Zara's forehead was unlucky', presumably because Zane was unemployed when she was born. They paid her hardly any attention, barely glancing in her direction, in marked contrast to the fuss they had made over our first two children. The idea that our beautiful little girl could be anything but a blessing infuriated me, especially as Zane found a job a few days after she was born. Most of the time, Mum and Layla behaved as if I had not had a baby at all and seemed to expect me to carry on with my share of the household chores as usual. One day I was upstairs tending to the baby when I was overcome by dizziness and fell over. As soon as I felt well enough I went downstairs and told them that I had just fainted; they merely looked at me for a moment and then carried on talking as though I hadn't spoken at all.

Summer and Ali were also affected by changes in the house. Sajida had returned to work whilst we were away, leaving her baby with Layla every day. During that time, Layla simply transferred her affections and most of her attention to her new charge. I found this very hard to understand, even though part of me welcomed it because it meant she interfered less in how they were raised. I could understand that the new baby must seem like a grandchild to her, as she had more or less brought Sajida up herself, and I understood that the family were doling out some 'tough love' because we hadn't listened to them, but it seemed very mean to punish us through the children. Anyway, with three children to look after now I had little time to worry about it – their spiteful behaviour simply made me more determined than ever to move out as soon as we could.

We still had to live through one or two more dramas before this was to happen, though. The first occurred just after lunch one day. I had finished feeding Zara and had settled her off to sleep when there was a commotion downstairs loud enough to make me rush out despite my reluctance to get involved in family matters. As I descended the stairs I was confronted by a totally black figure. It was jumping about and shrieking like a whirling dervish, while Layla and Nadia, also shrieking, tried to restrain it. It was like a scene from an old-fashioned film about Africa; the figure leapt and spun around, waving its arms and causing the long topknot of hair to swing from side to side. Despite the familiarity of that pony tail it still took several seconds before I realised that the figure was Sofia, Zakiya's eldest daughter.

It turned out that, after she returned from school she had decided to light the hamam burner in order to heat the water for the family baths. It was the first time she had lit the burner herself and she had several false starts. She was still wearing her school uniform of a polyester pleated skirt and tights and when it suddenly flared up after several attempts to get it going, it set her clothes alight. Sofia's first instinct had been to run to Layla and I have to say that she couldn't have done better because Layla was marvellous on that occasion: she calmed her down and took her into the bathroom where she helped take off her clothes and gently examined her injuries. Luckily, it turned out that it was mostly soot on her face and neck but her hands and legs were quite badly burned and the tights she was wearing had melted on her legs, making matters worse. She was obviously in need of medical attention, so Mum called for a taxi and took her off to the hospital for treatment. When they came home a couple of hours later, Sofia's legs were swathed in bandages and she was in considerable pain. For several weeks she was quite unable to go to school, let alone carry out her newly inherited role as housekeeper, so her younger sister had to take over. It seemed as though that family's suffering would never come to an end.

# Chapter Nine

In the meantime I was having my usual struggle with breast feeding. I was determined to complete the forty days of breast feeding which are supposed to provide a baby with immunity from disease, but one night I woke with a fever and excruciating pain in my right breast. It was throbbing and swollen and when I tried to feed the baby I found that it was not only an angry red colour but unusually hard. It happened that Emir was at home on leave and he had brought his friend Issam with him. I was very obviously unwell, and on hearing what the problem was Emir asked me if I would mind if Issam examined me. I would gladly have shown my boobs to anyone if only the pain would go away so I was duly examined by Issam, who after one glance said confidently that it was a breast abcess which would have to be lanced immediately. I would also have to stop breast feeding straight away, much to my secret relief. First thing in the morning, Zane took me to a nearby hospital where a young doctor gave me a whiff of chloroform before opening the abcess; as soon as he did the pain disappeared as if by magic. It seemed that Issam was always there waiting in the wings when I needed help, calm and efficient.

A few years later Zane was travelling on business and as he disembarked at Beirut airport he realised for the first time that Issam had been on the same flight. They greeted each other warmly, but as they climbed on the bus Issam said 'Zane, please don't come anywhere near me at the airport, I'm being watched and I don't want you to get involved'. That was the last time either of us saw him. He was shot and killed in Beirut quite soon after that and his younger brother, an aeroplane engineer, was also killed. It was rumoured that Issam was involved in secret negotiations with the Israelis in an effort to bring about peace between them and the Palestinians. This may well have been the case: there are always people on both sides of any conflict whose interests would not be served by peace. Whatever the truth, it was a tragic waste of a talented doctor and a good man; he was certainly a good friend to me. Issam had a third brother who gave up after that and went to live in America, where I hope he managed to make a good life for himself and his family.

Zane's new boss was a contractor who came from Mosul in the north of Iraq. Like the Scots in Britain, people from that area are reputed to be very careful with money and are said to be reluctant to part with it. We were looking forward to his first pay packet, but the end of the month came and went and still no pay was forthcoming, just a promise that the money would be available soon. The other engineers, who had been working on the project for several months, were also from Mosul. They did not seem to be unduly worried about the delay, so there was nothing to do but wait. Several days passed and there were the usual rumblings from the family, then a direct question from Layla. 'Is it true that Zane hasn't been paid yet?'

'Of course it's true, why would he lie? He would have given Mum her money if he'd been paid, wouldn't he?' Non-intervention was becoming increasingly difficult and my determination to maintain dignity in the face of these onslaughts was wearing very thin.

Every morning a car would come to collect Zane and off he would go, leaving me to face the gathering storm. That's the only way I can describe the atmosphere at home by then: there was a palpable air of tension and trouble brewing – the air felt thick with it. I took to going to bed early, partly because I was tired but also because I couldn't bear to be downstairs. In the end, Dad solved the problem. He resorted to the simplest and perhaps most obvious method: he threw us out.

He did this first thing one morning following a night when I had lain in bed listening to the wrangling coming from downstairs. When Zane came upstairs he lay on the bed staring at the ceiling. Although he refused to tell me what the row had been about, he was obviously very upset. This was totally out of character – in the past he had appeared to enjoy family rows, as I suspected they all did, but I knew from his demeanour that this was different. Despite my tiredness, it was several hours before either of us fell asleep that night.

For once I wasn't woken early by any of the children, so I stayed in bed dozing while Zane dressed for work. As he moved about the room we heard the sound of voices coming upstairs, then the door burst open and Dad and Hatim burst into our bedroom. For some bizarre reason Hatim was carrying a kettle of hot water. 'Get out, take your wife and children and go. Come on, come on, get out, leave as you came – with nothing.' I jumped out of bed, stunned beyond belief to hear my usually mild and reasonable father in law actually raising his voice.

As soon as I moved he directed his attention to me. 'Come on, take your brats and go – we don't want you here.' Summer was awake and beginning to cry, Zara was not yet six weeks old, and the family who had professed to love us so much were chucking us out. I was so shocked that I don't believe I uttered a word, apart from trying to calm the children. Hatim was making threatening gestures at Zane with the kettle, taking care not to come too close. 'All right, all right, we'll go, just wait until I come home from work'.

'No, you'll go now, I want you out now, you and your brood,'

'Just wait, I'll go and get a taxi. Leave her alone, what's wrong with you?' This was because I had begun to collect some nappies and other essentials, but when I moved to open the wardrobe Dad barred my way. 'No, leave those, don't touch anything. Come on, you're not taking anything with you. You came with nothing and you can leave with nothing'.

I found this not even worthy of a response so I gave him the most withering and disdainful look I could muster, brushed past him with my children and went downstairs. I don't remember passing anyone as I walked through the house and went out onto the terrace. The car which usually took Zane to work was already waiting outside and I watched as he leaned into the window to speak to one of the waiting engineers. I don't know what excuse he gave but he told them that he couldn't go to work that day and asked them to send a taxi for us when they reached the main road. One of the engineers, Adnan, was married to a Swedish girl and although they became life-long friends, they have never once asked about that morning and for my part I have never mentioned it to them either. As a matter of fact, although I had many close friends in Baghdad, I never told any of them what happened that day. When the taxi arrived we climbed in, put our arms around our crying children and drove to his eldest sister's house in New Baghdad. It wasn't until we were safely inside and the children had run off to play with their cousins that I allowed myself to cry. I doubt whether I'll ever know what really prompted their actions that day – perhaps they were as fed up with the atmosphere at home as I was. Eventually we did become reconciled, but I never felt the same about the family from that time and I no longer felt a need to respect their traditions and values. For their part, they always denied throwing us out of the house, saying that we wanted to leave anyway, and I could not in all honesty deny that this was true.

Despite their appalling behaviour that morning, I have never regretted the years I spent with them. I learned to speak fluent, if colloquial, Arabic and I developed an understanding of the society in which my children were to grow up. I had been involved in the dramas of everyday family life but also the happy times, helping with preparations for Moslem festivals and other celebrations. A few days before, the women would sit around the kitchen on their little wooden stools making pastries by the dozen, stuffing them with dates and nuts or spicy meats while they planned the menu for the family get-together which would take place on the first day of the festival. If one of the neighbours called in, she would pull up a stool and lend a hand, even though she might have spent hours making her own pastries earlier that day. Whilst they worked the women would swap cheerful banter over who produced the neatest, daintiest pastries, although I often suspected that a serious competition underlay the jokes. Whilst I lived with my in-laws I became a passably good cook, learning skills which I might never have done otherwise. I can still joint a chicken in a couple of minutes whilst my daughters stand cringing at the idea of touching raw meat. More importantly, whilst I lived with them I had the time to indulge my passion for reading and so was able to read most of the books which got past the Iraqi censors in those days – mainly the Penguin Classics. I read and usually enjoyed everything from Dickens to Chaucer, Zola to Dostoyevsky and this stood me in good stead later when I became a mature student back in Britain. I even read *War and Peace* twice, falling in love with the characters and unable to decide whether I would have gone for the heroic army officer or the bespectacled academic.

Perhaps I even recognised similarities between the characters I read about in Chekov's short stories and those of my in-laws. Despite her penchant for bitching and stirring up trouble, one could not help but admire Layla's devotion and loyalty, not only to her own family but also to her neighbours. When President Kennedy was killed, she wept like any American democrat at the tragic waste of a talented young life. They were emotional and passionate but also uncompromisingly honest and direct and this combination often made them difficult to live with. Nevertheless I learnt a lot from them and I was able to recognise that our relationship was based on completely polar expectations which were bound to cause problems. When Zane chose to live with them and announced his intention to be a 'good son' in the time honoured way, they thought that meant we would stay forever as part of the traditional extended family. However, I had made no such commitment; as far as I was concerned we were to stay with them only until we had a home of our own. In a sense we were all misled by Zane. His wanted to please everyone and ended up pleasing no-one, which is usually the way.

So there we were once again in someone else's house, this time with little more than the clothes we stood up in. My sister in law, Reema, assured us that we were welcome to stay for as long as we liked and set about clearing out a room for us. This was no easy task, as she had 9 children of her own, 8 of them still living at home. They ranged from her eldest son who was just a year younger than me and the youngest child, a little girl the same age as Summer. Reema had been a great beauty when she was young with green eyes and bright chestnut coloured hair which was set off by warm golden skin. For many years she was also the only daughter, so she was the spoiled and pampered favourite of her parents. However, when she was about 12 or 13 her father's cousin asked for her hand in marriage, even though he was already married with children. This suitor was an honourable man who was comfortably off and more than able to support two families. The fact that he was also a cousin clinched it, since cousins had first refusal in the marriage stakes in those days. As Mum put it, 'In the old days a girl could be one legged and cross-eyed, but so long as she had a male cousin she was sure of getting married'. In Reema's case, an agreement was soon reached. Reema told me that the first inkling she had that the proposal was being seriously considered was when she overheard Dad saying to Mum that 'marriage is a hole – you throw a girl in and if she's clever, or lucky, she'll find a way to climb out of it'. She was devastated when she understood that she was to be handed over by her doting father, apparently with so little concern, to take up the position of second wife to a much older man and I don't think she ever fully forgave him.

Her husband, Mohamed, was the manager of a blanket factory. It had originally been owned by a Jewish family, but after they emigrated to Israel it was taken over by the Government. He had worked himself up to the position of manager under the original owners, and had been running the business for a number of years by the time they left. After that he continued managing it as a government employee, earning a relatively good salary and pension rights in return. He was a quiet, amiable man who rarely interfered in household affairs, leaving Reema to rule the roost much like Mum did. His first wife lived with her three sons in the house next door and he was scrupulous about treating both wives in exactly the same way; although he now lived with Reema full time, he still regularly popped next door to make sure the other wife, nick-named 'Momma', had everything she needed. I once asked Reema whether she and Momma had ever been jealous of sharing Mohamed when they were younger. 'Oh no, quite the opposite: whenever he came near me – a euphemism for husbandly sexual advances – I would tell him to go to his other wife, and when he went near her she would tell him to come to me.' Momma must have said it quite often, judging by the number of children Reema had.

Reema's eldest daughter, Tala, was very pretty with a lively and irreverent sense of humour which sometimes got her into trouble. She had been married at the age of 17, also to a cousin, but the first years of her marriage were not happy ones. I think this was mainly because she had agreed to the marriage on condition that she was allowed to carry on with her education – it was not uncommon at that time for girls to marry while they were still in college or even high school. Add to that the fact that couples were expected to produce their first child as soon after marriage as possible, it often happened that a student became a mother before she was a graduate. Unfortunately, Tala's husband reneged on his promise almost immediately. He insisted that she stay at home and look after the baby born a year later. Despite her protests and the intercession of her family he refused to back down. Tala was deeply unhappy and felt she had been tricked into marriage, so it was hardly surprising that their relationship suffered as a result.

There were constant rows over trivialities which she suspected were instigated by her mother in law, who shared their home. Because of these she regularly left her husband to return to her family, taking her children with her, sometimes staying for weeks at a time. They had one of their arguments a few weeks after we arrived at Reema's, so the number of people occupying the house increased even further when she turned up one day with her two children, carrying all their clothes in two large bags. Luckily, it was summer-time by then and there were two large roofs which we could all sleep on at night. Obviously, her children were very happy to see their grandparents and aunties and uncles, but I didn't understand how she could voluntarily uproot them and take them away from their father. 'Why doesn't she just stay at home and sort out their problems? Surely it would be better for her and the children'.

'Because he'll become violent'. I turned in surprise to look at Tala's elder brother, a university student who was sweet and easy going, making him a favourite with Zane and the rest of the family. Reading my expression, he supplemented this answer with: 'Because she'll refuse to sleep with him'. Tala's husband might have broken his promise regarding her education but he was in all other ways a pleasant guy, with a reputation for being helpful and generous. There was obviously some elaborate ritual going on here which I did not fully understand.

One afternoon he arrived at Momma's house and sent a message that he wanted to see his children. Tala refused to let them go despite their eagerness to see their father and there was a spirited exchange between the couple over the garden wall whilst the children watched and wailed. In the end he gave up and left. However, this visit paved the way for a second and before long she was persuaded to return home, much to her mother's relief. I imagine that she was probably feeling the strain of so many extra people in the house.

The older children were all students either at university or high school, so they were at home for the summer. They were a lively bunch and good company, and, despite the over-crowding, that summer was great fun. They would have me in stitches with stories about university life, seemingly totally indifferent to the growing political storm which overshadowed every aspect of life for their elders. Young people from all over the Arab world went to Baghdad to study in those days, bringing with them a sense of freedom which was like a breath of fresh air for the straight-laced Iraqi students. Naturally, all those young people were very interested in the fashions and other events of the swinging sixties, as depicted in Lebanese and Egyptian magazines and it was noticeable that, as the summer got hotter, Reema's daughters' skirts gradually became shorter. One day a scandalised Mohamed demanded to know whether one of his daughters intended to go out in the dress she was wearing. 'It's all right, Dad, I've got tights on' was the ingenious reply. It was also the era when the PLO and the Palestinians featured regularly in international news reports. Although Reema's children were obviously preoccupied by events nearer to home, other teenagers looked further afield for their heroes. We heard one day that one of Shetha's nephews had run away to join the PLO, but had been hauled off the bus by his father at the last minute, just as it was about to head off for the occupied territories from Liberation Square.

We stayed about three months at Reema's. Whilst we were there, Zane insisted on paying her the same amount of money as he had previously given to his mother, despite her protests. I saved the remainder of his salary and when we left we had enough money to fully furnish the house that we had rented just two streets away. It was brand new, built as an investment by a middle aged teacher who lived next door with his widowed mother and unmarried sister. I can't remember how many bedrooms there were but there was a family room as well as a lounge and dining room and a very large kitchen with a huge utility area. Unfortunately, the kitchen had absolutely no fittings apart from the stone sink which was perched on a platform built out of bricks, so it looked very bare and I had no washing machine to put in the utility room. I tried to make it more homely by lining up my saucepans and other kitchen utensils along the walls. To tell the truth, there was nowhere else to put them. The other drawback was that it only had an eastern bathroom and toilet, but as they were brand new and therefore very clean I thought I could live with them.

For a time we were very happy in that little house. There was a large garden in the front and a smaller, enclosed one at the back where the children could play safely whilst I watched them from the kitchen. We had become friendly with Adnan and his wife, Marita, and had met one or two other couples, so our circle of friends was steadily increasing. There were a lot more Christian families living in New Baghdad than there were in Karrada and I was surprised to find that some of them were much more straight laced and conservative than my in-laws were. This may have been because many of them came originally from the north of Iraq, where people clung on to their traditions much more than people living nearer the capital. It was noticeable that the further away from Baghdad you travelled, the more people tended to follow ancient customs, leaving their way of life largely unchanged.

I had never given much thought to the subject before then, but it was obvious that behaviour which is often attributed to religion is in fact largely a product of culture. There were a bewildering number of Christian sects – far more than I had ever encountered in Britain. The most prominent were Christians of the ancient Chaldean sect, Assyrians, Syriacs, Greek Orthodox, Russian Orthodox, Catholics and Baptists. There were also Armenians, Jehova's Witnesses and even a sect which venerated Lucifer, the fallen angel whose members were consequently dubbed as 'devil worshippers' by the unenlightened. This belief may have been reinforced by the black flowing tunics the men habitually wore and their habit of allowing their hair and beards to grow long and wild. Despite this kaleidoscope of religions, there were core values which appeared to be common to all. Purity before marriage and female modesty were expected of all women, regardless of their religion. There was also a universal code of politeness, honesty and respect for others, particularly older persons, which applied in every religion and every sect.

There was a German girl living with her in-laws in the street behind Reema's. They were also Christian and quite well-off, with a large house and live-in servants rather than the daily char woman that most people thought themselves lucky to be able to afford. She spoke good Arabic and was said to have an impressive command of foul language which she used when she was shouting at the servants. She was also rumoured to have been a show girl, and she certainly had the figure for it, being very tall and slim with blonde hair and huge boobs. As soon as she heard that I was staying at Reema's she came round to see me, wearing a sun dress which would have been considered revealing even in Britain in those days. She had a little boy whom I never saw as she always left him with the nanny when she called. She came to see me several times, but for some reason we never really became friends, possibly because she lived such a different life-style from mine or maybe because I hadn't yet shaken off the prudishness I had acquired whilst living with my in-laws.

Another problem was that I never seemed to have a moment to myself, partly because Zara was proving to be the most difficult of babies; she always seemed to be crying, and despite frequent visits to the doctor, no-one could fathom the reason. In the end, one baffled paediatrician told me 'There's nothing wrong with her, it's just her personality. Don't bring her to me again unless she has a fever or other obvious symptoms.' I have always thought that the constant stress which surrounded me whilst I was pregnant must have transmitted itself to her. At any rate, she didn't settle down into the happy little girl she later became until she was well into the toddling stage.

School recommenced in September, and Summer started attending the local kindergarten every morning. There was a mini bus which, for a very small fee, went around the area collecting children and ferrying them to and from school. On the first day, Ali and I stood outside the garden gate, excitedly waiting for the bus to appear. After a while it became obvious that it was going to be late. Of course, I began to worry as I anxiously scanned the street for any sign it, but what could I do? If I started walking to the school there was a good chance I would miss the bus coming from a different direction. There was nothing for it but to wait, both of us standing in the midday sun which was still quite hot in September, Ali's excitement gradually disappearing as boredom took over. When at last the bus appeared, there was just one small face peering from the window. Thankfully it was Summer's, looking very worried, and there were tear tracks running down her flushed cheeks. Her face lit up like the sun when she spotted us and she jumped off the bus almost before it had stopped. The chaperone who always rode on the bus told me crossly that they had been driving round for 30 minutes because 'Summer didn't know where her own house was'.

Zane had filled in her registration form, which was obviously in Arabic, and I naturally assumed that it would include an address. I could hardly believe that a four-year-old child could be expected to know her own way home through unfamiliar streets, but she was obviously the only child left on the bus so I could only assume that the other children were able to do just that. Despite this poor start, we were soon receiving reports from the school that she was 'very clever'. Of course, we already knew that. Children in Iraq were tested every month at all levels, following which a monthly report was sent to parents. Most people were highly competitive over their children's education and I rarely met a parent who didn't tell me that his child was first in his/her class – I'm not sure how that was achieved. No-one worried about so much testing or wondered whether it was excessive, and woe betide the child who came home with a poor monthly report.

Once when Zane was very young he failed all his exams. He was terrified of what Mum would say when she heard but Emir, displaying his political skills very early in life, advised: 'Just tell her you've passed, she won't know' so he did just that. But his mother was not so easily fooled. Seeing his shifty expression, she hurried round to a neighbour with the suspect report. The neighbour read out his marks, subject by subject, confirming all Mum's fears– his results were below the pass mark of 5. Although they laughed about it later, Zane never forgot this early experience and would become instantly suspicious if any of our children was slow to produce their monthly school report. This was never the case with Summer, though. She was bright and extremely quick to learn almost from the day she was born, and hardly dropped a mark throughout her entire school life in Baghdad.

That spring we engaged a gardener and Ali immediately made friends with him. As soon as he arrived in the morning, Ali would go outside and stand chatting to him as he worked. Soon he was helping, passing tools for weeding then standing back to watch while the lawn was mowed and watered. It wasn't long before the gardener began taking Ali with him when he went to work in neighbouring houses, giving him an opportunity to make even more friends. Around that time Zara learnt to walk and she took to following Ali everywhere. When necessary, he would hold her hand to help her negotiate steps or clamber over obstacles, and they soon became inseparable. Inevitably, she soon joined the gardening crew and the little posse would trek from house to house several times a week, keeping the neighbourhood neat and tidy.

I never had any qualms about letting them go, it was a child-loving society and people were not given to suspicions about grown-ups who enjoyed the company of children. Our landlord was also very fond of Ali and turned up one day with an unusual present for him, a tiny, pure white kitten. Feral cats were plentiful in Baghdad. They bred like rabbits and even their kittens were scarily aggressive when cornered. I don't know where this one came from, but it was very sweet and surprisingly docile. All the children loved it, and it was often carried around with them on their gardening rounds. Sadly, it disappeared one day; whether it was stolen or whether it returned to the wild as it reached maturity we never found out.

Zane had a new job working for a contractor who was installing an integrated sewage system throughout Baghdad. At last the septic tank was to be made redundant, although our area was to be one of the last to benefit. Ironically, Karrada was the first area to have the system installed, so once the work commenced Zane began working near to his parents' house, something he had not been able to do during the three and a half years that we lived with them. The contractor came from a very well-known Iraqi family; his father and other relatives had been prominent in political circles during the monarchy, so I was surprised to discover later that he still had political connections and insider knowledge. For the moment, though, Zane was assured of having several years' work ahead of him, so we felt it was time to invest in a car for our growing family. I use the word 'growing' advisedly, because before Zara was 12 months old I found to my horror that I was pregnant again.

After the first few weeks of despair which I imagine accompanies every unwanted pregnancy, I became reconciled to the fact that I would be the mother of four children before I reached my twenty-sixth birthday. On reflection, I decided that it wasn't such a bad idea – it would be nice for everyone if there were two boys and two girls in the family. This pregnancy was also turning out to be much easier than the previous ones, and that helped enormously. Having the car also made life much more pleasant, enabling us to get around and visit friends. It was a huge American Dodge with leather bench seats, very like the one we had brought from Germany. Whenever we went out in it I would find myself sliding to and fro on the front seat as Zane hurtled round corners in his characteristic driving style whilst the children screamed with delight as they did the same in the back.

We could also make the most of Fridays, the only day off for most Iraqis, and join all the other families who were driving out of the city, heading for a day in the fresh air before the hot weather arrived. Even with three children in the back there was plenty of room for passengers, so Reema and one of her children would accompany us at first. Unfortunately, Zane decreed that, since we were providing the transport, she should provide the food, and sandwiches would not do. He wanted rice cakes stuffed with spiced lamb, stuffed vine leaves and similar picnic foods which took hours to prepare, so those weekends became anything but a picnic for Reema. She began to invent excuses not to go, and although I told him that it was only fair that I should take turns with the catering, he brushed my offer aside, making it clear to his sister that he was offended. The idea that she sometimes preferred the company of other friends infuriated him and before long there were tensions surrounding us once again. I couldn't believe it. Apart from welcoming us into her already over-crowded home, Reema had shown us many kindnesses and we had become good friends. I often popped round to see her in the afternoon for a cup of tea and a chat with her and the older girls. Now I felt awkward and unsure of my welcome. It was also infuriating that this happened just at the time when I had the chance of a lively social life if only I had an occasional baby sitter.

There was now quite a large team of engineers working with Zane and several of them had British wives. Someone suggested organising an informal social club, with regular outings and parties, but I just didn't feel comfortable asking Reema to take care of the children while Zane was being so stroppy with her family. In the end, I told him to go alone and was rather put out when he did just that. I did eventually meet some of those wives, one of them 40 years later in a very different country. We found we had many experiences and aquaintances in common and struck up an immediate friendship, but it seemed such a shame that it had taken so long.

As the pregnancy progressed I began to struggle to keep up with the never-ending housework. We didn't have a washing machine and, although our neighbour and landlady had told Reema admiringly that I was 'red hot' at housework and always had my washing out on the line by nine a.m. I was finding it increasingly hard to cope with everything. Things came to a head one rainy morning. Zane had been too busy to take me shopping and our food cupboard was almost bare. I desperately needed to go to the shops but they were at least twenty minutes' walk from our house – much more with the two kids in tow. I looked out at the rain. As yet there were no pavements in the area and the unpaved strips of dusty ground between the paved street and the houses had already turned into mud. Zara had just settled down for a nap, so I made a snap decision. I placed a couple of her favourite toys in her cot, put Ali's coat on and hurried off down the muddy street pulling him along behind me. At the shops I bought the items I needed as quickly as I could – not bothering to haggle – and headed back towards home, ignoring Ali's whinging that there had been no time to look at the stalls. His feet hardly touched the ground as I dragged him along, my heart racing with the knowledge that I had been really stupid to leave Zara alone. When we arrived home to find her sitting quietly in her cot playing with the toys I felt weak with relief and vowed to myself that I would never take such a risk again.

It was obvious that I needed some help at home. Luckily there was no shortage of people willing to oblige and within a very short time, Zane had recruited the daughter of one of his labourers to help with the children and housework. She arrived one morning with a big smile on her face, apparently delighted to get the job. Her name was Mullia and she must have been about sixteen – she herself wasn't sure exactly how old she was. Although she was stocky and rather masculine in appearance she possessed a very feminine willingness to pitch in and help with any household chore. Initially I planned that she could take over the back-breaking jobs like washing the tiles and maybe do some of the washing, but gradually she took over the house. 'You sit down, I'll do that for you' was her immediate reaction every time I started on a task. Within a few days it was quite obvious that when she set her mind on doing something, she had a remarkable ability to do it well, often much better than I could, so more often than not I was happy to sit back and let her carry on. She possessed unflagging energy and good humour and the children loved her. Before long she had taken over the evening bath, giving Summer and Ali a Layla-like scrub which left them red faced and spluttering at the end of the day. Once they were clean she would wrap them in towels before pushing them out of the bathroom door so that I could dress them, then take a bath herself before gathering up her dirty clothes and setting off for her bus ride home. Bath time was one of the jobs I was most grateful to hand over as I found my expanding middle made it very hard to squat down on the tiles of the eastern-style bathroom in order to give them a bath. I drew the line at handing over Zara, though. She was still far too little for such abrasive bathing methods.

Occasionally I let Mullia go to the souq, carrying a basket on her head just like Mum. Once or twice she took Summer with her, bringing her back with some dubious- looking sweets clutched in her hand. At first I was apprehensive about trusting her with the shopping, but it quickly became obvious that she had a very good eye for selecting fruit and vegetables and was also much better at bargaining than I was, consistently managing to buy more goods for less money than I would have spent. On the whole, though, I preferred to remain in control of the shopping and only let her go as an occasional treat. She was such a welcome addition to our household that I would have liked to keep her with us forever, but unfortunately fate took her away from us in the shape of a mysterious suitor and an arranged marriage.

The first I heard of it was one afternoon when Mullia and I were sitting in the garden enjoying a cold drink before she left to go home. 'I'm never getting married, what would I do with a husband?' Her remark came out of the blue, entirely irrelevant to whatever it was we were talking about. 'Well, you've got plenty of time, you don't have to worry about getting married just yet'. I must have been about 25 when I made this patronising remark, but by then I knew enough about traditional Iraqi culture to know that I should be careful what I said. Perhaps I should have been more switched on to her feelings and encouraged her to say more, but as I didn't the subject of marriage was never mentioned between us again. A couple of weeks later her father arrived one morning bringing with him a younger girl who he said was Mullia's sister. 'Mullia's married now, she can't work anymore: her sister will take her place'. For him, it was as simple as that. He hurried off, leaving me with little option but to take the girl indoors. She looked nothing like her 'sister', but was fair skinned with delicate bones and none of her predecessor's confidence. Added to that she was utterly useless at housework and seemed incapable of learning anything. It was partly my fault because she looked so young and frail that I was reluctant to ask her to do much around the house. Anyway, after a couple of days I felt as though I had an extra child to care for so I let her go at the end of the week and bought a washing machine instead.

# Chapter Ten

Whilst these everyday events were taking place, the Middle East was in turmoil. There were constant disagreements between Arab governments as they jockeyed for influence in the region, and then of course there was the Six-Day War. I remember watching lorry loads of Iraqi soldiers heading for the front. They were watched by largely silent crowds; Zane was the only on-looker near-by who applauded them, the others seemed to have sensed defeat already. In fact the Iraqi army never got the opportunity to fight in that war – they were forced to turn back by the squabbling generals. When Jamal Abdul Nasser resigned after the debacle, the general despondency was overwhelming – everyone in the country seemed to be depressed. Whatever one thought of his politics, he was the only strong leader in the region at that time and I think people felt that they had been thrown back into being quasi-colonial subjects once more. There were fears of invasion which I found particularly scary because I didn't have access to enough information to judge whether the threat was real or not. The government routinely blocked broadcasts from the BBC World Service and Voice of America, making reception impossible.

It also introduced civil defence measures; citizens were given instructions about where to shelter when the air raid warnings went off, and there were regular civil defence exercises. I remember sitting under the stairs, cuddling the children and dripping with sweat in the summer heat as the sirens wailed, rather like Americans in the 'Duck and Cover' films of the fifties. Once again, Selwa's family were called upon to cover up the plane on the roof, but the fears did not materialise and eventually it was uncovered as the country gradually returned to what passed for normality.

One afternoon Zane returned from work and went straight into the bedroom, where he turned on the radio. 'Have you heard the news today?' He was twiddling the dials as he spoke, trying to find the correct station. 'No why?' This was unusual because the children always rushed to greet him when he came home and he enjoyed spending time with them – he usually caught up with the news on early evening television or in bed. 'My boss was listening to the radio all morning; he said he was waiting to hear that the government has been overthrown. According to him, the CIA have organised and paid for the coup.' Although I knew that his boss probably still had some insider knowledge of what went on in political circles, I shrugged it off as self-glamorising nonsense. I thought no more about it until the next day when groups of army officers burst simultaneously into the presidential palace and the TV and radio stations where they proclaimed a new government. As usual, everyone gathered around their TV and radio sets, waiting to learn who the new leaders would be. I don't imagine we were the only people whose hearts sank as the names of the ministers were announced and they realised that the Baathists were back.

During that summer Zane also had his appendix removed. It was the perfect opportunity for him to kiss and make up with his family, but apart from Reema they stayed away. He was very hurt and phoned Mum to tell her what he thought of a mother who failed to visit a child who had undergone surgery. I believe she replied that, as far as she was concerned, an appendectomy is little more than a circumcision and therefore nothing to make a fuss about, but she hoped he was feeling better. Partly because of that and also because our new baby's birth was imminent, I couldn't believe it when he arrived home one day to announce that he had rented a house in Karrada and we were moving at the end of the month. He over-rode my protests: he had shaken hands on the deal and that was that. Our landlord and his family were very offended when they heard we were leaving. You would have thought that the house had been built specifically for us. 'We were planning to install a western bathroom for you next month,' the sister told me crossly. Zane ignored their disappointment and carried on with his plans, so when the appointed moving day arrived a lorry pulled up outside and our furniture and possessions were piled onto the back for our journey back to Karrada. This time we were going to the very outskirts of the area, close to a large parcel of land on the bank of the river Tigris which was ear-marked for a new university campus. At that time, although the area was already known as 'the new university', the only indication that a campus was to be erected there was a couple of paved roads which were mostly used by learner drivers to practice on. They were the only paved roads there at that time, and the new university building was not completed until after we left Iraq for good.

Our new baby was actually due in the third week of September, so for the first time I was glad that my babies were always born late. This one's tardiness allowed me two weeks in which to get our new house in order before it arrived. It was early afternoon when the pains first started, and for once Zane responded quickly (and caringly this time) to my phone call. He rushed home, picked up the children and drove them over to Reema, then returned for me. By the time we reached the hospital I knew that labour was well established – I was at last what my first mid-wife had called 'an experienced pusher'. Paradoxically, I felt less able to cope with the pain than I ever had before, and moaned and groaned like a true Iraqi wife. 'Don't you ever dare make me pregnant again', I gasped at my husband between the pains, then 'Don't you dare leave me' as the nurses came to wheel me into the delivery room. Walking beside the trolley Zane tried to accompany me, but he couldn't get past those nurses. 'This is no place for a man, besides, you wouldn't like it' they assured him as they closed the double doors resolutely in his face. He didn't put up too much of a fight and the doors remained firmly closed.

After that, things happened very quickly and in record time I heard the now familiar slap and then the wail of a newborn baby. What was also now familiar was the moment of silence which told me I had given birth to another girl. My heart sank; I had rationalised this pregnancy by imagining a perfect family of two boys and two girls. My mental pictures of them pairing off and playing happily together in perfect harmony had helped me through the bad days. I collapsed back onto the pillows, allowing my exhaustion to overcome all other emotions while the nurse quickly attended to the baby and wrapped her in a shawl. 'Oh look at her, she's beautiful' she cooed as she offered me the little white-wrapped bundle. Struggling to sit up despite my disappointment, I took the bundle and looked down at a chubby pink and white little face below dark chestnut hair. She was right. She was the most beautiful baby I had ever seen, immediately adorable, and my momentary disappointment disappeared. I couldn't wait to take her home so that I could introduce her to her sisters and brother, who I missed already.

As soon as the nurse came into the room the next morning, I told her I was going home. 'I'm getting dressed, call a taxi', I instructed as I climbed out of bed. Horrified, she rushed from the room and was soon replaced by a mid-wife. 'Our policy is that mothers must stay a minimum of three days', the doctor will never discharge you. Get back into bed and rest', she told me sternly as her glance strayed to my beautiful baby. When the doctor arrived he confirmed what she said. 'Dr Hydari (the founder and director of the hospital) believes that a minimum of three days' rest is essential after child-birth. You won't get any rest once you get home with three other children to care for, so be sensible and relax now while you have the chance'. I made several attempts to escape during the next two days but to no avail, even the cleaner refused to call a cab for me, so it was the standard three days before I returned to our new home.

This was, unusually for Baghdad at that time, semi-detached, with two bedrooms and a bathroom upstairs. The bath was extra- large and sunken into the floor with a tiled upstand about twelve inches high surrounding it. It was ideal for bathing all three children together and that's exactly what I did every evening. Later, when Tula started to walk she used to stand near the edge watching the fun as the others slid up and down the bath like synchronised swimmers. She leaned forward and fell into the water head-first on more than one occasion, to the great amusement of her brother and sisters and also the young couple who had built a house next door and could hear the noise from their kitchen window. Downstairs, there was a large through lounge and diner, a sitting room and a kitchen and bathroom. The lounge was sunken too, so that it resembled a swimming pool, with the dining area hovering over it like a huge diving board. There was also a locked door leading from the dining room into the house next door. Despite these oddities, it was an attractive house; there was a long balcony leading from the children's bedroom which they were very excited about. The room itself was large and rectangular so it perfectly accommodated their three single beds with bedside cabinets between them. When they were tucked up in bed with their story books, they closely resembled the three bears which they so loved to hear about.

The next few days were taken up with a stream of visitors bringing gifts for the baby: among them was one of Zane's colleagues with his English wife, Ann. We became firm friends and spent a lot of time together over the next few years. I think it was Ann who was responsible for naming the baby Ghussan after a pretty white blossom which flowers in the north of Iraq in the spring. It was so apt that it became her name immediately she suggested it, although for some reason we always called her Tula.

Summer was now old enough to start formal school and it so happened that a new girls' school was under construction just at the end of the street. It was supposed to open for the beginning of the new term, but there had been delays so it eventually opened a few weeks after we moved into the area. It was perfect: she would be able to walk there and would also make friends in the area, or so we thought. Everything seemed to be going well for the first week, but on Thursday she returned with a letter from the school in her bag. 'I don't think there are enough girls here, so they're giving the school to the boys instead', she volunteered as she jumped through the door – my daughters never walked if they could skip or jump. 'I don't think so, how can they do that?' She had obviously misunderstood what her teacher had said. Unfortunately, she had understood only too well – the girls' school was moving to a building on the main road, about twenty minutes' walk away.

There were two roads bordering Karrada, named the inner and outer Karrada roads. They were the main arteries leading to the city centre, but they more or less petered out by the time they reached our newly developing area. The main difference was that the inner road, which Summer's school was moving to, was actually paved up to the point where the school was. Apart from this it was like the other streets in the area, consisting of a deeply rutted mud track which differed only in being wider and straighter than the residential ones. Zane left for work early in the morning and I didn't see how I could negotiate the deep ruts with our high-wheeled pram loaded with a baby and toddler whilst dragging Ali at the same time. Fortunately, one of our new neighbours had two daughters who went to the same school. They were a few years older than Summer, so I gratefully accepted when one of their parents suggested they walk with her to and from school. For the first few days I was very nervous about letting her go alone. I would stand at the gate watching as the girls made their way down the street, the skirts of their school overalls swinging, white collars flapping as they jumped from ridge to ridge like little goats. Thankfully, my anxiety soon subsided as she settled happily into the new routine. In fact, she actually enjoyed walking to and from school with her new friends.

The friends were not sisters but cousins; their mothers were sisters and they all lived together in the house whose garden backed onto ours. It was an unusual arrangement brought about because the husband of the younger sister was an invalid and unable to work. I never found this story very convincing and later a more likely reason for his unemployment suggested itself. They were having some family celebration which was taking place in the garden and had employed a troupe of country dancers as entertainment. These dancers, known as 'Kowlia' were usually very young and it was rumoured that children were simply stolen from their parents by the dancers as they travelled the country, thus ensuring fresh recruits to the group. It was also commonly believed that male and female dancers offered sex as an additional service to clients.

In order to maximise their appeal, both girls and boys wore their hair long and flowing and were heavily made-up. It was rare to see these dancers perform in Baghdad except on television, so I went up to the roof to watch. As the long-haired girl and boy performers shimmied and whirled their way around the garden, a man leapt up from the audience and joined them, introducing some very suggestive moves of his own. One of the other guests went over and led him back to his seat, but within minutes he was up again. Another onlooker took him back this time, but the irrepressible dancer would not stay down and soon joined the entertainers again. This time it was the host who pulled him away with the help of another guy. Between them they frog-marched him past the other guests and escorted him into the house. From my vantage point on the roof I could see that it was the invalid husband and it was obvious from the way he moved that he was the worse for drink. I couldn't help but suspect that perhaps chronic alcoholism was the true reason for his inability to work!

If it was, no-one in the family ever acknowledged it; they stuck to their story, apparently all working harder to make up for his shortcomings. His brother in law ran a dry cleaning business on inner Karrada Road, and the entire family, including the six children the sisters shared between them, helped out. The two older girls, who no longer attended school, could be seen every morning in the garden bending over shallow metal washing tubs, washing clothes by hand in a petroleum-based spirit before hanging them out to dry. Later, after school, the boys would deliver the already crisply ironed clothes to customers on their bikes. The dry cleaner's wife liked to boast that she could do anything that a man could do, and indeed she would often be seen making running repairs on their house, including electrical work.

The person I got to know best in that family was the younger of the teenaged girls, Halima. She was tall and slim, a natural beauty, with golden, almond-shaped eyes and perfect features. True, her nose was rather strong but that simply gave her a regal appearance. Despite the simple, baggy house dress she normally wore she looked like an Arab princess, or at least how I imagined an Arab princess would look. I think she was fifteen when I first knew her and it was mainly because of Tula that we became friendly. But I am getting ahead of myself because that didn't happen until early the following summer and we had a difficult winter to get though before that.

The house beyond the locked door was more or less the same as ours, except that the ground floor was all on one level and didn't have the swimming pool effect in the lounge. It was occupied by a Christian lady and her daughter, Clare; the mother was tiny and round whilst the daughter was exceptionally tall for an Iraqi woman, well over six feet, with broad shoulders and fierce dark eyes. Sadly, I can't remember the mother's name so I shall call her 'Oom Clare'. She told me that her husband had been a British engineer who worked for the Iraqi railway company, but she was rather vague about what had happened to him. It was years later before someone told me that he was actually Indian. More recently, on a visit to India where I saw huge, fierce-looking Rajasthanis in their fabulous costumes, Clare's unusual physique suddenly made sense to me. There was another daughter who actually owned the house we were renting. She lived just down the road, but had fallen out with her mother and sister for some reason, and they had nothing to do with each other.

Clare worked as an administrator whilst her mother stayed at home and ran the house. She wasn't in very good health, although she was always rather vague about her ailment, so every day she would prepare lunch, then doze on the day bed which was set up in the sitting room, waiting for Clare to return. I never knew either of them to go out socially. Clare had been engaged once but had never married and there were rumours of some scandal associated with this; her sister had married a Moslem but I think she was divorced or separated – I don't know whether this was the reason they had fallen out. I thought they led a rather sad existence, but they were very kind to me and were particularly fond of Tula, who was only a few weeks' old when we first knew them. Every two or three days Clare would help her mother to climb into the car and off they would go shopping for food. It wasn't long before I was accompanying them on their afternoon shopping trips, leaving the children with Zane. This suited him because he hated shopping and it suited me because it not only gave me some time out from the children but also enabled me to take advantage of Oom Clare's haggling skills.

That winter it rained more often and more heavily than usual, revealing the reason for the deep ruts in the road. The parcels of land surrounding us were gradually being built upon, so there was much to-ing and fro-ing of delivery trucks and other heavy vehicles, apart from the cars belonging to people who had already taken up residence. This traffic churned up the roads, turning them into deeply pitted mud baths, but as soon as the sun came out the mud hardened into the ruts which were making it so hard for cars and pedestrians alike. The outer road, which was later to become a dual carriageway, was like a wide mud lake with cars sliding uncontrollably from side to side as residents tried to reach the safety of the paved section. It became so difficult to walk through the mud that Summer lost her little escorts. Their elder brothers began taking them to school on the cross bars of their bikes, skidding their way between the mud and the ruts like a circus act. There was no way that I would let her walk all that way alone, so despite my reluctance to put her safety into the hands of unknown strangers, I hired a local taxi firm to take her to and from school. Almost immediately, her friends joined her on the journey, preferring a free taxi ride to one on a bike. Clare was scandalised when I told her what was going on. 'They're taking advantage of you, why don't you just enrol her in a private school? They'll pick her up in their bus and that will be the end of it.' I agreed that the current situation was not ideal – the taxi firm had already let us down once, but private education was not something which had ever been an option for my family. The only thing I knew about private schools had been learned from the tabloids, and this knowledge consisted of the conviction that the aristocracy liked to send their children to one as soon as possible, while celebrities paid colossal fees to get their children into Eton or other British public schools. 'We can't afford that!'

'Why ever not? It'll probably be cheaper than paying for a taxi twice a day. Why don't you look into it?'

So I did and found to my surprise that, like everything else in Iraq at that time, it would be surprisingly cheap. The other advantage was that the school day ran from early morning to mid-afternoon, unlike the state schools where one building was usually shared by two schools, one occupying it in the morning and the other in the afternoon. The upshot was that for an easily affordable sum we would be able to put Summer into full-time private education, with a cooked lunch and transport to and from school thrown in.

After visiting a couple of schools I came upon one in a side street just off of the inner Karrada road which I liked immediately. It was run by a stout, artificially blonde lady who was both owner and headmistress – Miss Noele. The building occupied what had been a large, traditionally laid out Arab house. The rooms around the central courtyard made perfect classrooms, whilst the courtyard itself was used as the playground and the property was surrounded by high walls and secure gates. The school was named 'Home of Children', which was very apt because all my children, plus many of their friends, felt very at home there for the first eight years of their educational life. It had the added advantage of incorporating a kindergarten, named 'Little Flowers', which Ali joined the following autumn. Most of the teachers were Christians, although their pupils came from the usual cross section of religions. Although they were strict they were fair and on the whole got on well with the kids. There were also two sisters who acted as caretakers, keeping the classrooms clean and tidy and carrying out the less pleasant jobs like changing the pants of children who had 'accidents'. A very tall Armenian lady accompanied the children on the school bus; she appeared to be particularly fond of my children, but perhaps all the other mothers thought that. This efficient and caring team continued at the school unchanged until political events ripped it apart, doubtless ripping apart the lives of some of the staff at the same time.

Whilst we were still living in that house Zane took his first step towards becoming a contractor in his own right. In partnership with a close friend he took on a sub-contract to pitch stone for a well-known contractor. Zane was very happy to be his own boss and would arrive home at the end of the day tired and covered in dust but full of the good cheer and satisfaction which arises from a job well done. The kids would rush out to greet him, Tula shuffling along behind them on her bottom, to be swept up in turn by their father and swung around the garden until they were dizzy. Later, after he had showered he would get down on his knees on the Persian rug and play 'Tigers' with them, a game that involved him standing guard on the rug, growling menacingly and leaping forward whenever a child tried to step onto it. The penalty for being caught trespassing on the rug by the tiger was to be grabbed up and nuzzled until the 'tiger's' day-growth of stubble made their faces red. This game was always accompanied by screams which were only partly of delight, because the kids would get so into the game that the tiger became almost real to them.

After a few weeks, however, I noticed that he was cutting playtime short, using the excuse that he felt tired, then go into the other room and sit quietly – he obviously had something on his mind. It turned out that the contractor was trying to renege on their deal, and reduce the unit price which had been agreed. He had found someone who would do the job for less, and was trying to beat them down. Zane and his partner refused to back down and in the end the sub-contract was handed over to the other man who had undercut them, leaving Zane and his friend without employment. In typical fashion he just walked away, accepting a job from another contractor almost immediately. His friend, however, didn't. He tried to persuade Zane that they should apply to the courts but Zane thought it was a waste of time. 'You go ahead if you like, but I haven't got time. I've got a family to support and I can't afford to be out of work.'

I never expected to hear any more about it, but one day the friend arrived at our house bearing a large wad of Iraqi dinars. He had won the case and been awarded a generous settlement by the judge. After taking out his costs he had divided the remainder into equal halves, leaving us with around three thousand dinars if I remember correctly. It seemed a fortune to us at the time and I was not only very grateful to the Iraqi civil justice system but also filled with a very healthy respect for it. Sadly, once the Baathists consolidated their hold on the country, the civil courts were no longer able to function as an autonomous body. Like most of the other institutions in the country, they came to be perverted and corrupted in the years to come as high ranking party members found ways of using them to advance their own schemes.

I think it was during the time that he was supervising the stone pitching that Zane came home one day with the gift that caused such a hullabaloo in our kitchen. It was quite innocuous – a leaf-wrapped parcel containing what looked like the fronds of a palm tree. He was very excited, calling us all into the kitchen where he proceeded to lay out his treasure on the tiled floor. 'They were cutting down palms and I managed to rescue these – they're heart of palm. They call them 'millionaires' salad' because a tree has to be cut down to make just one salad. People pay a fortune for them in posh restaurants abroad'. We all crouched down, unimpressed, as he carefully unwrapped the parcel to reveal surprisingly white shoots at the centre of the bunch. 'Come on, taste it', he pulled pieces off and handed them around to us. I must admit that it tasted better than expected, but I wouldn't cut down a tree for it. As he reached the middle section he disturbed several black ants. As soon as they were disturbed they left the safety of the palm to scatter all over the kitchen floor. The kids moved back sharply as I told them: 'don't eat any more, I'll have to wash the salad first.' I scooped all the palm fronds up and threw them in the sink, but as I opened the tap and more of the tiny creatures emerged it became clear that they weren't ants at all, but tiny little scorpions, already lifting their tiny little tails as they sensed danger. 'Scorpions – get back'. I grabbed Zara and plonked her down on the kitchen table, then began lunging at the tiny insects with the broom head, whilst the other kids, who found the baby scorpion hunt much more exciting than Dad's boring present, took up the chase. I think I got some, but most of them disappeared into cracks or under the kitchen cupboards, leaving me to suffer from nightmares of being plagued by huge scorpions for weeks afterwards. 'Get that stuff out of here, and don't leave it in our garden'. I was never more grateful that we were surrounded by parcels of undeveloped land. Zane gathered up his bundle and slunk off, muttering that there was no pleasing this woman. I took him to mean me, but I was too preoccupied with catching scorpions at the time to take him up on the argument. Despite my fears, no scorpion ever materialised whilst we lived in that house. In fact, I only saw one other scorpion during the entire time we lived in Baghdad. It strolled past me one afternoon when I was hosing down the garden path, probably disturbed by the water. Luckily, heavy wooden-soled clogs were the fashion that summer so, almost as nonchalant as the scorpion itself, I ground down on it until I heard a satisfying crunch.

Apart from these minor excitements, the weather continued to be wet that winter, casting everyone into despondency, whilst the political situation did nothing to cheer people up. Zane came home from work early one day looking sick and pale – not something easily achievable with his dark complexion. 'Oh, you won't believe what they're doing in town – they've hung some people and their bodies are on display. They're rounding up people in the street and making everyone go to have a look, it's terrible. I had to pass the bodies but I didn't look at them.' We switched the TV on and there they were, the bodies of several men hanging by their necks, their bodies swinging round whilst a commentator screamed hysterically in the background that the men were part of a ring of Israeli spies; perhaps they were spies, who knows? Whatever the reason for those men's execution, the incident established the reputation of the Baathist government as being, inhuman and utterly ruthless. The TV coverage continued all day, with the party faithful making a big show of celebrating and cheering whilst the corpses swayed from side to side in the background. They were obviously trying to whip up mass hysteria, but I imagine that most of the passers- by were reluctant spectators who had been forced to take that route, like Zane. I'm not sure whether it was that night or the following day, but soon after the hangings, some sort of Baath party celebration was shown on TV, and the jubilation of the party-goers was obvious.

Suddenly, someone set up a cry which was immediately taken up by most of those present, accompanied by a loud, rhythmic hand-clap as they looked round the room. They all began cheering when a tall, loose-limbed and very handsome young man leapt onto the stage, brandishing an automatic weapon and grinning – obviously the hero of the hour. 'He seems very popular, who is he?' 'Oh, he's just a party thug ', Zane dismissed him with his characteristic reserve. It seems unbelievable now that I didn't recognise Saddam Hussein but at that time he was still working in the shadows, quietly but steadily increasing his influence and biding his time.

About a year later, still in that state of blissful ignorance, I was at the dressmaker's where I had a fitting for a suit. Zahara, our Turkish dressmaker, had very wisely left the country, taking her husband with her, so I now went to an Armenian lady near Mum's. She was more expensive but she could make up a suit or dress to a remarkable standard, all she needed was a picture. As I was getting into my suit I noticed a girl standing in her petticoat in the doorway across the room. She was quite attractive, tall and slim and fair skinned for an Iraqi, but the reason I noticed her was that she was wearing a Marks & Spencer bra slip – an innovation which had just come into fashion when we made our visit to Britain. Now it was forbidden to bring Marks & Spencer goods into the country at that time, so anyone who had ventured into their local M&S when they travelled abroad would carefully cut the labels off their merchandise before returning home. Being one of those non-conformers, I recognised the slip immediately. It must have been obvious that I was staring because the dressmaker whispered to me, 'That's Saddam's wife'. It meant nothing to me, even though I noticed an army vehicle with a soldier at its wheel waiting outside when I left. Later, recounting the story to Zane I learned that Saddam was a very important person in the Baath party; he also told me not to use that dressmaker again once my suit was finished. Saddam went on to increase his influence until he was able to exert control over nearly every aspect of life in the coming years, and creating fear in the hearts of Iraqi citizens, but at that point in history all I felt was that he should practise what he preached in the matter of ladies' underwear.

# Chapter Eleven

But I've jumped ahead again and haven't told you about Halima. Tula was normally a laughing, happy baby but she displayed her strong and very individual personality early in life. Typically, this often manifested in a refusal to accept anything she didn't like lying down. The first indication of this was when she started teething. I imagine my other children were probably grumpy and out of sorts whilst they were teething – I really don't remember anything specific, but when Tula was cutting a tooth there was no ignoring it. She would scream angrily for hours at a time, growing redder and redder and refusing to be pacified. One afternoon in early summer I could bear it no longer. The weather was hot and I was stressed out – keeping up with the housework and shopping and bringing up four cheeky kids was always more difficult in hot weather – and trying to do this to the accompaniment of her furious wails was 'doing my head in' as they say in Wales. At my wit's end, I grabbed my howling baby under one arm, picked up the little feeding chair she liked to sit in and stormed outside. The back garden was still in bright sunlight, so I went round to the front: mercifully it was already shady. Sitting her in her chair, I put the feeding tray in place, plonked a toy on it then resolutely turning my back on her screams I returned to the house. I waited just inside the kitchen door, listening. The screams showed no sign of lessening, but they didn't get worse either, so I left her there whilst I went to hang some washing out in the back garden. As I was doing this, a head popped up over the wall. It was Halima. 'What's wrong with your baby?' Is she ill?'

'No, just teething, I can't get her to stop crying, so I sat her in the front garden.' I was starting to feel a bit silly by this time, and wanted to end the conversation. 'Oh no, you can't leave her on her own out in the garden, give her to me, I'll look after her for you'.

'She won't stop crying, you'll soon get fed up with her.'

'Well, let me try.' I went back to where my little angel was still screaming her head off, yanked her out of the chair and returned to the wall where I handed her up to Halima. 'Good luck', I am ashamed to say that I was relieved at being able to hand her over to someone else for a short while. Of course, after about half an hour I started to worry, so I went back to the wall and called for Halima. She returned accompanied by her older cousin; both were beaming and more importantly, so was my daughter. From that time it became a daily ritual; Halima would finish her chores then climb up to look over the wall and call for Tula. Sometimes she would be accompanied by a cousin, but Tula would always be greeted by big smiles and would always come back smiling. Soon, Zara was going too and for an hour or so I was able to finish my own chores without having a child, or two, clinging to my legs, courtesy of my boundlessly willing unpaid baby sitters. As soon as Tula could speak she began going to the wall herself, calling in a lisping sing song for Halima to come and collect.

Teething wasn't the only reason for the outbreaks of crying though, for one day I noticed that they were often accompanied by a swelling on Tula's left chest. One day while Reema was visiting, I took the opportunity to show it to her. She pressed and prodded the swelling in a business-like manner, pronouncing that there was 'something not right in there' which needed investigating. We duly took her to a surgeon who carried out a similar examination and confirmed Reema's diagnosis. 'There's a lump there – I doubt whether it's anything to worry about but I'll have to remove it. I'll book her into the hospital for the day after tomorrow.' For the next few days we were in a state of shock and terror, particularly as the hospital somehow mixed up the sample sent for testing after the lump was removed, so we were initially told that the tumour was malignant. Fortunately, the surgeon was so confident of his own diagnosis that he contacted the pathologist himself, and within an hour or so he was assuring us that Tula's sample had been mixed up with one taken from an old lady. At the time we were preoccupied by worrying about our baby, but looking back two things strike me: the first is the speed and efficiency with which the whole course of treatment took place. We would have paid an initial consultation fee of a couple of Dinars to the surgeon, plus a fee for the operation itself in addition to hospital charges and pathology. I doubt whether the entire treatment cost more than around one hundred dinars and the whole thing was sorted within a week, including taking out the stitches. The second is the contrast to the Iraqi hospitals we see on television today. There is also a world of difference in the expectations of the doctors regarding their patients' ailments. Tula's surgeon was confident that he would not find a malignancy in such a young child, but nowadays a high percentage of Iraqi children are diagnosed with cancer early in life: it is thought that this change has been caused by chemicals released during bombing.

Whilst all this was going on, the drainage system had reached the streets surrounding us and every day I expected Zane to come home for lunch, possibly bringing a colleague with him. I would prepare a meal which could easily be kept warm, then spend a couple of hours waiting eagerly for him to arrive, possibly with a guest in tow. Every day I was disappointed: I would try to keep busy but my eyes would return constantly to the clock as I longed for the sound of a car pulling up in the driveway. Instead, it would be the sound of the school bus arriving which sent me outside, at which point I would give up hope of adult company for the rest of that day. Sometimes I was moved to tears of frustration and loneliness, but I would not cry openly in front of the children so those choked back tears became doubly painful. The truth was that the owner of the company had created a graph on which he charted the progress of the work of the various engineers, turning it into a competition. Zane was determined to outshine the others and in fact the chart showed that he was literally streets ahead of his colleagues. This led to his promotion to the position of Chief Engineer. There was no increase in salary, it was purely a matter of status but Zane found it ample repayment for working through his lunch hour. Personally, I would have preferred some company in the middle of the day.

I had another reason for craving adult company – I had fallen out with Clare and her mother. This came about because of my wild and boisterous children and, although I do not blame them for the event nor regret my initial reaction to it, I still feel ashamed to this day when I think of how I allowed it to ruin our friendship. A rainy afternoon had prevented the kids from going out to play and after a morning cooped up in school they were full of energy which needed an outlet. I sent them up to their bedroom to play but instead they went out onto the balcony, where the driving rain had formed puddles on the tiles. They were happily splashing through the puddles, shouting 'rain, rain, go away' and similar songs at the top of their voices when Oom Clare stormed out onto her balcony, yelling at them to be quiet. As I ran up the stairs to see what the noise was about I was met by a very indignant Summer and Ali, followed by a very wet Zara, rushing down to complain that Clare's Mum had come out onto her balcony and shouted at them. Outraged that anyone had dared to shout at my beloved children, I went outside to find an equally outraged Oom Clare waiting for me. 'Why do you let them make so much noise when we are trying to sleep? Have you no consideration for others?' I can't remember exactly what was said, but we were both angry and exchanged a few heated words before walking back into the house, both of us slamming our door at the same time if I remember correctly. After that I avoided both Clare and her mother; I never spoke to either of them again and in return neither of them spoke to me. If the quarrel had taken place now

I would probably pop round the following day as usual and hope my neighbour had calmed down enough to have a laugh about it, but I had little sense in those days, only emotions. Oom Clare was merely treating me as a surrogate daughter but I was too inexperienced to recognise that. I was socially inept and my isolation had caused me to cling to my children probably more than was wise. I was the loser. I bumped into Clare in a shop a few years later, but whilst I was trying to muster the courage to speak to her she turned away from me – another failure on my part.

Because of the difficulty of reaching the house throughout the winter, few people could be bothered to risk the road at that time. Tala and her husband had built a house in the area but on the inner Karrada side. We did visit each other from time to time but she was in the same position as me. She now had three young children of her own and was without transport during the day, so it was difficult to walk across the ruts and mounds which comprised the still undeveloped scrub between her house and mine. By the time you arrived it was almost time to turn around for the return journey if you wanted to get back for the kids' bedtime. Ann and her husband did make the effort when the road was passable. Their two little girls were around the same age as Summer and Ali, and they all loved playing together. They were very lively little girls, impetuous and fearless, which is probably why they got on so well with my volatile brood. Almost as soon as they arrived, the kids would be racing round the house and garden yelling like banshees, whilst we settled down for a gossip over beers and a bottle of wine.

One evening our conversation was cut short by an almighty crash coming from above, followed by an uncharacteristic silence. We rushed upstairs where we found children scattered all over the floor of the children's bedroom. In the centre of this circle, up-ended on the floor, was our large, solid wooden wardrobe. The only child still standing was Zara. It turned out that the four older kids had climbed on top of the wardrobe, which they were using as a boat. As their imaginary ocean voyage progressed they became more and more enthusiastic, rocking the wardrobe to and fro as they tried to reach their imaginary destination. Zara, being too small to climb up, had remained on shore, shouting encouragement up to the voyagers until she was narrowly missed by the 'vessel' as it crashed to the floor. Luckily, no-one was hurt apart from the wardrobe, but we took to checking up on them more regularly when they were playing after that.

I don't want to give the impression that my kids were deliberately naughty, but they could think of foolhardy things to do before you could think of telling them not to do them. Sometimes this scandalised strait-laced passers-by, like the time Summer decided to swing across an exceptionally wide irrigation ditch in the field near the river by clinging to a branch, displaying her underwear to all and sundry before losing a shoe and eventually falling into the water. Girls were expected to guard against accidentally flashing their pants from a very early age and it was considered ebb for girls to ride bicycles. Later, when we moved to a different area, there were other girls who rode bikes and even horses, but back then Summer often caused raised eyebrows. One of the things I will always be grateful for is that my children grew up in a place where kids could play out in the street, free to roam, always subject to the dreaded word 'ebb' of course. I suppose they were luckier than others in that I never said 'ebb'.

Whilst we were still living in that house a couple Zane met while he was studying in the Midlands turned up on our doorstep. They arrived out of the blue one Friday afternoon, dropping in whilst on their way to lunch at his parents', who lived nearby. Once they had tracked us down they frequently popped in on their way to Friday lunch with the family. Their names were Pauline and Munim and they were a handsome couple. Pauline had big blue eyes and a voluptuous figure which she always emphasised with tight skirts and wide clinched belts. She also had an acute sense of humour and ready smile which made her easy to talk to. Munim was tall and dark and always impeccably turned out. He was unlike most men in that he actually enjoyed talking to women and would happily chat to them on a wide range of subjects. This made him very good company and we frequently became so engrossed in conversation that they stayed far beyond the time when it was polite to turn up as guests for lunch. In fact I imagine that his mother must have often cursed us because her cooking must frequently have been well and truly spoiled by the time they arrived to eat it. Pauline and Munim lived in the refinery compound at Dorra, where Munim worked as a chemical engineer. They had a son and daughter but we rarely saw them in those early years because they usually stayed over at their grandparents' on Thursdays so that their parents could enjoy a night out. Munim worked just as hard as he partied, though, progressing steadily upwards in the Ministry of Oil until he reached a position of significant power and influence. Despite this, his story and that of his family ended in tragedy like that of so many other Iraqi families.

Although these visits from family and friends made the weekends pleasant, I still suffered tremendously from loneliness at this time, so when we had the chance to move back to a more established sector of Karrada I jumped at it. It came about because Zane was offered a job out of the city; it wasn't better paid or in fact better in any way than his current job, but he wanted to take it. By then I was beginning to recognise the pattern that was emerging in his professional life. He constantly needed a new challenge, so once he felt fully on top of a job he became bored with it and began looking round for something else. This latest job would entail him staying away overnight again – obviously not an ideal situation given our isolated location. Luckily, we had made up with the family quite soon after Tula was born – I can't remember exactly how it came about. Anyway, Dad offered to come and stay with us on those nights when Zane was away but it was a long way from the coffee shops of Karrada and after he had stayed over twice it was obvious to me that it was a great inconvenience, so I told him not to bother any more.

From that time, Zane's work regularly took him away from home, finally forcing me to grow up. I became totally responsible for running our household, organising the children, the shopping and every other aspect of our lives completely unaided. This was unusual in Iraq in those days, because most women could rely on quite a lot of support from members of the extended family. The males in the family usually did the bulk of the shopping, too, but Zane hated shopping. I was often without transport during those early years so he had no alternative but to drive me to the market when he came home, but he would usually stay in the car with the younger kids whilst I haggled over vegetables and fruit. He couldn't wait until I had my own car so he could hand this last duty over to me. This may not appear to be a particularly onerous situation to women in Britain, but for an English girl living in Baghdad at that time it was often a hard slog, particularly as the children got older and the political situation became more and more complicated. What made it worse was that Zane never phoned whilst he was away, even though he complained about how much he missed us. Usually I didn't even have a number where he could be reached, so I often felt that I was truly alone, trying to bring up my children to follow the rules of a culture which was quite alien to the one in which I had grown up.

But before I could become truly independent I had to be able to move around. I had managed to improve my driving skills by practising on the new university site whenever possible. Work on the building had not yet commenced, but a preparatory system of roads had been laid out which turned out to be very useful to learner drivers, myself included, whenever the site was accessible. We would load all the children into the back of the car, sometimes accompanied by family members who might be visiting, and off we would all go for a practice drive. Zane was the most impatient of teachers, always urging me to go faster so that I could overtake the other learners who were whizzing around the area. On one occasion he became so irritated with me that he put his foot on top of mine as it rested on the accelerator and pushed down hard, leaving me unable to control my speed or even brake as we hurtled along. He only removed his foot when we narrowly missed another novice driver who was coming around a bend on the wrong side of the road, (all the rear seat passengers cheered when I managed to avoid this collision).

After that, I declined any more free tuition from him. Instead I would put the children in the back of the car then drive carefully around the area until I felt confident enough to venture onto busier roads. This may seem a highly irresponsible way of learning to drive but it was not unusual. A friend of mine knew someone who lost her husband but inherited his large American car. The car was an automatic model but as she had never mastered the reverse she was reluctant to use it. My friend devised a cunning plan to get her on the road – they would work out a route which would not necessitate reversing. They used to drive the huge car to the busy centre of Baghdad and park at the rear of Orosdi Bach, the capital's main department store. Once they arrived, they would speak nicely to any passing shopper and get him to reverse the car into a parking bay so that she could drive straight out again when they were ready to leave. I don't know how long this went on for, and my friend never said whether she ever learned to go backwards as well as forwards.

For my part, once I felt confident on the road Zane took me to the driving test centre. The test was a fairly simple one involving carrying out a figure of eight around a set of barrels. They had to be negotiated both forwards and in reverse and if you hit a barrel you failed the test. I never passed it for the simple reason that I never took it. When we arrived at the centre the police office responsible for testing took one look at me and asked, 'Can she drive?' 'Well give her the test and see' was my husband's non-committal response (he has never recognised me as a competent driver). 'It's OK, that won't be necessary, all foreigners can drive'. He was already reaching for the form needed to issue a driving licence as he said this and a few minutes later I drove away, my new licence securely tucked into my handbag.

Anyway, once I had learned to drive properly the next step towards independence was to move to somewhere more accessible. Mum had told us about a house which was available for rent with an option to buy if we liked living there. It was a couple of streets away from the family home and – luxury of luxuries – it was on a paved street. Unfortunately, I disliked the landlady and this was a major disadvantage as she lived next door. She was nosy and critical, constantly trying to interfere in the way I cared for what she considered to be her house, even though we were paying rent for it. I might have been able to overcome my dislike of her but I could not overcome my dislike of her house. It had been tenanted before so it was a bit scruffy when we moved in but I thought I would be able to scrub it up. I couldn't. Whatever I did, it remained a basic, uninspiring box which had been built solely for letting purposes. Even worse, I could not eradicate the cockroaches which seemed to lurk in every dark corner. We had to go, and as soon as we found a suitable home we did just that, moving to the house which was to be our home for the remainder of our years in Baghdad.

It was in Jadriya, an up-market suburb about a mile up the outer Karrada road from Mum's house. It was on a bus route and although the side street itself was not yet paved, I didn't feel this would be a problem as all the plots had been built upon some years before and the area was already well-established. There was a small palm grove opposite the house which could not be built upon because of green belt restrictions, so the house had a 'country' feel to it, particularly as the river Tigris was at the end of the road.

By dwelling on these trivial domestic details, I may have given the impression that the political situation had stabilised. On the contrary, by the time we moved to Jadriya we had lived through the trauma of various coups and counter coups and to make matters worse, for most of that time the country had also been involved in a sporadic war with the Kurdish population in the north of the country. The truth was that for the last few years I had been so busy with my growing brood of children that I was only vaguely aware of political events. Nevertheless, whilst I was busy reproducing, the Baathists had been busy eradicating all opposition to their rule. They started with the communists, purging them from all walks of life, particularly from the army. When senior career officers voiced their concerns over the loss of experienced army personnel, they were purged in their turn.

At the same time, throughout every ministry and government department, employees, especially teachers, were under constant pressure to join the Baath party. The party also established a youth division whose primary function appeared to be to wean children off their loyalty to their parents and replace it with loyalty to the party. Traditional values instilled by parents were discouraged as outmoded instruments of imperialism and the tight bonds of social control which bound children to their parents began to loosen. Youth party divisions were set up within schools which even the youngest kids were put under pressure to join.

Zane made it very clear to the children from the time they were old enough to understand that he considered it to be dangerous to dabble in politics in Iraq; he strictly forbade them from joining any political association. We couldn't isolate them completely from these developments however. One example was the 'raising the flag' ceremony which was traditionally held in every Iraqi school once a week – a bit like school assembly. This ceremony involved one of the pupils hoisting the national flag up the flagpole whilst the others sang nationalist songs. The child who was chosen to carry out the job was usually being rewarded for having done well that week – it was the Iraqi version of being given a gold star or merit. Gradually, the traditional songs began to be replaced by new ones extolling the virtues of the Baathist party, emphasising in particular the 'fatherly' qualities of its leadership. All these policies were regularly and loudly publicised as steps towards a more 'just' society, whilst behind the scenes the cloak and dagger activity aimed at eliminating any opposition to Baathist domination continued. Not that the general public was unaware of it, on the contrary rumours of people disappearing, or being tortured and raped were widespread, but they were only spoken of in whispers to trusted friends. Gone were the days when irreverent jokes about politicians and political events spread around the capital like wildfire – the party was now sacrosanct and its leaders were elevated to a level so high that no humour could possibly touch them. If anyone felt unable to join in the praise which was routinely heaped upon the party by its members, the best course was to say nothing at all.

Meanwhile, behind the scenes Saddam directed operations, casting his net then inexorably drawing the entire country into his grasp. Import and trading licences were cancelled and government departments took control of many basic commodities, crucially including food supplies. In those early years he was still known as Saddam Hussein Al Tikriti, signifying that he came from the town of Tikrit. As his power increased he began promoting his close relatives until they gradually took control of all the major positions of power in the country. They set up trading companies and appropriated property until the name 'Al Tikriti' not only inspired fear but also became synonymous with corruption. Although Saddam held the position of deputy leader of the Revolutionary Command Council, everyone knew that it was he who really ran the country. He preferred to be addressed as 'Mr Deputy', in fact he insisted on it, so when one day it was announced that all surnames were to be banned, most people assumed it was because he was embarrassed over the associations his surname had attracted to. The remainder of the population felt that the ban had been imposed because of the rumours that 'Al Tikriti' wasn't a real surname at all. A few even whispered that his mother had been unmarried when he was born so he invented the name to cover up his illegitimate status, although I always thought that to be very unlikely given that the requirement for female chastity before marriage was even stronger in the countryside. Whatever the true cause for this latest edict, by the time we moved to Jadriya my children, like everyone else in the country, were known only by their first names followed by their patronym.

A day or two after we moved into our new house, Zane invited three couples to dinner. They were friends from work and as they were all Iraqi I decided on a traditonal Iraqi meal, and spent most of the afternoon preparing it. Early in the evening I was out in the garden, rounding up the children and making sure that everything outside was ship-shape when I noticed a young woman in an unusually short skirt passing by. She was slim but shapely and as she walked by she glanced over her shoulder at me with the kind of studied nonchalance adopted by my grand-daughter when she thought she had spotted Alan Sugar in a restaurant in Marbella. She was obviously very interested in what was going on in our house and she looked European, so I went out to the gate and called 'Hello'. She came forward immediately and introduced herself in very precise but accented English, 'Hello, my name is Erica, I live next door. I'm so happy to have a European neighbour'. So was I, but I hardly had time to say more than a few words before my visitors arrived and I saw to my dismay that each couple had brought their entire families with them – parents, some brothers and sisters, children and assorted other relatives. Putting on a brave face I welcomed our guests and settled them all comfortably in our sitting room, but my mind was racing. I calculated that I had enough food for everyone – Iraqi food is the kind that can easily be made to stretch to feed a few more people – all that is needed is a little more rice and salad, some extra savoury pastries and other dishes which are usually to be found in every household freezer. The reason for my dismay was more concrete – I didn't have enough plates to go around. Once everyone was seated with a drink in their hands (soft drinks for the women and beer or whiskey for the men) I retreated to the kitchen on the pretext of checking on dinner. After banging a couple of saucepan lids together then running the tap for added effect, I opened the back door as stealthily as I could and raced round to Erica's house. She was rather surprised to see me on her door step so soon after our brief meeting, but she was even more surprised when I blurted out, 'Hi, could you possibly lend me some plates?' Luckily, she did so our guests were able to enjoy their dinner and I was able to maintain my reputation as a competent and hospitable hostess.

The next day I returned Erica's plates and she invited me to come inside for a coffee. It was to be the first of what must have been a million cups of coffee we drank together in the course of the next few years. I quickly discovered that Erica was totally without reserve. I had made hardly any headway on my coffee before the floodgates opened (conversationally speaking) and she was giving me the complete history of her life and the events which led to her coming to live in Baghdad. I suppose it was because I had grown used to Iraqi reticence when it came to personal and family matters, but I was shocked at how indiscreet she was with a total stranger. It turned out that she was from Germany, where she had met her husband, Saidi. He was an Iraqi Kurd who had originally gone to Germany to study medicine. Finding himself unsuited to that profession he had left university and enrolled in an agricultural college; he was now employed by the ministry of agriculture, although it was never clear what he actually did except that he found it very stressful, according to Erica. She said that he often suffered from depression because of his job, which caused him to become withdrawn and sleep a lot. I never saw any evidence of this depression: in fact he was a very jolly man, always smiling and joking. As I got to know them better I privately felt that his retreat into sleep was his way of getting away from Erica's constant complaining, but perhaps that was unkind of me. At any rate, before we were half way through that first cup of coffee I knew that she had been pregnant but not yet married when she first arrived in Baghdad. Her in-laws welcomed her as Saidi's wife and they moved into their house for a while. Saidi had been so ashamed about living there under false pretences that after a few days he dragged her off to Samarra to get married. I don't know whether her in-laws ever knew about that, but knowing Erica, I doubt whether she managed to keep it a secret for long.

As I came to know Erica better I found that she was equally indiscreet about political events; she was very highly strung and excitable and during the years that we were neighbours she was on and off the Valium all the time. Whenever she was het up about something, she would stalk up the road, on the lookout for some hapless neighbour so that she could launch into a tirade of complaints – never a wise thing in Baathist Iraq. Happily, this never seemed to come to the attention of the authorities and she got away with it. I know that some of our Iraqi neighbours thought she was crazy, which she certainly wasn't, so perhaps she was ignored by the local party spy network on that basis, rather like a madman in an Indian tribe. Anyway, we became friends and before long we were in the habit of getting together for coffee and cake nearly every day.

Despite her excellent English, Erica found my name difficult to master, so I suggested she call me 'Dot' instead, but she could never quite get the hang of that either. The nearest she ever got was 'Doss' which is what she always called me. She had two sons, well built, sturdy lads who soon became pals with our kids. Whilst we were chatting they would be making up games, falling out and making up at the drop of a hat. The area had originally been developed by brothers whose wives were all English and it still seemed to be a magnet for families with foreign wives. There were so many diverse nationalities living in the neighbourhood that, as Ali grew older and began playing street football with the local lads, they could all boast that they knew how to say 'Shit' in about ten different languages. But it was great for me. For the first time since arriving in Baghdad I had easy access to friends who came from abroad and experienced the same difficulties as I did. It was wonderful and despite the fact that life became harder and harder from that time, they were my happiest years in Baghdad.

Although Erica was our next door neighbour, her house was actually situated to the rear of our back garden because our house was on a corner. The couple who lived next door to us on the other side were related to the original owners of the area, but they rarely had anything to do with the rest of us, possibly because they had so many relatives in the neighbourhood. The two houses which were actually nearest to ours were in the street running along the side of our garden on the opposite side of the road. When we first moved in they were both let to foreign embassies; one was occupied by the Czech cultural attaché, a job description which we all assumed to be shorthand for 'spy' and the other by a Hungarian vet who was on secondment to the United Nations. The Hungarians had a teenage son, a tall handsome boy with big blue eyes who was the object of Summer's first crush. The Hungarians kept themselves very much to themselves, although the vet was quite helpful later when we had dogs and needed advice. The Czechs, however, were a different story. The wife, Antonia, was stout and friendly; when she wasn't cooking delicious soups and cakes she was chatting over the garden wall to one or other of the neighbours. She told me that they were ethnic Slovakians and therefore second class citizens in the Czechoslavian republic. According to her it was quite unusual for a Slovak to progress so far in the diplomatic corps. This tended to reinforce our opinion that her husband must be a spy, but as being close mouthed was by now second nature to all of us except Erica, it didn't interfere with our friendship with Antonia and in fact we rarely saw her husband. Antonia had two children, the eldest being a boy who was a little older than Ali. He was the best football player in the neighbourhood and went on to play professional football when they returned to Czechoslovakia.

The other was a daughter, Zushka, who was the same age as Tula and they quickly became best buddies. Zushka was impulsive and fearless, qualities which made her the perfect playmate for Tula, who was also impulsive and fearless but with the added feistiness that comes from constantly competing for attention with three older siblings. Nevertheless, despite the similarities in their personalities, the pair made an unusual sight as they played outside together because they were very different in appearance. For a start, Zushka's hair was fine and blonde, whilst Tula had a dark-auburn, curly mop which defeated all my attempts to control it; similarly, Zushka's deep golden-brown skin contrasted beautifully with Tula's peaches and cream complexion. Because they were so striking, they attracted a lot of attention when they were outside, particularly as they rarely obeyed the rule not to venture out into the street on their own. Obviously, both Antonia and I tried to keep a sharp eye on them, but the main reason they were allowed to stay outside was because of the huge yellow dog which had come down from the river and adopted Zushka. Whenever she was outside he would stalk along two steps behind her, silently daring anyone to come near. It was the strangest thing – he appeared out of nowhere and appointed himself as her guardian. Whenever Zushka left the street and returned to her house or garden he simply lay down in front of the gate and waited for her to re-appear. So far as I know, he never tried to go through the gate and he seemed to know when it was time to go home at night, wherever 'home' was for him. Luckily for us, as her constant companion Tula was guarded too. Perhaps he related to Zushka because her yellow hair was very similar in colour to his own fur – who knows. All I know is that after they returned home we never saw the dog in the street again.

Anyway, there I was in Jadriya with friends close by and children old enough to bring their own friends home from school. Summer had two best friends whilst she was at the Home of Children and the older they became, the closer they grew. Their names are Izhar and Farah and although the girls all came from quite different backgrounds they were inseparable. Izhar came from a Christian Baptist family and lived in a different part of the city, but she and her brother still managed regular after school visits to our house courtesy of the school minibus. Farah on the other hand lived just five minutes' walk away. She came from a well-established Karrada family: they were 'good people'. This made her very acceptable as Summer's best friend from Zane's point of view, but he did have qualms about the politics of some of her relatives. I got on well with Farah's mother; she was unpretentious and down to earth and we would call round to each other's houses for coffee occasionally. Her brother in law was Saddam's best friend, although I didn't know this until later, so she led quite a hectic social life. People who needed someone to 'put a word in' for them were keen to be her friend so I met other people through her, some of them British. As the girls grew older, Farah came to our house nearly every afternoon, except on those days when Summer went to hers. This relationship was to impact on our future in totally unexpected ways in the years to come.

During those years we often drove out of Baghdad on day trips or short holidays, so I was lucky enough to see almost every part of Iraq, although we never passed through the town of Tikrit. We saw all the antiquities and remains of great cities – Babylon, Cestiphon and further north the ancient city of Nineva, which was amazingly intact considering its great age. I was intrigued to find that the features on the faces of the statues which lined the streets were recognisable as the ancestors of people walking the streets of Baghdad today. I found it enthralling to walk along ancient avenues which had been trodden by historical figures like Alexander the Great or Salahaddin, while the kids just loved scrambling over the ruins and being free to run in the sun. Zane, on the other hand, was not particularly interested in his cultural heritage but he loved spending any free time he had with the kids and enjoyed taking them on these days out.

On one such occasion we went to stay in Kirkuk with an old college friend of Zane. He was known as 'Ginger' for the usual reason and I had originally met him when he was a student in Birmingham. He came to visit after Summer was born and spent a weekend with us, bringing with him his British girlfriend – a lovely girl from the Midlands. Now he had a lovely Iraqi wife who had given him two children, neither of whom looked remotely like him, not being ginger. He worked as a petroleum engineer at the oil refinery, so they all lived on the residential compound in one of the houses provided for refinery staff. The compound also boasted a club house with a restaurant which served such good food at such a reasonable price that compound residents rarely bothered to cook at home. There were also regular social events at the club which were very well attended. Alcohol was cheap and all in all they lived a very pleasant life-style, particularly as the climate was much less extreme than that of Baghdad.

Because of the on-off conflict with the Kurds, there were often restrictions on travel to the north of the country, but a cease-fire had recently been declared and for the time being it was considered safe to go there. We were taking advantage of the temporary lull in fighting to make our first visit to the area before the inevitable resumption of hostilities. A large hydro-electric dam had just been completed and Zane was eager to see it whilst he had the chance, so one day we decided to drive out there to have a look, taking a picnic lunch with us. Things didn't work out as planned, however, because the area approaching the dam was restricted and armed guards turned us back before we were close enough to catch sight of the dam. We still had our lunch to enjoy, though, so we turned off the main road and began looking out for a good picnic spot. What we had in mind was a grassy area dotted with some of the wild spring flowers for which the area was famous, perhaps with a shady tree and a stream nearby. We drove for a quite a while without finding this idyllic location, so in the end we gave in to hunger and the children's boredom and simply pulled off the road onto an open, uncultivated area.

The weather was perfect for a picnic, sunny and warm so after we had finished lunch we loosened our belts and settled back to doze in the sun whilst the kids began an energetic game of chase which took them in ever-increasing circles further and further away. As we relaxed in the sun, our conversation flagged and their voices began to fade into the distance; I think I would have slept if it had not been for the sound of a motor vehicle pulling up on the road with a screech of brakes. Rather sleepily, we all began to pull ourselves up into a seated position from which we could see that the vehicle was an army jeep. We were immediately on edge, and stood up as two very smart army officers jumped out of the jeep and began walking quickly towards us. Zane and Ginger went over to meet them, rather warily I thought, so after a moment's hesitation I followed, just in time to hear one of them call out 'Get those children off there – it's a minefield.'

I doubt whether any of us had ever run so fast – I certainly hadn't. As we ran we called out to the children but unfortunately they thought we were joining in their game. They turned, waving and jumping up and down before running on even faster. We caught up with the younger ones fairly quickly and immediately swung them up off the ground but the older children went careering on, suddenly swinging around to the right in an arc like a pack of hunted animals, before heading back towards our picnic spot. The men told us to take the little ones back to the cars whilst they rounded up the others, but with Tula on one arm and Zara slung under the other, head and legs dangling, that appeared an impossible feat. With the children safely in our arms I was suddenly acutely aware that with every step we were in danger of triggering a land mine. It became clear why the soil managed to look so unnaturally loose and loamy without any trace of anything growing, cultivated or otherwise: it had been dug up, possibly blown up. Fortunately this meant that our footsteps were clearly visible in the loose soil, so with great trepidation we retraced our steps as carefully as possible. By some miracle, Zane and Ginger also managed to round up the other kids and bring them safely back to the roadside. As soon as they were satisfied we were all in one piece, the officers turned and jumped into their jeep, causing it to bounce up and down on its springs, and drove off without further comment. I couldn't help wondering whether stopping tourists from blowing themselves up was a regular part of their army duties, or whether it was pure coincidence that they passed when they did. Needless to say I didn't waste too much time thinking about it as we followed their example and got out of there as quickly as possible.

That evening there was a dinner dance at the clubhouse. Zane rarely wanted to get up on the dance floor, he much preferred good conversation and a couple of drinks, but quite early in the evening the band began to play a slow tune so we got up to dance. We had just made a space for ourselves in the throng of other dancers when the enormity of what might have happened that afternoon hit home and I started to shake so badly that Zane thought I was ill. 'What's the matter? You're trembling. Come on, let's go and sit down'. It was rare for him to show as much concern as he did as he led me back to our table, so I must have been shaking really badly. During those years in Baghdad it sometimes felt as though life was like making your way through a building site, trying to dodge large heavy objects which were constantly falling off roofs. Some people seemed to be able to weave their way between the falling debris without ever being hit, whilst others got flattened every time. I will be forever grateful that we were among the lucky ones, unlike many people we knew.

# Chapter Twelve

We made two or three more trips to the north of Iraq in the following years and each time the scarcity of food in the shops was more obvious, even though the area was renowned for its production of fruits, nuts, other foodstuffs; even fine wines used to be produced in monasteries nestling among the crags but local market stalls looked increasingly empty and it was noticeable that the hotels struggled to provide decent meals for their guests, often to the embarrassment of the waiters. It was also impossible to ignore the fact that every man and boy in Kurdish dress was armed to the eye-balls, with weapons slung over their shoulders front and back. Layla accompanied us on one of these trips and soon after we arrived at the hotel she had a panic attack over a cup of tea which we were all enjoying on the terrace. 'Let's go home, they're all Kurdish here' she begged, panting and fanning her ample bosom with a scarf at the same time. It took all our powers of persuasion to convince her that we would be perfectly safe and that the locals always dressed like that. However, despite my assurances, I couldn't help noticing that there were a lot more weapons around than before.

Once, we drove high up into the mountains, nearly reaching the Turkish border. I watched the locals striding up the steep slopes as easily as we walk along a garden path, envying their straight backs, strength and fitness. The road got steeper and steeper until it was little more than a beaten track which eventually ended at a village which took up the entire area of a small plateau; anyone who succeeded in reaching the top was rewarded with spectacular views of the surrounding countryside. Perhaps this vantage point was the reason the village had the reputation for being a smuggling centre. It was said that all kinds of goods smuggled in from Turkey were available there, so we hoped to be able to pick up some bargains. What we were particularly hoping for were Rothman cigarettes which were hard to come by in Baghdad, causing the price of a pack of twenty to rise to an extortionate quarter of a dinar (about 25p). Perhaps it was a symptom of the tension which increasingly accompanied every aspect of life, but I had become a regular smoker by then, getting through at least 20 cigarettes a day whilst Zane needed at least two packs, so we were always on the lookout for cheap cigarettes. In addition to smoking, everyone drank a lot, particularly the men. Looking back, this was a bit foolhardy given the need to constantly watch what you said; after one particularly heavy drinking session at our house one of the guests was so drunk when he got up to leave that the more he tried to move towards the front door, the more his feet took him backwards, much to the amusement of Summer and Ali, who were still awake. In the end, he managed to get through our front door with the help of both his wife's hands placed firmly in the small of his back.

There were other ways in which people were affected by the chronic insecurity and fear which was gradually taking hold of the country, even among Baath party members. Some of my friends complained that their husbands had lost interest in sex: one could only have sex when he was out of the country, which obviously placed great strain upon the marriage, particularly as he was away on government business a lot. Zane's outlet was more straightforward – he shouted a lot. He would lose his temper at the slightest thing, ranting and raving and never giving me a chance to get a word in. He would often begin shouting as he walked through the door on arriving home, working himself into a rage about some triviality: his evening meal might be too hot, or the shirt he felt like wearing not ironed. Anything could set him off and he would start yelling and storming about the room, sometimes even throwing his knife and fork down on the table and abandoning my carefully prepared meal. Having let off steam he would return ten minutes later as though nothing had happened, rather like a child having a tantrum. The shouting was always directed at me, never the children, but it obviously upset them too. What's more, it was not the behaviour I expected from a husband who had just returned from working away for several days. I would usually bite my lip and take it whilst the children were around, but my resentment would simmer until it found an outlet later, frequently ending in a furious row. On the whole, I think I would cheerfully have settled for less activity in the bedroom if we could have enjoyed some peace and quiet in the rest of the house.

Up until then, people always said that things could only get better whenever there was a coup or some other political drama, even though the reality was that things usually got worse. Now, despite some innovations which gave the outward impression that life was getting better, such as a vastly improved public transport system of smart new buses, most people felt that the country was free-falling towards catastrophe. It was if we were living parallel lives: on the surface our kids were enjoying a hurly burly street life which epitomised what childhood should be and we enjoyed a good social life ourselves, but at the same time our lives were gradually being squeezed into pre-determined moulds by the pressure of Baathist doctrines. The next few years saw the country change so quickly that I am no longer sure of the sequence of events, so I will simply recount them as I remember them even if I have got some of them in the wrong order.

The government was involved in a flirtation with the Russians, presumably in the hope of being supplied with armaments which were not forthcoming from other quarters, and a delegation of high ranking Russian army officers had arrived for celebrations to commemorate the establishment of the Iraqi army. Army day happened to coincide with the day on which one of the Christian sects celebrated Christmas – I think it might have been the Assyrians – anyway it was the sixth of January and usually cold and miserable in Baghdad. Tula was the only child still left at home with me by then, so I wrapped her up in a coat and we set off for the shops in the little VW Beetle which I drove at the time. Later, when we were ready to return home I found that every side street I tried to take was closed, forcing me onto roads which would take me further and further from home. I tried to turn into a street which I thought would take me towards Jadriya, only to be met by a man coming in the opposite direction who told me to turn back because the street was closed at the far end.

I was getting further and further away from my destination and also getting more and more frustrated, so when I found a main road at last I put my foot down hard and pulled out into the traffic as soon as there was a gap. I wished I hadn't because I realised at once that I had jumped into the middle of a convoy of army vehicles. They were all heading very briskly in the direction of the Rashid Barracks – the largest and most important army barracks in Iraq. The vehicle behind me closed the gap, forcing me to keeping going even though I now realised that I had just joined the procession ferrying the Russian Generals to the celebrations. We travelled in this way for several miles with me contemplating what would happen when we reached our destination, my heart sinking with every mile. I knew the road quite well, as Omar had built a factory in the area which Samir now managed and my only hope was that I would be able to turn off onto the road which led to the factory. I wasn't sure that I would be able to pull this off at speed because the jeep behind me was so close, but it seemed to be my only option. There were police cars stationed every so often along the route and I could hardly believe my luck as I approached one of them when a police officer held up his hand and signalled to the driver behind me to slow down then directed me to pull off the road. Once the convoy had closed up and sped off again he came over and looked into the car. 'Where do you think you're off to?' He was having a good look into the back of the car, having ascertained that Tula was the only passenger. 'Jadriya, the roads were closed and I lost my way.'

'Hm.'

He was obviously a man of few words, which suited me fine as I felt such an idiot. I imagine someone must have radioed ahead to tell him to get the uninvited guest out of the way and for my part I couldn't wait to get out of there. By then the convoy was safely past and the road was clear. 'Go on then, off you go,' he extended his hand outwards in a rather courtly gesture, as if giving way to me in a door way, so I did brisk U turn onto the highway and headed back in the direction of home. I arrived without any further complication, but I didn't waste time taking in my shopping. Instead, I hurried round to Erica's where we had a good laugh about it over a cup of coffee. Nevertheless, I knew that I had been lucky: the incident could have ended very badly for me. When I told Zane about it later he didn't find it at all funny, nor could he understand how I ended up in the middle of the convoy in the first place. Sometimes I got the feeling that my husband was entirely lacking in a sense of humour.

Now that I could get about more easily I started to take the children swimming. I had wanted to join the Alwiya Club that summer. It was an elite club, always open to foreigners but Iraqis needed someone to 'put a word in' for them before they could become members. We had someone who could do this for us but Zane would not join, saying that there were now too many Baathists among the membership and he didn't want us mixing with them. We often went there in the evening for dinner dances with friends, but I think he was OK with that because he was there to keep an eye on me, which may sound mad, but was perhaps understandable in view of the rumours which circulated about top Baathists forcing husbands to hand over their wives for an evening's entertainment. Not only that, but Summer was growing up, and growing up very pretty, and he certainly didn't want her catching the eye of the wrong person. Instead we started going to the Baghdad pool, a huge public pool with all the attendant facilities, although if I remember correctly there were actually two pools on the site.

We often went with Erica, either cramming ourselves and our kids into a tiny VW (she had one too) or going by taxi. If we took a taxi, Ali and Erica's boys would scramble to get into the front seat first, pushing and shoving each other out of the way. For once, none of the girls joined in the scrum because they didn't want to sit in front with the driver; I suppose this showed that they were affected by local culture more than they realised themselves. Erica was a member of the Mansur Club, which had been started by rich Iraqis in the days when they weren't welcome in the Alwiya Club. We didn't like going there because the pool was so small, but obviously she felt she had to go there sometimes to get her money's worth. When she did we would go with other friends or on our own – many of the people we knew were likely to be there anyway. Sometimes Nadia would come with us, or she would go with friends and meet us there and we all spent many happy hours swimming together.

All my kids were fearless in water and both Zara and Tula could swim happily in deep water by the time they were two. We used the Baghdad pool for several years until one day we turned up to find it closed because army personnel were using it for training. We all waited outside in the boiling sun until they came out, a bevy of fit-looking, often handsome young officers with water still dripping from their hair. Some of the foreign wives set up the piercing 'halleluja' sound traditionally made by women at weddings, and they were soon joined by laughing Iraqi women. The young men slunk sheepishly away, but unfortunately that was not the end of the matter. From that time on, whenever we went to the pool we had no way of knowing whether we would get in or whether it would be occupied by the army. Things continued in that way for the rest of the summer until the following year when it was officially appropriated by the army. There was another pool which we occasionally used, but it was much smaller and wasn't half as clean; it didn't really matter because by that time I could afford to bring the kids home to Britain every summer, so we weren't in Baghdad much in the swimming season anyway.

Once Tula joined her brother and sisters in school I became very bored and began looking for other things to occupy my time. Because of the scarcity of goods available, I was already sewing most of the clothes for myself and the children. I also made home-made jam and pickles, even producing home-made squash every year with the Seville oranges which grew plentifully in our garden, but I needed some other outlet. Life was no longer as cheap as it once was and many women who had formerly stayed at home were increasingly going into employment, often taking jobs which they would have considered beneath them and consequently 'ebb' a few years before. This included some of the foreign wives; one began making Danish pastries which she sold to grateful friends. An American who was married to someone from a farming background brought corn seed back from the States and sold the product as corn on the cob to fellow foreign wives, managing to produce the most delicious corn on the cob I have ever tasted to this day.

Since no such inspiration occurred to me I began filling my extra spare time by going to coffee mornings more often, taking up first bridge and then mah- jong, both of which I was rubbish at. I also played Scrabble with local friends, sometimes far into the night, often accompanied by a glass or two of wine whilst my children slept at home in the next street. We had no qualms about their safety because Baghdad was still the safest place in the world to live. That summer, Zane accompanied us on a trip to Britain and we left in such a rush that we forgot to close the front door. The following day, one of the neighbours noticed that both the garden gate and the front door were wide open; she closed the gate and phoned Mum, who called round at her convenience, gave the house the once over then shut the door on her way out.

Since all those coffee mornings involved a lot of extra baking, I dabbled in having a live-in maid to help with the never-ending household chores, as many people did in those days. With the assistance of a friend I found and hired an Assyrian girl who would do all the housework and ironing and only go home once a week. I think I paid her 25 dinars for this, which I suppose wasn't bad when you consider that a teacher still only earned about 40 dinars a month. Now that Summer was growing up she slept downstairs with the other girls, leaving Ali as sole occupant of the room upstairs. Since he was only about 9 I saw nothing wrong with the maid sleeping in his room, so an extra bed was duly installed for her. She proved to be a good worker when she was there, but had the unfortunate habit of failing to turn up for work after the weekend whenever she attended a wedding. It soon became apparent that weddings were a very regular occurrence among the Assyrian community, so when it happened once too often, I let her go. After she left, Ali told me that she often used to entertain him by belly dancing in the bedroom after he had gone to bed. In view of this, and taking into account the limited size of our house, I decided that all I needed was daily help after all and never repeated the experiment.

The next and last person I employed to help with the housework was a skinny mother of several children named Oom Khalil. At that time she lived in the slums of central Baghdad but she came originally from the north. Zane was convinced that she came from Tel Kafe, mainly because of the outlandish outfit she always wore. It appeared to consist of several lengths of cloth tied together around her body, with an extra fringed one which went around her head. Her husband did not appear to do much in the way of work and I think that she was the main bread winner at home. She was a very good worker and soon learned to do things around the house exactly the way I wanted them to be done. In fact, she was a treasure and I gradually entrusted her with more and more of the housework. Although she stayed with us for quite a long time, she was very reticent and rarely spoke about her husband or children. It was obvious that life was really hard for her and I tried to help her out in the usual ways, like giving her all the children's cast-off clothes. On several occasions I also bought her material to be made up into dresses for herself but she never turned up in anything but her usual outfit and I suspected that she used the fabric for her children instead. Once we got to know each other better, she also refused to eat the lunch I dished up for her, saying she would take it home to share with her children, so naturally I felt obliged to cook larger quantities so she could eat herself after finishing the housework and still have something left over to take home.

It was while Oom Khalil was working for us that we had the mercury poisoning scare. We first became aware of it as a vague rumour, but it was later confirmed by a doctor friend of ours. The official story was that the government had imported a large quantity of grain which had been treated with mercury to prevent it deteriorating before it was sown. It had been distributed to farmers in the north of the country who, out of sheer laziness it was alleged, had eaten the corn themselves and also fed it to their livestock rather than go to the trouble of planting it. Mercury poisoning causes a terrible illness and almost certain death, so everyone was naturally anxious to avoid it, yet every day more items were added to the list of foods we were warned to avoid as the full extent of the problem became apparent. First we were advised to remove any locally produced meat from our freezers and dispose of it – Oom Khalil eagerly requested that she should be allowed to take ours home, but I could not in all conscience allow this. I left it in the freezer until she was safely out of the way, only to have the bin men come knocking on our door to enquire whether we had any poisoned meat that we wanted to get rid of. It then became apparent that milk would also be unsafe and that flour used to make bread might have been produced using the poisoned grain; the list continued to grow until in the end we were afraid to give our children anything except fruit and vegetables whilst we waited for the government to import foodstuffs from abroad to tide us over until the threat of poisoning had passed. The scare went on for several months, during which time Oom Khalil was a great help, suggesting ways of preparing a meal without using meat, dairy or cereal products – broad beans can be very useful in those circumstances. Nevertheless, I worried continually that the children weren't getting an adequate diet and was convinced that they weren't as healthy as usual in the months that followed.

Looking back, I don't think we even knew anyone who was acquainted with anyone who was directly affected by mercury poisoning, although there were newspaper reports of foreign scientific experts visiting the country to determine the extent of the problem. With hindsight, I can't help wondering whether it was an elaborate hoax on the part of the government, because the mercury scare must have occurred around the time that food shortages began to pose a daily problem. In fact, all commodities became a daily problem as the government was proving to be unable, or unwilling to ensure that they imported a steady and consistent supply of goods to fill the shops and meet the needs of the increasing population. The most basic commodities like eggs were scarce and when there was a delivery word would spread like wildfire around the capital, causing large crowds to gather outside those shops which were thought to have received goods. For the first time Iraqis came to grips with the concept of queueing, although once the shop doors opened the queue often disintegrated into a struggling mob as everyone tried to get their share. It wasn't only foodstuffs which were in short supply, it was everything, elevating the work 'marcoo', literally 'there aren't any'- to the status of being the most often used word in the language. The entire population became obsessed with tracking down scarce items of food and other goods, just at the time when strict limitations were placed on travel abroad. These were probably introduced in an attempt to halt the brain drain, but were universally viewed as just another attempt by the government to make life difficult for its citizens.

Iraqis became fanatical shoppers and for many years those who were lucky enough to be able to travel could be seen throughout the summer snapping up anything they could get their hands on in Oxford Street and beyond. At the airports they would go to great lengths to hide some of their bags and parcels so they could take excess baggage as hand luggage, leaving their possessions with other travellers whilst they checked in, then returning the favour so their fellow passengers could also avoid paying for excess baggage. As a foreigner I was free to travel so long as Zane gave his permission and there was the additional incentive that Iraqi Airways now flew direct to Heathrow, meaning I no longer had to use the country-hopping Czech airline. Following one particular summer visit to my family the plane was so crowded with parcels and plastic bags on the return flight that we could hardly make our way up the aisle to find our seats. When we reached them Summer and Ali had to climb over parcels which had been placed in front of their seats by a woman seated next to the aisle, leaving them unable to sit straight.

She was also holding a long narrow box and as soon as they were seated she slid it across their laps, effectively restricting their movement even further. When I protested she begged, 'Darling please, it's a wedding dress for my daughter, I can't let it be spoiled'. Whilst we were negotiating over a way to store her bargains without endangering the comfort and safety of my children there was a commotion near the door. It was the pilot and he was furious: 'I'm not taking off until all this stuff is out of here, put it all in the hold' he yelled at the dumbstruck cabin crew. Not waiting for his staff or passengers to respond, he began grabbing parcels and other items and chucking them in the direction of the crew, who quickly formed a chain gang to pass the items out of the plane. It was like being in the forerunner of the *Airplane* movies without the comic effect. Eventually he was satisfied that the plane was safe to take off and left the cabin with a straight back and a satisfied air. I can't remember what happened to the wedding dress.

Anyway, despite those who said that the mercury poisoning affair was just a rumour started by the government to distract everyone from these chronic shortages, it can't be denied that Baghdad always abounded with conspiracy theories. All I know for sure is that I became paranoid about my children's diet from that time, forcing milk on them after every meal and probably leaving them with life-long eating disorders.

The Hungarians left and their house was rented by a Scottish nurse, Carol, who was married to an Iraqi doctor. She was unable to have children so they were planning to adopt, which had apparently made her very unpopular with his family. There were few babies available for adoption in those days because extended families were still very close and supportive, so most orphaned children would have a relative who was willing to take them in. Because of this it took them a little while, but eventually they adopted a little girl who was healthy and cute and quickly settled in with her new parents. This encouraged them to add to their family, so they went on to adopt a baby boy with finely drawn features and a solemn expression. Sadly, within a few days the medically-trained couple recognised that the baby had all the symptoms of a terminal illness. They were devastated and couldn't decide whether it would be best to keep the baby for the short period remaining to him or return him to the adoption authorities; the next day, Carol's husband took the decision out of her hands by rising early and taking the baby to the hospital before she woke up. This incident made them even more determined to have a brother for their little girl, so they tried once again but tragically lost their next baby to cot death. In the end they were lucky enough to adopt a sturdy, dark-skinned little boy who was unmistakably bursting with health. It was obvious from his appearance that his natural parents probably came from the south of the country, so they would most likely have been Moslems. When he was a few weeks old Carol took him to church to make arrangements to have him christened, but the old priest was scandalised. 'I can't christen him, he's a Moslem child'. He refused even to discuss the matter further and Carol was sent packing. I'm not sure what caused him to respond in that way, whether it was out of respect for another religion or merely fear that there would be repercussions, but I found it an interesting example of how boundaries must be observed if one is to get along in a multi-cultural society.

That autumn Antonia and her family also left to return home to Czechoslovakia. The new Czech Cultural Attaché who replaced him was a middle-aged man with a much younger wife. She was said to be a model, and was certainly very pretty with long blonde hair and a slim but very shapely figure. She spoke hardly any English and we saw very little of her until the time when she was forced to spend the night at our house. We were all very sad to see Antonia go, particularly Tula, who I knew would miss Zushka even though she saw less of her now that they both went to school. A few weeks after they left, a parcel arrived for Tula from Czechoslovakia containing a pair of bright red fur-lined boots; they were identical to a pair owned by Zushka which Tula had always admired. She was so happy with them and wore them constantly regardless of the weather until they more or less fell apart.

I think that was also the year that Summer left the Home of Children to go to high school. She received very high marks in her final year and so could pick and choose which school she wanted to go to. She didn't even need anyone to 'put a word in' for her. We wanted her to go to the girls' high school in Mansur district; it had an excellent reputation and creamed off the best teachers. It was originally founded as a sister school for the Jesuit College for boys and was still known locally as the American school. It was quite a long way from home, but there was a school bus which would pick her up from the end of the road very early in the morning. As an added bonus, Farah was going to the same school so they would still be together. Sadly, Izhar was not accompanying them because, unlike Farah, she did not have the luxury of an influential uncle who could help her get a place. Just before the new term started it was announced that private education was to be abolished and all private schools would be taken into the state sector. I have no idea whether the owners were compensated, but initially the schools carried on as before with the same head teachers and staff. They also continued to offer a full school day and a school bus service, so we were delighted because the cost of living had been rising and it was no longer so easy to pay school fees for four children on top of everything else. Of course, the new law also meant that children of prominent Baathists would gain places regardless of their academic ability, but I didn't give much thought to that at the time.

At the end of her first day at her new school I was busy preparing lunch when I received a phone call from Summer. 'Mum, can you come and collect me? I can't find my bus'. I dropped everything and drove to the school where several buses were lined up, their drivers all standing around smoking and waiting for the girls who were milling around them to get organised and get on board. I found Summer and we went straight to the headmistress, an impatient and waspish woman, typical of the head of a girl's grammar school. She told us the number of the bus for our district, shaking her head and muttering to a nearby staff member 'and she's one of the clever ones'. I couldn't help but share her impatience – my daughter seemed fated to have problems with the buses on her first day at school. Notwithstanding her impatience on that occasion, the head teacher proved to be a terrific leader and the school maintained an excellent standard of education in the next few years. The daughters of the president, Ahmed Zane al-Bakr, Michel Aflaq, Syrian founder of the Baathist party and several ministers' daughters attended the school whilst Summer was there. Naturally, everyone knew who they were but so far as she was aware they were never given any particular privileges. Later, the head was suddenly and unexpectedly replaced by a woman who was a solid member of the Baath party. Even later, I heard that Saddam's wife, also a qualified teacher, had taken over the job, though apparently she rarely actually turned up for work. However, Summer had left the school by then so I don't know whether this was true.

There were staff changes at the Home of Children too and the first to go was Miss Medeeha, the chaperone on the school bus. She was replaced by a young man with bright blue eyes and a friendly manner who got on well with all the children. He often stopped the bus at the bread stall at the end of our road to buy rounds of hot bread for the last children still remaining on the bus. He was also very good-looking, so I gathered that there was quite a competition among the girls to sit next to him. One day over lunch Tula took advantage of a rare lull in the conversation to get a word in edgeways – as the youngest child she was always demanding to know 'when is it going to be my turn?'

'One of the girls was crying in the playground this morning. She said that the chaperone did something very rude to her'.

'Oh, what did he do?' Apparently the girl said that he put his hand up her skirt – all the way. I was flabbergasted; up until then I had little knowledge of the realities of child molestation and had always had complete trust in the adults who cared for my children. I knew that the bus was always crowded, with as many children as possible squeezed onto the bench seats. 'It was probably an accident; I expect she was mistaken'. Just in case,

I instructed Ali to keep an eye on his sisters whilst they were on the bus and make sure that neither of them sat next to the chaperone. He thought I was crazy; he thought the girl must be crazy too, but he was at that age when boys tend to have a poor opinion of most females. But the girl wasn't crazy: within a week or two the father of another little girl paid a visit to the school early in the morning before lessons started. He went straight to Miss Noele's office where he could be heard quite clearly from the play-ground, shouting at the head. Although the children couldn't make out his words, the upshot of the conversation was that the chaperone was sacked and that was the end of the matter, although it left me with an irrational distrust of men with bright blue eyes. After that I occasionally heard of other incidents of children being molested and it seems strange now that I never did before. Perhaps the changes in society made people more willing to talk about things which would have been 'ebb' to discuss before, or perhaps the incidents occurred as a result of those changes. Who knows?

The fact remained, however, that Baghdad did not feel quite as safe as it had before. The children had already told me about the girls at a large house which we often drove past. It was on their way to school and it stood out not because it had very spacious balconies but because the pretty young girls who lived there always seemed to be out on them, dressed in bright nylon kimonos. I'd never given it much thought until the one of the children announced one day that they were 'naughty ladies'. Of course there had always been prostitutes in Baghdad but they had been mainly confined to a specific area; in fact I believe that at one time this area was walled to protect the prostitutes from attacks by relatives bent on honour killings. Now it was rumoured that the security forces were buying up houses as they became empty so that they could have wild parties and entertain prostitutes without being interrupted. There was a house near the end of our road which had been on the market for ages, but had not sold because the owner had gone to live abroad and wanted to receive payment there. An Iraqi neighbour told me that this house was used by the secret police, adding that they brought girls there late at night for immoral purposes, but I found it hard to believe because I never saw or heard any sign of life in the property, so they must have been the quietest wild parties ever held.

One area where steps were being taken to improve safety was the roads. New highways were being built and traffic police were cracking down on driving infringements. The main road leading to our street was now a fully paved dual carriageway with flowering shrubs planted at intervals along the centre. The filter allowing us to do a U turn back to our exit was several hundred metres up the road so most people, including us, had always been in the habit of leaving the carriageway at the roundabout and completing the last part of their journey by driving up the wrong side of the road. Now a spanking new police station had been built a hundred metres along the carriageway with occupants who always seemed to be on the lookout for drivers coming along on the wrong side, so we no longer had any option but to keep to the right side of the road and take the long way round.

This didn't stop me falling foul of the traffic police one hot afternoon right at the beginning of summer. I had pulled over and was waiting in the car with the fan running whilst Summer ran into a shop to buy something she needed for school. Whilst I waited a police officer tapped on the window, motioning that I should move on. Since I expected Summer to come out of the shop at any minute I was very reluctant to do this, so I fell back on the time-honoured evasion tactics used when caught out in a foreign country: 'Sorry, I don't understand'. He was ready for me though and replied in perfect, if obviously exasperated, English 'Madame, you are not allowed to stop on a pedestrian crossing'. I apologised, put the car into gear and moved forward.

The Iraqi police and armed forces had always sent some of their more promising officers to Britain for further training, so that particular police officer may well have received training abroad. Increasingly, however, it was rumoured that the reason they were sent abroad was to learn new torture techniques, although not necessarily in Britain – rumour had it that Canada and East Germany were the best places to go to learn these. I have no idea how true this was but it was widely accepted that torture inevitably accompanied any period of detention, no matter how trivial the alleged crime. In addition to the traditional establishments dedicated to ensuring law and order and national security, there were now also several security forces, each one monitoring activities in specific walks of life: there was one for the army, one for the civilian population and so on. A huge network of informers made up of people from all walks of life was reputedly employed to pass on information to these agencies about colleagues, neighbours and friends. Although we usually referred to them as 'secret police' very little effort appeared to be made to keep them secret. On the contrary, security men could be spotted at a hundred paces because they usually wore very smart imported suits, were often tall and well-built and, most importantly, always sported the trade mark 'twenty past eight' moustache, so called because it was large and drooped down at the sides of the mouth, causing the face of its wearer to resemble a clock which has stopped at that time. They could also be recognised by the cars they drove; initially they were provided with Mercedes saloons which always had curtains in the rear window – Mum said this was so they could rape girls on the back seat undisturbed – but later other cars were imported for their use.

I found this out one evening when I stopped off at some shops in Mansur district, parking my car head-on to the kerb. When I returned I found a Range Rover parked behind it, blocking me in. Since I wasn't prepared to wait for its driver to finish shopping I turned my key in the ignition and leaned on the horn in time-honoured Baghdad fashion, expecting the driver of the Range Rover to come rushing back to let me out. Within minutes this had the desired effect and a man emerged from one of the buildings and walked briskly up to the car. He was giving me the middle finger and thumb sign which means 'wait a minute' all over the Middle East, but the main reason I stopped tooting was because I knew at once by his 'twenty past eight' that he was a member of the secret police

There was no apology, he simply got in his car and drove off – very quickly followed by myself, heading in the opposite direction. This incident may not seem worthy of mention, but it demonstrates the fear inspired by the secret police. Rumours of on the spot beatings/rapes and other assaults on innocent passers-by – even children- for the most trivial of reasons were widespread, fuelling the chronic insecurity which was taking over the nation. On this occasion, I was so grateful to be still in one piece that when I arrived home I began telling everyone about the incident. Ali, who has been a car fanatic since the age of eight and makes it his business to know everything there is to know about cars, interrupted me: 'Oh yes, they've just imported some Range Rovers for the secret police – they had special souped-up engines fitted'. He was probably about 10 or 11 then but it didn't occur to me to ask how he knew because, as I said, the government didn't seem to try very hard to keep these things secret.

A large area had also been either bought up or appropriated near the centre of Baghdad and the former residential area was now occupied solely by the security forces. Citizens could no longer drive through those streets unless they were on the list of people expected by the guards that day: no-one wanted to be on those lists. Unfortunately, Zane would be forced to pay a visit there before we finally left Baghdad. On the whole, though, we weren't personally bothered much by the secret police, it was just that it was impossible to ignore their presence. They were always in the background, waiting for someone to slip up and say or do the wrong thing. Traditionally, students graduating from high school with the highest marks had gone on to study medicine or engineering, but now it was said that they were encouraged, even forced, to join the security services instead. I have no idea whether this was true, it may have been part of government propaganda to scare its citizens into towing the line, but there was no getting away from the fact that most people did live in fear of a visit from one of the security agencies.

The first time I came into direct contact with them was when my car went on fire. It burst into flames on our hard stand one morning during the university's winter reading week. The day before, which must have been a Friday, Zane and Ali had been tinkering with the engine, arguing as usual about the right way to do it, so they must have failed to screw something back correctly, leaving oil or petrol to leak out overnight. Tula was at home with a sore throat, so when I went out to visit a friend I took her with me, well wrapped up in a coat and scarf. I think she would have been about five or six at the time. As soon as we were both settled in the front seats I pulled out the choke and started the engine, but instead of the usual cough and splutter which signalled my car was being required to start there was a loud 'whoosh' and flames shot up into the air followed by thick black smoke. Needless to say, we both jumped straight out of our seats and I ran for the hose which was attached to the garden tap, very mindful of the gas cylinders which were lined up against the wall. I threw my keys at Tula. 'Go and phone the fire brigade, quickly'. She rushed back into the house as I opened the tap and began spraying water onto the bonnet of the car. Some of the local lads were university students and therefore on holiday; they had been standing around a neighbour's gate, chatting and tossing a ball in the desultory manner of teenagers. This was just the diversion they needed and they made the most of it, rushing over in a race to take command of the garden hose, whilst some of them began moving the cylinders to a safe distance. I left them to carry on and went to check whether Tula had in fact managed to phone for a fire engine. 'I've phoned them: they're coming'. She appeared to have fully recovered from her sore throat as she rushed back out of the house, cheeks restored to their normal pink and obviously eager to see what was happening. As I entered the phone rang. I picked it up and heard a male voice asking whether we needed the fire service and if so, would I tell him where the fire was; Tula had obviously neglected to pass on that information in her excitement. I gave him the necessary directions and promised to send one of the students to the end of the street to direct him to the fire, although anyone could have found it by following the black smoke. But I was puzzled. This was long before the days of telephone call back systems or automatic exchanges and it seemed odd that they knew which number to call. Within a short time two fire engines arrived and the fire was put out, leaving only the metal shell of the car intact. The firemen were very business-like, storing away their equipment and leaving as quickly as they had come as soon as their job was done.

Once they had left I thanked the boys; one of them was a medical student who was to spend many years in prison, first as a prisoner of war in Iran and later in solitary confinement at Abu Ghraib. His only crime was that he managed to escape from Iran and make the long trip over the mountains to Pakistan. When he eventually returned to Iraq he should have received a hero's welcome; instead, he received a visit from the secret police, who viewed him as a security risk because of his years in captivity. Tragically, his long imprisonment effectively brought an early end to his medical career. Of course none of us knew this then, nor did I realise that he was the elder brother of my future son in law.

After the boys had left, I went back into the house with Tula to wash the oily black marks from our faces and hands and change out of our smoke-blackened clothes, but before I could do so I was interrupted by the door-bell. As soon as I answered it, the man at the door immediately began to question me about the fire. He did not introduce himself and even though I had never seen him before I did not ask who he was because it was immediately obvious that he was 'security'. He wanted to know how the fire started, who I thought started it, whether I suspected any of the neighbours of being involved and whether I had any enemies. I explained what had happened, pointing out that my neighbours, far from trying to set me alight had rushed to my aid and probably prevented the fire from spreading. 'Was there a loud bang before the car started to burn?'

'No, only a 'whoosh'. I hoped I didn't sound sarcastic, but the idea that anyone would put a bomb under my car was ludicrous.

He stood there looking at me, obviously mulling over what he had heard. 'Well, where were you going?'

'Shopping.' The conversation was getting ridiculous but I had no intention of telling him any more than I had to about my business – it had become common practice by then to give as little information as possible to strangers, on the basis that any snippet might be used to incriminate you. This guardedness became such a habit that, years after we returned to live in the UK, I found it impossible to give a straight answer to telephone enquiries such as 'Who's speaking', and would counter with 'Who's calling?' or 'Who did you want to speak to?' My answer obviously satisfied him, though, because he left, possibly because shopping was what people spent a lot of time doing by then.

From that time I was convinced that our phone was tapped because it seemed to be the only way the fire service could have known that Tula had phoned from our house. We suspected that they tapped the phones of every foreigner, but in our case it may have been because Pauline and I regularly had long conversations over the phone. Her husband, Munim, had been rising steadily up the ladder of the ministry of oil, eventually becoming a minister himself. His phone calls would definitely have been monitored and as regular calls to our house were made from their phone, ours may have been too. If this was the case it worked in our favour on that occasion: 'It's an ill wind', as they say.

The next encounter was much more serious and I still wonder how we walked away from it unscathed, or perhaps I should say drove away. It happened after a party at the house of a contractor Zane worked for at the time. A French consulting firm was supervising their current project, so the contractor had invited some of the senior French engineers and their wives to dinner. These engineers were responsible for approving every aspect of the construction work, so the boss was very anxious to impress, as indeed Zane should have been. Neither the contractor nor his wife spoke fluent English, so we were probably included on the guest list to help with the conversation. Hatim and his wife had finished building their house by then and had already moved into it with their children. As it happened to be quite near to where the party was, we were leaving our kids with them for the evening.

It was the era of the maxi dress and I was wearing a high-waisted, pale blue maxi in a soft, silky material which fell in graceful folds to the floor; although I had made it myself it was one of my better efforts and it certainly didn't look home-made. I wore my hair up exposing long, dangly earrings which were very much in vogue at the time and I knew even before we arrived at the party that I looked pretty damn good. The other guests at the party all spoke very good English, and I seemed to arouse a lot of attention – probably because I was a bit of a novelty to the French as the foreign wife of an Iraqi. The hospitality was very lavish with a wide selection of alcohol on offer, including some absolutely excellent wines and the other guests were very convivial so it didn't take long to establish the party mood. Our host had a good record collection, including some which were currently in the charts in Britain, but as the evening wore on he began playing Arabic music. This apparently delighted the French party who began clapping loudly and enthusiastically before they progressed to trying out what they fancied were Arabic dances. Our host urged the rest of us to join in, and made a point of urging me to leave the circle of sedate guests who were content to watch and join in the shenanigans. There was no danger of my complying because I was far too self-conscious to dance in front of an audience, even if I could have pulled off the required hip wobbling, which I couldn't, so there was absolutely no need for Zane to turn on his boss with a loud 'Leave her alone, don't tell her what to do.

I was suddenly stone cold sober just as most of the other guests reached the stage where the slightest absurdity seems hilariously funny, and I had good reason. Zane had never been able to handle alcohol and could change from being slightly jolly to very argumentative in seconds once he'd had too many – something it was wisest to avoid in a country where you had to watch what you said. He seldom needed any provocation, anyone present might trigger a stream of insults and on this occasion it was obviously going to be his boss. There was no point in telling him to slow down, I had learned from past experience that it would only spur him on to drink more, so it came as a great relief when our hostess chose that moment to announce that dinner was served. We all made our way into the dining room, where I hoped some solid food would mop up the alcohol in my husband's stomach.

The dinner was laid out in traditional Iraqi style as a hot buffet. Among the selection on offer was a variety of meat dishes including game, which proved very popular with the French guests. For some reason this prompted our host to produce a little stuffed bird from another room; they seemed very taken with the tiny little creature, leaning forward to stroke its soft breast feathers; seeing this he took it away only to return with a slightly larger one. This time the bird was passed round from hand to hand as the guests admired its bright plumage before directing their attention back to their plates. It took him a little longer this time, but our host soon came back carrying an even larger stuffed bird and was rewarded with a cheer as he held the bird high before handing it over to his guests. At my side Zane began muttering and re-filled his glass, ignoring the bird as it reached our side of the table. 'Idiot, is that supposed to be funny? Does he think they haven't seen birds before?' It was apparent that there were two things going on in the room: half the guests were in danger of doubling up with mirth as larger and yet larger stuffed birds made their triumphant appearance (God knows where he kept them all), whilst some of the other guests had become aware that Zane was drunk and likely to cause trouble.

There were two things going on inside me as well, a combination of cold, furious anger with my husband for spoiling the evening but also embarrassment that he had let the side down by being the only Iraqi present who couldn't handle his liquor. It was obvious that we had to leave before he caused a scene: I'm not sure how I did it, but I managed to persuade him that we should go – I think I even made some kind of farewell to most of the people in the room before I hustled him out with a very firm hand on his arm. As we passed one Iraqi lady I just caught what she was saying sympathetically to her neighbour: 'Poor thing, she's embarrassed because her husband's drunk' above the assorted cheers, whistles and uproarious laughter which greeted our host, who had somehow managed to stagger into the dining room carrying what looked like a stuffed eagle.

As soon as the cool night air hit him, Zane became worse and had to lean against our car for support as he took his jacket off and fumbled for his keys. I grabbed it, took the keys from the pocket and unlocked the door of his white estate car. 'I'm driving, get in,' I snapped as I jumped into the driver's seat very quickly, expecting resistance. To my relief, he got into the car on the passenger side, though not without mumbling a few very uncomplimentary things which I assumed were directed at me.

I ignored him and started the car, heading towards Hatim's house. By that time I was absolutely furious but I knew there was no point in saying anything whilst he was in that state. I just wanted to collect my children and go home but I was also grateful that I had managed to get Zane away before he openly insulted his boss or caused a row with another guest, so perhaps the evening had not been a complete disaster, I reflected as I tried to find my way back to Hatim's house.

I couldn't go back the way we had come because the drainage system which Zane had worked on a few years earlier had reached this part of the city, so several side streets had been closed off. 'How do we get to Hatim's from here?' Even my inebriated husband should have been able to answer this simple question, but he had completely lost the plot. 'Take me home, I'm telling you, take me home, can't you understand?' It was obviously him who was incapable of understanding, but there was no point in saying that, so I decided to go straight home and ring Hatim when we got there to let him know that the kids would be staying overnight.

First we had to get back to the main road, though. The first street I tried was closed at the far end, so I turned into the open driveway of a large building with the intention of backing out onto the street. The car was a French model which Zane used for work and I had never driven it before, so I was dismayed to find that it did not have the usual H style gear shift I was used to. 'How do you put this into reverse? Show me'. My head was bent forward as I tried to work it out for myself so I didn't realise he had opened the door until he got out of the car and started up the drive, probably thinking he had arrived home. I was really losing patience as I got out myself to go and bring him back. Before I could reach him a policeman appeared: he had obviously been guarding the building. I hurried towards him to explain why we were there but I didn't get a chance to speak because Zane shoved him aside and carried on walking. The officer yelled out and un-holstered his gun – all policemen were armed in Iraq – and several others came running out of the building, taking out their weapons as they went. The evening was turning into a nightmare. 'No, stop, it's all right, my husband's drunk, I can't get the car into reverse, we didn't mean to come in here'. I was babbling, but I had never been threatened by guns before, and Zane had reached the other officers by then. Most people would have sobered up, but not my husband. 'What do you want? I want to go home'. At least they could see I was telling the truth about him being drunk. The first officer gestured towards the building with his gun, 'You'll have to come inside and answer some questions.'

Strangely, I wasn't scared: I was too angry to be scared and all my anger was directed at my husband, the man who was supposed to protect me. How could he be such an idiot? Not only had he got us into this mess, he was totally unaware of the seriousness of the situation and seemed hell bent on causing even more trouble. Inside the building we were taken into a room where several police officers were sitting, some drinking tea and some playing a card game which involved slapping the cards down hard on the table. I explained again exactly what had happened, including the fact that we had been to a party. 'Probably been to the Hunting Club', a portly middle-aged officer glanced up at us before directing his attention back to the game. The Hunting Club had been started by Saddam for the exclusive use of government employees; it was much more ornate than any of the existing clubs in the capital and its stated purpose was to provide its members with the facilities which they might not otherwise have access to.

Hatim and his wife had taken us to a dinner dance there not long before; it had been a disappointing experience with much more emphasis on the dinner than the dancing. Everyone present at that event seemed stiff and uncomfortable, decidedly on their best behaviour. The liveliest bit of the evening was when everyone scraped their chairs back so that they could stand up and applaud enthusiastically when a high ranking government official entered the room. I don't know who thought up the name of the club, but I can't help thinking he must have had his tongue in cheek because there were absolutely none of the high jinks which most British people would associate with the name. I can honestly say that the entertainment on that evening was a far cry from the excesses which Saddam's sons and their entourages were later widely reported to have indulged in.

Nevertheless, I think that the police officers' treatment of us was tempered by the fact that we might have been at the club and therefore Zane might have been a person of influence. I said nothing to dispel the idea since I had not been asked and felt it was better to leave them to their own conclusion rather than tell them that we had been to a private party which had been attended by several foreigners, an event much more likely to give rise to further investigation. 'You'll have to send for security. You can't let them go until they've been questioned by the duty officer'. This was from the portly officer again; he seemed to have a lot of influence with his colleagues, even though he didn't appear to be any higher in rank than the rest of them. The guard who had first spotted us outside went off, I imagined to make a phone call and we waited for the dreaded security man to arrive. At least, I waited. No-body offered us a seat and I stood in icy silence with my husband's jacket slung over my arm while he mumbled and cursed at the fact that he was being kept from home. For the most part nobody spoke to us either, although every so often one or other of the card players would speculate on what we had been up to as he threw down a card. 'Look at the state of him, and he's an engineer'. I couldn't help but agree as I looked at my dishevelled husband. 'Oh, come on, everyone has problems sometimes, and when that happens you have a few drinks to drown your sorrows'. This was from an admirably philosophical young man who I felt was speaking from experience. 'He must have had quite a few problems then, he's had more than a few beers by the look of that belly'. It was undeniable that Zane was no longer the slim young man he had been when we first met. Over the past few years he had developed a noticeable beer gut.

One policeman did sidle up and speak to me. I still remember what he looked like, thin faced and shifty and I knew instinctively that he was up to no good. 'Are you really his wife? Only it will be very bad for you if it isn't true.' Intuition told me that he was longing for me to admit that we weren't married, that I was a mistress or maybe some kind of hired escort. I was convinced that he wanted to drag me off to another room for a spot of illicit sex before the security man arrived. I fixed him with my iciest stare. 'Do you really think I'd be standing here with him in that state if I wasn't married to him?' I stared him down and he backed off, slithering away back to his corner. We continued to wait, and Zane continued to ramble, until, incredibly, he started on Saddam. 'Saddam, Who does he think he is? What has he ever done for anyone?' The room became very still and the card players were all paying attention now, whilst I was thinking, 'Oh no, we're going to die'. 'Do you know Saddam?' It was Officer Portly who asked the question but I awaited the answer with equal interest. 'Of course, known him since he was in... I can't remember where he was supposed to have known him. I do remember dreading what was coming next. 'What about Barzan? Do you know him?' Barzan was one of Saddam's half-brothers – he had recently been given control of all the security forces and was reputed to carry out his job with great enthusiasm and brutality. 'No, never met him'. That was obviously the right answer, because everyone visibly relaxed and the card game continued.

I waited some more, reflecting that it was a good job that we weren't a threat to national security because they were certainly in no hurry to question us. I was just reaching the stage when I would have welcomed being locked in a cell for the night, so long as it had a bed, when a short, plumpish, cheerful-looking man positively bounded into the room. He came as a bit of a surprise to me because he was so unlike the stereotypical security men we had become accustomed to seeing around the city, but more surprising was the reaction he received from my husband. 'Hello, hello, welcome, how are you?' These were the first intelligible words he had uttered for hours and as he spoke them he held out his hand to be shaken, then lunged forward and enveloped the man in a bear hug. For one crazy moment I actually thought he knew the man, until he stepped back and lapsed once again into drunken ramblings.

The newcomer took it all in his stride, obviously identifying me as the other detainee with one glance. 'So what happened?' I went through the story again, hoping it sounded less nonsensical to him that it did to me. 'OK, identity card?' The smile was still there but he was all business. I took Zane's ID card, still in its little black cover, out of the breast pocket of his jacket and handed it over. Whilst he studied it he threw a question over his shoulder to the room in general. 'So, where's the car?' It struck me that he must have been in the building all along as he would have seen it in the driveway if he had come that way. I couldn't help wondering if he had come straight from roughing up a suspect. 'We haven't moved it, it's still outside where they parked it'. He turned and left the room, leaving me convinced that I was experiencing the 'good cop, bad cop' routine, and that a very different interrogator would be taking his place. I waited there for what seemed another age, imagining them carrying out checks into Zane's background and probably searching the car. The cause of all this trouble had collapsed into a chair by then, but I was frozen into the standing position, unable to move my feet. At last the smiley security guy returned with our car keys in his hand. 'OK, you can go but I'm coming with you, I can't let you drive alone with him in the car in that condition.'

He turned to speak to the police officers: 'A couple of you can drive him, I'll go with her in their car.'

'I'll go with you if you like', the young philosopher offered, obviously never having learned the maxim 'never volunteer'. I suppose any distraction was a welcome relief to sitting out the night in that room, but it was clear from his answer that the security man had other important goings-on to attend to: I suspected that they might involve searching our house, or taking us off to be tortured somewhere. 'How will you get back? I won't be able to bring you.'

'That's no problem, I'll get a lift back with the patrol car'. (there was usually a police patrol car stationed at every major roundabout in the city, particularly at night. Perhaps they would welcome something to do, too).

So we all went outside and Zane was helped into the back of one vehicle while I walked with my escort to our own car, which was still sitting on the driveway where I had left it. As I approached I was somewhat relieved to see one of Zara's dolls sitting on the parcel shelf of the rear window. She loved her dolls and rarely went anywhere, apart from school, without taking a couple with her. This may seem ridiculous, but I hoped the sight of the doll would substantiate my story that I was on my way to collect my children. Because I was under no illusion that the ordeal was over; on the contrary I expected, if we reached our house at all, that the man sitting beside me would metamorphose into the raping, torturing monster who featured in every Iraqi's worst nightmare.

Once I had managed to put the car into reverse with the help of my jolly secret policeman, I backed out into the street, then waited for the other car to drive out so that I could pull in behind it, as instructed. Our little convoy then set off briskly towards home, stopping only once on the way so that Zane could be taken over to a patch of waste ground in order to answer a call of nature. It was rather a lengthy stop – he was probably being sick as well. Whatever happened, the two police officers who had escorted him returned to the car grinning.

Dawn was just breaking as I pulled up onto our hard stand, parking the car neatly behind my little VW – more evidence that my story was true, I felt. The policemen had already unloaded their passenger, who was striding up the path towards the front door with the righteous air of a man who had been forcibly kept from home for far too long. 'OK, goodbye'. The security man joined the others in the car, which immediately began to execute a U turn so that it faced back up towards the main road. I couldn't believe it – was it some sort of trick? Were they just waiting for me to open the door so that they could come back and push their way in? Or had he just wanted to check that we lived where I said we did? Well, there was only one way to find out, so I went round to where Zane was fumbling in his trouser pockets for a non-existent key, and opened the front door. I stepped inside warily, half expecting to be jumped by people waiting for us inside. The house appeared to be just as we had left it: one of the children had left a pair of rubber flip flops just inside the front door and Zane had dropped a damp towel onto the chair near the bathroom. Both lay undisturbed. I stood for a moment trying to absorb the atmosphere of the silent house, but Zane showed no such hesitation, pushing past me and heading straight for the bathroom. By the time I went into the girls' bedroom, slamming the door behind me, the sound of violent retching was already audible through the bathroom wall.

It turned out that the building which we had inadvertently entered was some kind of local party headquarters – obviously its precise function wasn't public knowledge. The very few people we told about the incident could not believe that anyone could walk into it, curse Saddam and get away with it. For my part, it was several weeks before I was able to relax and believe that there really weren't going to be any repercussions. It took a bit longer before I could feel anything but cold anger towards my husband.

# Chapter Thirteen

As the party's control on the country increased, its ability to ensure an adequate supply of foodstuffs and other commodities continued to decline, whilst the man on the street continued to believe that it was a ploy to distract people from scrutinising the government too closely. Even locally produced and processed foods which had always been readily available became very hard to find. I particularly missed the dairy products which had been marketed under the trade name of Alban'. I think that they were produced under licence by the government, although I'm not absolutely sure about this, but they had always been on sale in most grocery shops, and could even be purchased from a chilled van which delivered regularly to city suburbs. Suddenly they were hard to find and people were forced to go back to buying their milk, cream and other products from the vendors who had traditionally offered their unpasteurised goods door to door. In our case it meant that large tins of dried milk took the place of the crate of long-life milk which had always stood in our kitchen.

Although the children hated the milk which I insisted they drink every day, and actually preferred the dried milk because they liked eating the powder, I knew that it could not be as good as drinking fresh milk. For my part, I found it hard to manage without Alban butter and cream; not only did I enjoy it at breakfast-time but its absence made baking very difficult, so I had to bite my tongue and hide my irritation when Summer told me that Farah's fridge and freezer were still full of the Alban products and her Mum said that there was no problem finding them in the shops. This was another ploy of the Baathists – they made sure that party members, particularly high ranking ones, had access to foods and other commodities not available to the general public. I suppose it was a way both of rewarding loyalty and ensuring that it continued; confirmation that the practice existed came to me because of Mah Jong, not that I ever doubted it.

Some of my local friends and neighbours had formed a mah jong group which met weekly, taking it in turns to provide the hospitality in the form of coffee and cake. As usually happens with these things, numbers fluctuated as people became bored with the game, so someone invited some German women whose husbands were also German to join us. Normally, most people avoided socialising with foreigners – wives of Iraqis were not considered to be foreigners – but the German girls were pleasant enough and I quite liked going to their houses to play because they made fantastic cakes. They also organised events which we wouldn't normally have thought of, like the evening we all went out to a rather nice restaurant at Christmas time. It seems funny now, but it was not customary for Iraqi women to enjoy girly nights out in public places at that time, they normally got together at home, so I got the impression that the waiters enjoyed the event almost as much as we did.

One morning we were playing at the home of one of the Germans whom I particularly liked. Her husband was the local manager of Lufthansa and she was much jollier and less formal than the others, who took their game very seriously. Whilst the English girls at such events gossiped and joked and took it with good humour when they lost, the Germans played to win. Understandably, they also tended to lapse into German whilst they were playing; during one such interlude our hostess turned to me and brought up the subject of the shortages in the shops, surprising me by asking: 'Do you know that the people in government have everything they want?' Every day a plane arrives from Germany with everything you can imagine on it – foods, delicacies, clothes, perfume, medicine, everything. I've seen them.' I wasn't surprised by what she said, only that she had said it to people she didn't know very well. English eyes met over the mah jong tiles but no-one said anything until we were driving home. 'What do you think, shall we give mah jong a miss from now on?'

'Yes, I think we'd better'. There was no need for further discussion – too many people had been dragged away from queues and beaten up for publicly acknowledging that there were shortages in the market.

I think it was around that time that a story began to emerge about the slaughter of a doctor and his family. It seemed that their home had been broken into by burglars who had gone on to butcher the whole family, including several children. It was said that the person who found their bodies discovered a scene of horrifying carnage. At first everyone shook their heads and wondered what the world was coming to, but then another family was found murdered in similar circumstances, then another. Apparently the capital had a serial killer on the loose, something which I imagine causes general uneasiness at any time, but because this killer went on to butcher women and even children he evoked especial dread. Although it was not known whether an individual or a gang was carrying out the crimes, the perpetrator was universally known as the 'Axe Man' and just mentioning that name caused strong women and naughty children to shake in their shoes. Similar crimes continued to be reported throughout the summer, scaring families who normally slept on the roof into retreating down into their bedrooms. Although I was sceptical of the stories, being among those people who thought they were yet another government ploy to terrify the population, I still took the precaution of telling Ali to sleep downstairs on one of the settees in our open-plan hallway so that he would be near to the rest of the family.

Of course the children were affected by the stories; one night we were woken by the girls screaming that the Axe Man had tried to force open the bedroom window. Ali, who had jumped up and rushed into the bedroom when he heard the screams, also swore he had seen a man outside the window. In the morning we went out to the garden to investigate, and there were indeed footprints in the soil outside the bedroom window, but I always assumed that they had been left by the gardener or even Zane. I did expect the adults to show a bit more bottle, but one evening our immediate neighbourhood reached a state of near panic as yet another butchered family was reported to have been discovered. We were sitting out in the garden, enjoying the cool evening breeze when Carol, our neighbour from across the street, rushed over to tell us the news. Her husband followed, Erica and Saidi were summoned and a mini conference was held – Carol had been a staff nurse in the UK and liked to boss people around and organise things. Various suggestions were put forward, such as clubbing together to hire a night watchman to patrol the street, but that wasn't enough for Carol. 'None of us are safe at home, we should all move in together'. I felt that to be the most ridiculous suggestion of the evening and I think Zane agreed, but he managed to get this over quite tactfully: 'I'm not moving from my house, but anyone who wants to come and stay here is welcome'.

And so it was agreed; they all went home to collect the things they would need for the night whilst I set about getting out all the spare mattresses and bedding. Luckily, every Iraqi household kept a plentiful supply of these in case of visitors so it was an easy matter to plan where everyone would sleep. Carol and her husband and baby would take over Ali's room and Erica and family would sleep on the floor in the sitting room. When they came back it turned out that Carol had insisted on roping in the Czechoslovakian couple who had replaced Antonio's family. We allocated them the floor in the hallway but I can't remember where we put Ali.

By the second night the watchman had been recruited – a local man who worked as a foreman on building sites. He marched up and down the perimeter of our garden wall while we were awake with a heavy stick balanced on his shoulder like a rifle, but I suspected that he went off home to bed once he judged we were safely asleep. I doubt whether any of us slept any better for all these precautions. Those people who were sleeping downstairs had to step over the Czechs to use the bathroom, and the mere fact that people were sleeping all over the house gave it a siege-like atmosphere which was hardly conducive to rest. Carol reported that one morning she had got up very early to get the baby a bottle. On her way downstairs she had seen the diplomat reaching for his lovely young wife only to be pushed away, understandably given the lack of privacy. Perhaps this was why they were the first to break, returning to their own house after only three nights. The others stayed a little longer. Erica and her family left first, then Carol returned home the following evening, roping in Saidi to help her husband carry the baby's cot down the stairs and across the road. I still picture it now, Carol walking regally across the road followed by the two men lifting the cot up high like ancient slaves carrying a royal barge. Once they had gone Zane dispensed with the services of the night watchman. Needless to say, no-one offered to cough up their share of his pay.

Meanwhile the police were doing their best to capture the villain, or so we were told. Apparently they had a profile of the killer which included how tall he was. He would be hunted down, and to this end a full day's curfew was announced so that a house-to-house search could be carried out. It made little difference to the children, who were on holiday from school anyway, but the adults spent the day at their garden gates chatting across the street to neighbours while they waited to be inspected – it was almost like having a military coup. Our inspection team, consisting of three armed soldiers led by a man in plain clothes, obviously security, eventually arrived and we were all ushered up to the roof where our names and ages were recorded. Then Zane, Summer and I were made to stand in the mid-day sun, taking it in turns to hold a pole in the upright position whilst a photographer took pictures. Apparently the pole was the same height as the Axe Man but all I can say is that he must have been very tall. Mercifully, none of us reached high enough up the pole to be considered as suspects. After that the house was searched from top to bottom. They went through everything, cupboards, wardrobes, the lot. I accompanied a young soldier to my bedroom and waited whilst he looked under the bed and on top of the wardrobe before he turned his attention to its contents. Our wardrobe took up an entire wall of the bedroom and was divided into four sections, each of which had a wooden shoe rack in its base. Unfortunately we didn't have enough shoes to fill them all, so one of them was unused and I had folded some winter clothes on top of it. I stood and watched as the soldier reached that section, suddenly becoming visibly excited as he felt the shoe racks, which must had seemed to him to be deliberately hidden. He threw the clothes aside and scrabbled under them, keeping a wary eye on me while he did so. No doubt he thought he had found a rifle, or maybe even an axe, and was probably already fantasising about promotion. If he was his hopes were sadly dashed once the wooden rack was revealed.

Later that day Mum phoned; she was furious when we told her about the photo session on the roof, particularly when she heard that they had photographed Summer, who must have been about thirteen at the time. 'Why did you let them in? Why didn't you tell them where to go?' Amazingly, she had done just that, refusing to allow them entry and even more amazingly, they had gone away and left her in peace.

It must have been quite soon after that the Axe Man was reported to be captured. A photo of him standing alongside his main accomplice, his wife, appeared on TV and in the newspapers. Dressed in traditional Arab costume, both of them were middle-aged, stout and decidedly unfit-looking. I couldn't imagine them being able to chase anyone with an axe, let alone catch them. In addition they were both singularly ugly, but with the ugliness that comes from a lifetime of hardship and poverty rather than evil intentions. I doubt that anyone would suspect them of being mass murderers if they passed them in the street and I found it very hard to believe that they had carried out the atrocities they were accused of. In due course they were reported hanged along with their other accomplices and there was no more talk of an axe murderer being on the loose in the city.

The idea lingered on in the popular psyche, though, as we were to learn one evening. It was early in the new school year and the weather had at last cooled down. Little homework had yet been allocated and the girls were bored, so I took Zara and Tula and drove over to Pauline's for a couple of hours before supper. My girls got on really well with her daughter, Neda, and they were always glad to see each other. It was such a lovely evening that we decided to go out for a stroll leaving the girls at home. On our way we passed the house of an English girl while she was hosing down her driveway; we both knew her so we stopped for a chat and ended up staying out longer than we intended. By the time we walked back to Pauline's it was already getting dark. The house was very quiet as we approached the kitchen door but as it was children's TV time we didn't think it odd. Pauline opened it and stepped inside but as she switched on the light we both froze at the scene in front of us. The three girls were lying motionless on the floor, apparently asleep except for the bright splashes of red which stood out starkly on their light-coloured summer dresses. There were also red streaks all over their limbs. If they could have kept it going a little longer we might have fallen for it and started screaming, but their bodies began to quiver as they tried to hold back their giggles just at the same moment that I realised that the 'blood' was much too red. Of course, it was tomato ketchup. They jumped up shouting 'Fooled Ya, fooled Ya!', waving their arms and leaping around the kitchen like banshees.

'Yes, you scared us to death'. But they would not have thought of playing that particular trick before the advent of the Axe Man.

# Chapter Fourteen

That autumn Ali left the Home of Children for high school. He was going to Baghdad College, a very prestigious boys' school which had been started by Jesuit priests at the time of the monarchy. When the Baathists first took power in the sixties, one of the things they did was to expel the Jesuits apparently believing that they exercised a seditious American influence on their pupils, and install local management. Originally tuition was in English, but by the time Ali went there things had changed, and most of the lessons were in Arabic. The school even had recognised status with some American universities and Iraqi-born graduates of Baghdad College still hold regular reunions in the States. Nadia's husband, also an old boy of the college, still goes to them when he can.

As the school was right over the other side of the city Ali had to leave very early in the morning to get the bus, even earlier than Summer, but he refused my offer to walk with him to the end of the road – something I initially did with Summer when she first started high school. He set off down the deserted street, refusing to look back at me as I watched from the gate, very much the young man as he set off for his first day at high school. When he returned he was bubbling with excitement as he described the fantastic science labs, huge playing fields and the new friends he had already made. Sitting in our sunny kitchen he chattered on about his day whilst I dished up lunch, but by the time the meal was over a cloud had descended over me, or more accurately it hung from my chest like a heavy weight as I listened to what he had to say:

'And I spoke to Oday. Well, I didn't know it was Oday at

first, I just saw this boy playing with this really expensive football, so I went over and asked him where he got it. He goes:

"What do you mean? I bought it of course"

"Where did you buy it from? You can't get that make anywhere in Baghdad'." That was my son, ever the connoisseur of luxury items.

"'Why not?"

And then I realised I had all these men standing round me, all big security guards scowling at me.

"What do you want, kid?"

"I don't want anything".

"On your way, then".

'I got away as quickly as I could, but after that all the other boys kept coming up to me and asking what Oday said to me, so now everyone in the school knows me'.

Like every parent we wanted the best for our children, including the best possible education, but it had never occurred to me to wonder who my son's classmates would be. I suppose I assumed they would be kids like ours, bright kids with aspirational parents – 'good folk' to use the Iraqi social measuring stick. Oday was of course Saddam's eldest son. It turned out that Oday's cousin had also joined the school that year. The boys were very closely related since Saddam had married a cousin whose brother was a career army officer, very respected by his fellow officers. Along with the sons of several other top ranking Baathists, the group of boys literally formed a class of their own. They hung around together, always accompanied by the bodyguards, and there was an armed guard stationed at the windows and doors of their classroom during lessons. Later they were joined by Saddam's younger son and the boys were accorded much higher and more overt security than any prince at Eton. The kids would arrive at the school in a convoy of speeding vehicles and other boys would have to leap out of the way as the cars sped up the driveway. I even heard that a couple of boys who had not been quick enough were actually run over, but I think this may have been childish exaggeration.

Oday did have one thing in common with most of the other boys at the school – he was fanatical about football and played whenever possible. Unfortunately, he had something wrong with either his foot or leg which gave him a curious, rolling gait and made it difficult for him to run. Whenever he joined in a game the other boys had to hide their smiles as he desperately tried to reach the ball before the other side got to it. On one occasion he succeeded only to lose the ball again via a determined tackle. This was too much for the watching bodyguards; they went onto the pitch and marched the offending tackler away, leaving the players to continue their game. The boy-tackler was back in the classroom later but he never spoke about what happened to him during the time he was taken away by the minders. It was generally supposed that he was given a strong warning not to repeat the offence, perhaps with a slap or two to reinforce the point. Nevertheless, the incident served as a reminder to everyone at the school that Oday was not to be messed with. All we could do was to remind Ali to be very careful of what he said and did, to stay well away from Oday's group and above all, not to succumb to being bullied into joining the school's youth party unit. It wasn't long before this advice proved to be only too wise.

Ali had always been a very friendly, popular kid; he didn't stick to boys of his own age but got on well with boys of all ages, even when they were quite a bit older than he was. This was largely because his neighbourhood friends all had older brothers, so when one of Ali's friends went somewhere with an older brother, he would often tag along too. It wasn't something I was particularly happy about because, as the only boy in a family of girls whose father was away a lot, he often tried to play the 'head of the house' and boss his sisters about. I felt that mixing with older boys made this tendency worse and I was also reluctant to allow him the same freedom to come and go as he pleased which older boys in our area enjoyed, since he didn't have a big brother to look out for him like the others. It didn't surprise me, then, that within a short time one of his best mates at school was a year older. He was in Ali's class because he had missed a year of school owing to illness. Although I didn't know it then, he came from a highly political family and was chairman of the youth division of the Baath party at the school; his name was also Ali – a very popular name in Baghdad at the time.

Anyway, one day Ali returned from school with the tale of how his friend had 'wiped the floor with Oday at a youth party meeting. Apparently, at a lunch time meeting, Oday and this boy had disagreed over some item on the agenda. They had not been able to reach a compromise so, failing to win the argument, Oday had arbitrarily announced: 'That's it, this meeting's over'.

'You can't do that, I'm the chairman and I'm the only one who can pronounce the meeting over. It'll end when I say so.'

So the meeting went on for a little longer, with Oday glowering at the chairman but forced to stay. By the end of the day the story had been passed all round the school, much to the secret amusement of many of the pupils. I can't say I took much notice at the time; although I didn't want my kids to join the party, if I thought about these youth meetings at all I imagined them to be boy scout stuff, or something like the young farmers' association.

A few more weeks passed and the half yearly school holiday arrived; it was in February, always a cold, wet and fairly miserable month in Baghdad, so Ali was quite jealous when he told me that his friend Ali was leading a youth delegation to Cuba where he would be meeting Castro and other so-called 'non-aligned' leaders during the school holiday. I think I even felt a flash of jealousy that none of my own children were exhibiting any signs of early leadership skills, and then the holiday was upon us and I thought no more about it.

The first day of the new school term, Ali was quieter than usual when he returned from school. Usually he would be either winding up one of his sisters or making us laugh with tales of playground scuffles and one-upmanship, but he waited for lunch to be over before telling me the news. 'Something terrible happened in Cuba: Ali had an accident in the hotel swimming pool and drowned'. How do you tell your twelve-year-old son that one of his best friends has almost certainly been murdered and that nothing would be done about it? In this case, the answer was 'you don't'. I followed my first instinct which was to behave as though I really believed it was an accident. I didn't ask any questions which might suggest I suspected foul play, or which might encourage him to voice any suspicions at school. He was obviously very sad but I didn't think it had dawned on him that his friend had been murdered because he had stood up to Oday. 'Oh, that's terrible, I'm so sorry to hear that, what an awful thing to happen.' It was probably very cowardly of me, but discussing what was politically unspeakable in front of children was a sure fire way of bringing disaster on both them and their families. Everyone knew the story of the little boy who told his teacher that his dad spat every time Saddam appeared on television – the teacher reported it and the entire family disappeared. So I played dumb, as Iraqis all over the country did every day of their lives. Later that day I bumped into Saidi and asked him into the house so that I could tell him the story. I expected him to be shocked and saddened, but his reaction took me by surprise:

'What was his name?' I told him the boy's full name, which meant nothing to me, and was quite taken aback when the normally easy-going, jolly Saidi remarked:

'Just as well he's been killed now then, he'd have grown up to be even worse than his father'.

When Zane came home I repeated the story of the tragedy. He was shocked but agreed that it was best to say as little as possible and to leave Ali to get over it in his own way. Although his reaction was different from Saidi's, he couldn't stop himself from admitting some time later that he had not been happy about the friendship. Obviously, you can't choose your children's friends but he had been worried that the dead boy might drag Ali down into the dangerous water of Iraqi politics. He didn't say any more than that, but I had the sneaking feeling that deep down he couldn't help feeling a tinge of relief that the boy would no longer be around. I never found out who his father was but I have often wondered what he had done to produce such extreme and sad reactions to his son's death.

Despite the over-arching menace posed by our leaders, the city and countryside continued to improve on the surface, with smart new restaurants and hotels springing up everywhere. Family-oriented leisure pursuits were also being developed. One of these was a large natural lake with sandy shores which made it feel like the seaside, about an hour's drive from the capital. Saddam was developing a holiday centre nearby and we spent some happy days with friends at the lake. Later it became too popular with the Baathists, particularly Saddam and his kids, so we stopped going. The presence of government officials and other notables often put a damper on evenings out, like the time we went out for a meal with Marita and Adnan at a recently opened restaurant. The décor was impressive, the food and service was excellent and we were just debating whether we should order another bottle of wine or just have coffee. Our waiter joined in, trying to persuade Marita and me that we would really regret it later if we passed up the chance to try one of their delicious desserts, a speciality of the restaurant. Whilst he was doing this his attention wandered as it became obvious that something was up among the restaurant staff. The manager had gone into a huddle with one of his waiters and others were leaving their posts to join in. There was a lot of whispering going on, then the waiters fanned out back to their tables. Ours returned with a surprising volte-face, leaning over Zane to say quietly:

'I'm sorry, Sir, but if you want dessert you'll have to eat it really quickly because we have to clear the restaurant.' Apparently a government minister had just phoned to announce his imminent arrival at the restaurant with a large party of friends. Presumably he didn't feel the need to phone ahead and book a table like we mere mortals, nor did it seem that he wished to mingle with the hoi polloi. For their part, the hoi polloi obviously did not wish to mingle with him either because all over the restaurant diners could be seen gulping down their food with one hand whilst they signalled for their bill with the other. There was a genteel stampede for the door on the part of the diners whilst the waiters could hardly wait for them to vacate their seats before grabbing the plates and cutlery and whisking off the table cloths. We had made an early booking because we had left the kids alone at home, so our dinner wasn't completely ruined. Actually, the evening wasn't even disrupted much, because we had planned to go back to our house for drinks after dinner anyway, but even so we never went back to that restaurant.

Looking back, it seems amazingly irresponsible that we used to leave our children at home alone whilst we went out at night, but from the time that Summer was about fourteen we did just that. In those days it wasn't at all unusual for the eldest child to become the baby sitter as soon as they hit their teens, and despite the ever-present fear of the secret police arriving on your doorstep, Baghdad still felt remarkably safe. In our case, we also had our Alsatian dog, Tiger; at least he was almost an Alsatian apart from his ears which were a bit too floppy and refused to stand up properly. He was the terror of the neighbourhood because he loved to lie in wait for passers-by behind the garden wall then launch himself at the ornamental metal gate, snarling and barking like a demented wolf. Once he had scared his victim half to death, he would race across the garden to the garage gates where he would leap up and scare him or her all over again if this person was unfortunate enough to have turned the corner into the side street. Day or night, he never failed to play this game, causing people who regularly passed our house to make sure they walked on the other side of the street. For years our home was known in the area as 'the dog house' – it became a local landmark just like the corner shop at the end of the road. We never did anything to discourage the idea that he was ferocious, but close neighbours and friends all knew that he was in fact gentle and friendly and never hurt a fly, with the possible exception of the wild cats which lurked in the area scavenging for food. If one of these cats was foolish enough to venture into our garden it would be lucky to escape unscathed. Tiger would launch himself at the unfortunate animal and there would be a wild chase around the garden, often ending in a frenzied skid as he tried to avoid a tree trunk that the cat had managed to climb. If he did manage to catch up he would leap upon the terrified little animal then pin its head down with one paw whilst he worried it like a terrier. Alerted by the commotion, it would then fall to either me or one of the kids to rush out and pull him off by the collar, allowing the spitting, yowling cat to make its escape. So far as I know, he never seriously injured one so perhaps it was just another of his games, like the one he liked to play with the hedgehogs.

Baghdad nights were mild for most of the year, so Tiger usually slept outside. Once dusk fell the bats would start to swoop between the trees, looking for their nocturnal prey and among the animals visiting our garden at night were hedgehogs. When they sensed danger they would roll themselves into a ball, spikes pointing out as hedgehogs do, much to the fascination of the kids when they were young. I often used to bring one into the kitchen as a nature lesson for my children; I would put out a saucer of milk to tempt it into unrolling while the youngest child of the moment stood spell-bound. First its little nose would begin to poke out and quiver, then its head would gradually appear as it metamorphosed from a hard spiky ball into a hungry little animal.

Tiger liked to keep control of the hedgehog situation himself, however. Whenever he found a hedgehog rolled up in the garden he would pick it up gently in his mouth then carry it to the terrace where he would set it down before lying down beside it in the 'on guard' position. After a while he would appear to lose interest and begin to drop off to sleep, which was the cue for the hedgehog to start to unroll. It never got far, though; just as the little legs were starting to peep out Tiger would give one sharp bark and cuff it with his paw, causing the ball to reinstate itself. This could go on for hours, often until either Zane or I got fed up and went outside to scoop up the hedgehog with a spade and chuck it over the garden wall. If the kids were awake they would be furious and accuse us of being cruel, particularly if the animal had been thrown into the street where it ran the risk of being run over.

Our children were all staunch animal lovers, forever trying to save the life of some fledgling bird which had fallen from the nest – attempts which inevitably ended in failure. I don't think any of them ever really forgave me for the incident in the kitchen with the milk crate. It happened at breakfast time one cold winter morning. For several days, a little field mouse had taken to coming into the kitchen through the gap under the door, looking for a place to build a nest. I had no wish to play host to an entire family of them and had already cleared out its efforts from behind the cooker once. On this particular morning, the kids were playing up, we were running late and I was feeling very stressed. Just as I was yelling at them to cut it out and get a move on, I saw the little mouse out of the corner of my eye. First its head appeared under the door, then, with barely a glance around, it strolled across the kitchen towards the cooker with an infuriatingly nonchalant air. I know mice like to make themselves at home, but this one had all the appearance of a returning family member. I blew my top: picking up the milk crate, I swung it at the tiny creature, yelling 'And you can get out of here, too.'

By an amazing fluke, the crate hit it, causing all four kids to let out a synchronised yell of: 'MUM!!!', which was almost drowned out by the cries of the mouse as it limped back towards the door, yelping like a puppy whose tail has been stepped on. I never knew mice could cry before, and I must admit I felt a little ashamed as they all rushed outside, only to find it had disappeared. On the plus side, it never came back.

Like the mouse, Tiger preferred to sleep inside during the cold winter months. If Zane was at home he would constantly interrupt my sleep by getting up to check whether the dog was sleeping on the sofa in the entrance hall rather than on the Persian rug on the floor. Invariably he was, in which case he would be ordered off with a stern 'Get down'. Tiger would respond immediately, getting down and lying on the rug with a sigh, but as soon as the house settled down we all knew he would be up on the sofa again. The rest of the family didn't mind at all, but Zane still had the residual idea that dogs were unclean and shouldn't be allowed to use the same seats as humans. Or so he said, but I always felt that there was a bit of a power struggle going on, with each of them trying to mark out their territory as leaders of the pack. Needless to say, when Zane was away Tiger slept on the sofa undisturbed. I'm glad he did when I remember how his life was cut short a few years later.

One of the innovations introduced by the Government was a state contracting company, aimed at reducing and eventually eliminating the need to use foreign companies for very large construction projects. Zane was invited to serve his country by working for this new company and although he was considering becoming a contractor himself by then, he was more than willing to postpone his plans for a while to help get the company off the ground. Within weeks he found his new bosses impossible to work for. He never really said why, except that he didn't agree with what they were doing and feared that if he stayed he would end up in prison. All I know is that he couldn't wait for a reasonable time to elapse before handing in his notice. However, the fact that he had worked for this company in its formative years was eventually to become one of the factors which triggered our leaving the country for good.

In the meantime, life was becoming more and more expensive as the capital expanded. The traditional elitist disapproval of women taking work in low skill jobs had all but disappeared by then and Erica applied for a job at the Lufthansa offices. No-one was more surprised than her when she got it because she had worked as a medical technician in Germany and had no office experience whatsoever. She told me that she spent the first couple of weeks running up and down the stairs because, when instructed by the manager to carry out a task she had to run down to the staff working in the reception area below and ask them to explain what he wanted her to do. Tula was also finding that she was no longer able to manage on her husband's earnings so she took a job in the now state-owned store, Orosdi-Back. Several new branches were opened and because there were still desperate shortages of consumer goods, huge queues formed outside Orosdi-Back whenever they received a delivery. People would start to queue before they even knew what had arrived, sometimes waiting hours before finding out that there was nothing that they needed at the store. I have to say that, when they did arrive, the goods were usually of very good quality and relatively inexpensive. On one occasion I bought three watches at once just because they were available: one each for me, Summer and Zara. Mine was automatic and to this day it starts almost immediately whenever I choose to wear it. These may seem trivial hardships, but I still sometimes dream that I have been let loose in Orosdi-Back with all manner of luxury consumer items which are there for the taking.

What I found most frustrating were the continuing food shortages. By that time I didn't need to sew our clothes myself because we regularly visited the UK in the summer, so I concentrated my efforts on learning how to make those foods which, though not essential, made meals more interesting. With the aid of a cook book I learned how to make marmalade, jams, chutney and pickle, but despite all this kitchen activity I was becoming very bored with being a housewife, particularly as the children grew older. When the time came for Zara go to high school she didn't get high enough grades to get a place at 'the Americans' and we no longer knew anyone with enough clout to help get her in. In recent years she had not fulfilled her early promise in school, mainly because she couldn't memorise her arithmetic tables. Zane couldn't believe that a child of his, born into the race which invented the decimal point, could not master the basics of maths; he would go over the tables with her for ages when he was at home and I took over when he wasn't. I also made large posters of all the tables and positioned them all over the house. One hung on the bedroom wall opposite her bed so it was the first thing she saw when she opened her eyes in the morning and there was another above the kitchen table. I would stand at the kitchen sink simultaneously washing dishes and firing multiplication questions at her, to which she invariably answered 'equaaaaaals', drawing the word out as she struggled to remember the correct answer. It was hopeless. We would reach the point where she could tell us that five times five equalled twenty five one day but invariably she had forgotten it the next. We probably made her life miserable, but we had no idea what dyslexia was, let alone that the inability to recognise patterns was one of its symptoms. It wasn't until she was tested at university in the UK that her dyslexia was confirmed. Anyway, we opted to send her and later Tula to a convent which was situated a short drive along the river near to the city centre. It had the advantage that I was able to drop them off and collect them, and if for any reason I couldn't pick them up they could simply jump onto one of the new buses which now served our area and be home in ten minutes.

Erica's eldest son was also going on to high school and when we returned from the UK that summer I was astonished to learn that he was going to a Jewish school, since I had no idea that it even existed. In fact, I had the impression that there were hardly any Jewish people remaining in Baghdad by then, let alone enough to fill a school. This was typical of how personal relations in the city had become: Erica was usually so outspoken, she never hesitated to blurt out the most intimate and personal details of her life of and that of her family, but choosing a Jewish school for her son was potentially a dangerous decision so she kept it quiet until she knew it was safe for him to go there. I'm sure she would first have taken informed advice, probably from the husbands of her two sisters-in-law, both high-ranking army officers and therefore Baathists.

My parents had been talking about visiting us in Baghdad when my father died suddenly of a heart attack, leaving my mother a relatively young widow. A few months after his funeral the plan was revived: my brother and recently divorced sister would now accompany her on the trip. We were anxious that they should come in the spring so that they could make the most of their visit, so they applied for their visas before Christmas and waited; and waited. They made numerous telephone enquiries to the Iraqi consulate, all of which evoked the response 'your applications are being processed' and time was running on. Exasperated, my brother drove up to the Iraqi Embassy where he was astounded to hear that their visa applications had been rejected. They were, as he told me only half-jokingly, 'persona non gratis'. Fortunately, Zane was now working as a contractor, so he issued them with an invitation to visit the country for business reasons and their visas were issued almost immediately; such was the importance of potential 'business' to the government.

Naturally, they wanted to see as much of the country as possible but they were also keen to experience Iraqi customs and culture at first hand. We planned to take them to as many of the historic sites and other places of interest as we could, but they also wanted to meet our friends and family. A couple of days after they arrived, they were given an unexpected taste of one local custom whilst they were lingering over the breakfast table. The kids had just left for school and I went to have a shower, leaving my brother to make another cup of coffee. When I returned to the kitchen he had a big grin on his face.

'A strange lady just came in and helped herself to some butter from that tin. She said she wouldn't be able to make us a cake for this evening without it. She asked me to give you her regards: at first I thought she was German, but after she had filled her bowl she called out Ciao as she was leaving'.

'That would be our neighbour, Erica – she's invited us to dinner tonight'. Although my brother and sister found the casual way she helped herself to our groceries very amusing they also thought it was a bit cheeky, but my mother said it reminded her of her childhood. However, they all agreed on one thing – the cake we were offered that night was quite delicious.

When we weren't going anywhere my siblings enjoyed sitting out in the spring sunshine, so one afternoon my sister put on her bikini and spread a blanket on the roof in the hope of getting a better tan; she was soon joined by Zara and Tula, also in their bikinis. They weren't up there long before an army helicopter started circling overhead, obviously enjoying the view. After several minutes my sister couldn't stand the racket any longer and retreated downstairs. I was secretly rather relieved as it was better not to attract the attention of the authorities in any way. It was bad enough being known locally as 'the dog house', I didn't want our house to be known as the 'the bikini girls place' by the armed forces as well.

Everywhere we went, my family were met with smiling, friendly people, many of them eager to practise their English. They always made a particular fuss of my mother as an older woman. When we went to the old souq in central Baghdad she was offered tea and given small gifts as souvenirs by the stall holders. By the time we left to return home she was feeling the heat, so I managed to get a traffic policeman to stop a taxi for us on Rashid Street. It was an unheard of achievement in that high-speed traffic, made possible only through his consideration for an elderly visitor from abroad. Because their experience of Iraq was made more enjoyable by the friendliness, charm and hospitality which they encountered, I think they found it hard to believe that there was a darker side which residents were only too aware of. To those people who say that people get the kind of government they deserve, I would have to reply that, sadly, they usually don't.

Because they found everyone so friendly, my siblings reacted with amusement to all the outward signs of repression – the omnipresent photos of Saddam and the President, the overwhelming bureaucracy, the need to watch what you said. The first time we drove over the suspension bridge near to the presidential palace I heard clicking sounds from the back seat of the car and turned round to find my brother taking photographs. 'No, you can't do that, we'll be arrested, put the camera down – quick.' He was only doing what any tourist would do, photographing what was in fact a very beautiful view of the palace nestling among the palm trees just across the river. He dropped the camera into his lap just before we reached the armed soldiers who were always stationed around the palace, but I'm sure he thought we were over-reacting.

One weekend we drove with Hatim and his family to an ancient mud-built city situated in the middle of nowhere, but closer to Saudi Arabia than I had ever been. The city was not on the grand scale of others such as Babylon, so most people hadn't even heard of it. Consequently, it had not received much attention from archaeologists and it was rather desolate, with crumbling walls and gaps where the roofs had started to collapse. These defects were immediately clocked by our kids, and within minutes they were using them as footholds to clamber up onto the roofs. Once up they had a whale of a time, leaping over the gaps and in some instances jumping from one roof to another, closely followed by my brother, who was fit enough to keep up with them and terrified that one of them would fall. When we judged that that they had let off enough steam we started calling them down. They eventually obeyed, arriving back on the ground at about the same time as two strangers, obviously secret police.

After one of them had clicked his fingers for Zane's ID card – I sometimes wondered whether they were trained to do that – they went on to ask the usual questions: what were the foreigners doing here; what was their relationship to us and so on. I don't think they could have had too many foreigners to investigate in that area and they seemed rather at a loss as to what to do next. In addition, they both lacked the imposing figures and smart get-up of their Bahgdad equivalent, so when one of them turned to Zane with the question 'Are you Iraqi?' he blew his top.

'Didn't you just check my ID? Can't you hear how I talk?'

'Thank you, Sir, just checking'

Having exhausted their investigatory repertoire they withdrew rather humbly, much to my family's amusement, but Zane would have got a very different reaction had he tried that on in Baghdad. Now that he is retired, Zane spends a lot of time reading up on Iraqi history. He has recently discovered that the dilapidated mud city was an ancient emirate of his clan, so perhaps it was some deep-seated tribal impulse that drove him to visit that little-known place.

Zane couldn't always make it home whilst my family were visiting, and one night whilst he was away we had no arrangements for the evening, so I took our visitors for drinks at the Engineers' Union. Because we were on our own, we fell to reminiscing about our childhood, and my brother happened to mention that he had been fascinated with the idea of Mesopotamia ever since he first started school. He recalled his first teacher, a stout, elderly spinster who entertained her class not only with traditional Bible stories but also tales about the ancient country between the two rivers. 'Ever since then, I've always wanted to see it and I still can't believe I'm actually here'. I remembered being taught by the same lady in the tiny Methodist Primary school where all my siblings began their education. She is undoubtedly long dead now, but I hope she rests peacefully in the knowledge that her stories inspired at least two of her young pupils to go out and see a bit of the world.

My brother and sister returned home leaving my mother with us for an extra two weeks. On the first morning I decided to devote some time catching up on the huge pile of ironing which had accumulated during their stay; my mother was feeling the heat again and said she would be quite happy to spend the day quietly. I set the ironing board up and had just made a start when Erica appeared, distraught, and began ranting to my mother about the difficulties of living in Baghdad under the current regime. As she got into her flow her voice became shriller and her accent more pronounced, so I switched off the iron and put the kettle on, recognising that this was obviously something she needed to get off her chest. We were all used to these outbursts and sometimes even found them funny: the incident I recall most vividly happened one morning just as Zane was leaving for work. Whilst he stood checking his pockets for cigarettes, matches and keys Erica burst through our front door.

'Zane, I'm so depressed I could hang myself from that punkah,' she announced, pointing dramatically upwards towards the ceiling fan as she spoke. The children were busy getting their things together for school, so luckily they could bend over their school bags to hide their grins, but what made it funny was my husband's reaction. One might have thought that suicidal neighbours waylaid him on his way to work every morning because he continued walking towards the door, hardly missing a beat as he replied: 'Yes, well, never mind Erica, go and sit down and have a cup of coffee.'

I can't remember what triggered this latest outburst in front of my mother, but by the time Erica had got it off her chest we had to go and collect the girls from school. Unused as she was to both hysteria and repression, I expected some kind of reaction from my mother, but what she actually said was a bit of an anti-climax:

'You'd have been better to have got on with your ironing'.

# Chapter Fifteen

After my mother returned to the UK the house seemed very quiet during the day time, but the unaccustomed peace was soon shattered by noise from the street outside when workmen and machines unexpectedly arrived to pave the dusty road. I say 'unexpectedly' because few suburban residential side streets were paved in Baghdad in those days. Since ours was neither at the beginning nor the end of the main road it seemed a rather random place to start, particularly as there was nothing of importance at the end of our street except the Tigris river. People said that the street was being paved because a minister was building a house nearby; they eventually turned out to be nearly right when a whole complex of palaces for high ranking Baathists was built along the river bank, but at the time we were just grateful that we would be spared the muddy walk up to the main road which was a regular feature of Baghdad winters.

The work was completed and the men left, leaving the manholes which had been created uncovered. Local residents joked that, when the road was designed, the engineer had 'forgotten his pencil' and so had neglected to order all the materials. The jokes petered out as it became obvious that the holes in fact posed a serious threat to health and safety when someone broke his jaw by falling into one as he was walking home in the dark one night. From that time on I regularly heard loud bangs as the wheel of a car descended into the manhole outside our house. The bang would usually be followed by the screech of tyres and the smell of burning rubber as the unfortunate driver tried to extricate his wheel.

It happened to Pauline one day; she had come round to have a cup of coffee but also to have a moan about her husband.

Although I liked Munim and always enjoyed his company, I can't say that he was the best husband in the world. Pauline was so stressed out that she completely forgot about the hole in the road. She had her foot down hard on the accelerator of her little French car, and as she drove over the manhole her nearside front wheel went down into the gap. Unfortunately, it fitted perfectly; we both had a go at reversing the car out, but the wheel was well and truly stuck. Luckily, a car with two men on board happened to pass as we stood there metaphorically scratching our heads. All the locals knew the drill by then, so one of them performed a synchronised lift and push whilst the other put his foot down hard and within minutes the little car was back on the road. Not every driver was so lucky though, and more than one was forced to abandon his car in the middle of the road, where it would stand drooping dejectedly into the manhole until help arrived.

Had I been more alert to the signs, there were other indications that something major was being planned for the area on the banks of the river. There were still several undeveloped plots of land in the neighbourhood, usually unfenced, so people felt free to use them as short-cuts. Sometimes they would even position their rubbish bins on neighbouring empty plots, so when Ali and his friends organised an informal football league in which all the boys from one street played the boys from another they had no qualms about using a nearby piece of land as a venue. They even erected make-shift goals for their daily matches. Consequently, when one of the local 'characters' tapped at my kitchen door for 'a quick word', I was rather surprised by what she had to say.

The woman lived locally with her two daughters, who did occasional cleaning jobs for local housewives. She was a tall, well-built woman and didn't hesitate to do any odd jobs which came her way, anything from clearing out an overgrown garden to helping housewives with their laundry. She always seemed to be somewhere about, striding purposefully around the area with her substantial belly protruding above the low-slung belt she always wore, as though bent on a mission of great importance. Although the family lived near-by in a mud-built house it was rumoured that she was actually quite a wealthy woman, owner of several modern properties which she rented out. It was also rumoured that she was an informer for the secret police. Anyway, she had come to complain about Ali. One of the things she did was act as a 'watchman' and she had gone to speak to Ali in that capacity. Apparently the owners of the land objected to the goal posts so she had told him that the boys must remove them and find somewhere else to play football. She told me that all the boys had been upset and argued with her, most of all my son, who had apparently shocked her by his cheekiness:

'I couldn't believe it, Ali's usually such a gentleman. He even asked me what it's got to do with me. I never expected him to argue, let alone speak to me like that.' I tutted something about 'kids today' in response to her pained expression, but privately I was vowing to kill him when he got home.

'So, can I rely on you to have a word with him? Make sure he stops playing football there?' I assured her that she could and also promised her that Ali would get a good ticking off for being cheeky when he got home. In contrast to my visitor's reaction, I wasn't at all surprised when he put up an argument, but I insisted that the football ground must be moved, since the plot did after all belong to somebody else. I did feel for them, because the boys had spent quite a lot of time levelling the plot, but as the new school year was about to begin, their football league was effectively coming to an end anyway. Nevertheless, this objection to the boys' games left me feeling uneasy, although I couldn't quite put my finger on the reason. It wasn't until much later that I made the link and recognised that she was following orders to keep the land clear. Eventually it formed part of a complex of villas which led down to a private marina; the villas housed some of the regime's most influential members, including Tariq Aziz. Once building commenced, that section of the river bank was closed to the general public, although none of this happened whilst we lived nearby.

There were other changes taking place along the river bank. Further down towards the city centre the lovely old houses, most of them traditionally built around a central courtyard, were being bought up by the authorities amid widespread rumours that tunnels and underground bunkers were being constructed beneath the city. One day we drove further along the river bank than motorists usually ventured – I can't remember why. In that section the river was bordered only by orchards and palm groves, so we were surprised to suddenly come upon a large camp of prefabricated buildings. I think it must have been a Friday because there were large numbers of men lounging around outside, their body language clearly indicating that they were in the 'day off' mode. They were obviously foreign labourers, all black, very tall and powerful looking. I have no idea where they came from and no-one I asked seemed to know anything about them. The camp made sense of something which had recently occurred, though. Although the dusty path along the river bank was unpaved, it was wide enough to drive along and local people also used it as a short-cut to the residential streets further down. We sometimes used it to walk to Mum's or Sajida's house, so we felt quite comfortable strolling along the river bank, often quite late in the evening. As long as it was light enough to see where you were going on the unlit pathway, we would go for an evening stroll along the river.

A couple of weeks before, Erica and I had done just that, enjoying the cool evening air before going home to put the kids to bed. Whilst we were walking we were approached by a policeman who warned us not to walk along the bank at night because it 'wasn't safe'. This was also worrying because it happened near the wide, steep slope which led down from the bank to the road – a favourite spot for local kids, ours included, to play on their bikes. They used to take turns in speeding down the steep incline, often coming a cropper and grazing elbows and knees in the process. It wasn't necessary to own your own bike, particularly in those days when everything was hard to come by. Any of the kids could take his turn and have a go on those bikes which were available, sometimes spending hours in this pleasant occupation.

There had also been another incident near there recently. At a time when most people should be at work, I saw a car descending the slope carrying two young guys who were obviously involved in much less innocent pleasures. One was driving along very slowly while the other kissed and fondled the naked breasts of a very pretty teenaged girl in the back. She was staring out of the window looking very bored, but the man with her looked quite the opposite, forcing me to parry inquisitive questions from my two young daughters as to what he was doing. Later, I told a friend who lived nearby what we had seen. She said that the spot seemed to have become a venue for young prostitutes who brought their clients there in the early afternoon. Apparently, a couple of weeks earlier one of these girls had woken local residents from their siesta by running up the road, screaming demands to be paid at the occupants of a car which was speeding away from her – obviously customers who had left without paying. There was an area near to the centre of town which had always been known as a pick up place for prostitutes. A friend who lived in a block of flats which looked out on that street told me that the girls could often be seen waiting on the pavement with a box of tissues in one hand and a brick in the other; it was quite obvious what the tissues were for, but even after lengthy discussion we couldn't agree on what they might do with the bricks. Anyway, I suppose that the girls must have been forced to look for other places to ply their trade if that area was really being taken over by the government.

It was also becoming increasingly difficult to remain aloof from politics. Farah's uncle had been elevated to the job of

Minister for Planning. He was also reputed to be Saddam's best friend, privy to the most sensitive state secrets and closely involved in negotiations for military equipment and the procurement of armaments. He had immense power and influence, so on more than one occasion Farah's mother invited Zane to call in and meet the great man when he was invited to her house for a family dinner. I'm certain she did so with the best of motives, since it went without saying that no-one was better placed to 'put in a word' for you. 'Why don't you just pop in for a cup of tea and then you can meet him', she urged, to which Zane would reply with a non-committal 'In sha Allah'– God willing – or a simple 'Thank you' which was considered to be the polite way of refusing an invitation. He always thought it wise to keep away from anyone who was involved in politics and was very annoyed when he heard that Summer had accompanied Farah and her family on a visit to her uncle's home one evening.

Nevertheless, the minister did unwittingly give Zane a helping hand, through the good graces of his brother. Farah's father had been appointed as the Director of a state company which built heavy engineering and construction equipment under licence, no doubt with the help of his influential brother. There was a huge demand for this equipment because of the ambitious building projects taking place and as it happened Zane and his partner were in dire need of some lorries for their latest contract. The only way to get them quickly was to petition the state company in the hope they would agree to supply them as a priority. Zane duly applied for an appointment to see the Director and went along to make his request. Before he could do so and almost as soon as he had sat down, the Director interrupted to ask: 'You're Summer's Dad, aren't you? How can I help you?' It was as simple as that – he made it possible for Zane to purchase the equipment he needed, without the usual delays which sometimes dragged on indefinitely, frequently spelling disaster for unlucky businessmen.

Tula was less fortunate. Like all our children, she had resisted every attempt to persuade her to join the party and now she was paying the price at school. A new incentive had been introduced in the form of an extra ten per cent added to the marks achieved by youth party members in the monthly tests. Since teaching was based on a 'learning by rote' method, the marking system in primary and junior school was very simple – you either knew the answer or you didn't – so it was perfectly possible to gain nearly one hundred per cent in most subjects. Tula usually did very well, but she had a rival who also got consistently high marks. Month by month the girls would engage in good-natured competition, taking it in turns to be top of the class, but the extra ten per cent would clinch it, making the friend (and party member) impossible to beat. The first month that the bonus marks system was implemented, Tula came home incandescent with rage, not because she had come second but at the injustice behind it. It took all our powers of persuasion to convince her not to go to the head to complain – she had been known to barge into Miss Noele's office before when she wasn't happy about something at school. Now things were different and we had to make her realise that. In the end she accepted that it didn't really matter as she would be going up to High School at the end of the year.

Oday had his own method of coming out top of his class, as Ali witnessed first- hand. He had been off school with tonsillitis and had missed the monthly Maths test; coincidentally, so had Oday. On the first day that they returned to school, both boys were sent to an empty classroom to take the test. The maths teacher gave them both their exam papers then settled down at his desk with some work of his own. There was the usual shuffling of papers and sighs which accompany the start of any exam and it was several minutes before Oday spoke up: 'Sir, I don't like these questions!'

Ali looked up in time to see the teacher suddenly turning very pale. He jumped up immediately, taking back the offending paper with hands trembling as if it were a time bomb about to go off.

'Don't worry, my son, I'll go and get you some better ones'.

He left the room and returned shortly with two different sets of questions, one of which he handed to each boy, presumably to retain the appearance of fairness. I imagine he also felt that it was the only way he could be seen to exercise some control over the situation and maintain at least a semblance of dignity. The new test made my son very happy because the first questions had apparently been quite difficult while the second ones were very easy, but despite this he told me that he had felt sorry for the teacher, who was good at his job and popular with the boys. He hated seeing him humiliated by a kid in that way. Innovations such as these gradually eroded the quality of the Iraqi education system, destroying the notion of free, equal educational opportunity for all of which it had previously been justifiably proud.

Paradoxically, it was around this time that Saddam decreed that anything less than one hundred per cent literacy was unacceptable, and introduced the 'Ummia' centres, 'Ummia' meaning illiterate. Now any adult who was not able to read and write must attend one of the literacy centres which were being set up all over the country; no excuse was acceptable. Every afternoon all over the capital, women who had been taken out of school early, or maybe who had never been fortunate enough to go at all, could be seen setting off to the local Ummia centre. Most of them had big smiles on their faces as they walked along with their friends. In fact, they reminded me of kids on their way to school, enjoying the company of their peers and temporarily freed from the jurisdiction of their parents (for parents read husbands or elder brothers in this case). Illiterate males were also forced to attend, and not all of them were happy about it because it impacted on their livelihood. Zane said it caused problems on site when half the workforce had to down tools and go off to the Ummia, leaving their colleagues to tear their hair out and try to carry on without them, but no contractor or foreman would dare to ask them to stay for fear of a visit from the secret police. Admirable as the concept was, there were large sectors of the community who felt that it had come too late for them, particularly when they had to take time off from their only means of earning a living to attend classes. Nightly television programmes were broadcast to help the new students with their homework, reinforcing what had been learnt that day and providing revision for those people who were finding it harder to learn. I know Layla sat down at home to brush up on her literacy skills every evening with the help of these programmes. She never actually attended the Ummia, but I don't know whether that was because she had been to school for too many years to make attendance compulsory or whether there was an age above which it wasn't mandatory to attend.

Other friends also took advantage of these programmes to learn to read Arabic. They approached the task with great enthusiasm, much to my shame. I had learnt the Arabic alphabet many years before but had never taken the trouble to persevere enough to be able to actually read, using the feeble excuse that everything that was available in Arabic would be censored anyway. I really can't remember whether the classes continued for any length of time, or whether total literacy was ever achieved but I did recognise the essential dilemma it raised: it could only help those it targeted if it was made compulsory but the very fact that it was compulsory made it unpopular, particularly because it actually made life harder for some people.

I think it was around that time that we began to hear talk of the resurgence of a political party called 'Al Dawa', a party which apparently sought to restore a religious dimension to the politics of secular Iraq. It was alleged that Al Dawa had links with Iran and, though it had been in existence for several decades, appeared almost overnight to replace the communists as the favoured object for political suppression. More than one religious leader from Iran had taken refuge in Iraq over the years, the most well-known probably being Ayatollah Khomeini, but these relationships usually soured as it became apparent that the refugee could be just as intolerant and critical of human rights abuses in Iraq as he was in Iran.

Sajida had two brothers in law whose wives were also their cousins, a commonplace practice among traditional families. Both these men were arrested and imprisoned on suspicion of being members of Al Dawa. One was later executed and although the other was eventually freed from prison he felt it expedient to leave the country as soon as possible, probably never to return. Naturally, these events devastated the entire family who found themselves grieving for a husband, cousins, sons in law and nephews in one fell swoop. I have no idea whether the men were in fact members of that party, or whether the body of the executed man was ever returned to his family. If it was, one can only hope that it wasn't by the latest method, which was simply to throw the corpse over the garden wall in the night, leaving the unfortunate family to find the mutilated body of their loved one the next morning.

By this time Zane was working on a project in Amarah, where he had become friendly with the local bank manager named Faleh. Faleh was originally from that city but was married to a British girl who lived with their children in Baghdad. I liked his wife Sheila immediately – she was a down to earth Mancunian with a ready sense of humour – but I wasn't quite so sure about her daughters. There were two of them, both very beautiful girls in their late teens, with a younger brother who was around Ali's age. The eldest girl was already married with a baby and since her mother had unexpectedly conceived at around the same time as her daughter, there were two babies in the house. Sheila looked after her grandson while her daughter was at work and as the son in law was a newly qualified doctor currently rotating as a house officer, she and her baby also stayed at her parents' house while he was on call.

His sister was married to a very high ranking Baathist so I imagine that both he and his wife were also party members.

Although the girls were pleasant and friendly enough, I felt they took advantage of their mother, leaving her to do all the housework whilst often caring for both babies at once. Of course, I hadn't experienced the ego-centric selfishness of the teenaged child then, so I may have been rather unfair, but what I really disliked was the way they bullied her in political matters, often laying down the law on what she should think. On one occasion one of the girls criticised her mother for some imagined failure, telling her that she 'should do more to serve the country'. She responded with typical cheery bluntness:

'Serve the country? I've never done anything to serve my own country! I've got enough to do at home.

Despite these short-comings, they could be good company and they were very hospitable, even if it was often at their mother's expense, so when Faleh invited us to join the family in a trip to the marshes I jumped at the chance. I had been waiting for an opportunity to go there ever since I read Wilfred Thesiger's account of the unique culture of the Marsh Arabs, called 'Madan' by Iraqis, years before. The picture he painted had stayed in my mind and I couldn't wait to see at first-hand how they lived in their floating world on islands built of reeds. The marshes also provided a habitat for many species of birds, thousands making the long flight from Europe every year to spend the winter there and adding to the area's attraction for visitors. When we went their ancient way of life was flourishing, with the locals living by fishing, producing dairy products from the water buffalo they reared and growing rice. Men, women and sometimes quite tiny children could be seen travelling up and down the waterways between their reed islands, as comfortable in their hand-built boats as a Londoner on the Tube.

We were to go first to Faleh's family for dinner before going on to the house he lived in when he was working in Amarah, where we would spend the nights. They welcomed us with typical southern hospitality; the entire family came out to greet us at the door, bestowing two hearty kisses on each cheek for every member of the party, regardless of whether or not they had ever met before. After these lengthy greetings were over we were ushered inside and offered cold drinks before going to the dining room to enjoy the meal they had prepared. They must have been cooking all day because there was a huge variety of meat, chicken and fish dishes as well as different kinds of rice, salads and vegetable platters. When we had finished eating we returned to the sitting room where tea and cakes were served. Whilst we drank, Sheila and her daughters caught up with their family news and fielded questions about our family from their curious aunties, who were all traditionally dressed with covered hair. At one point, Sheila's eldest daughter asked her aunt whether she thought I was pretty, to which she replied 'No, what's pretty about her?' in such a matter of fact way that I couldn't take offence, particularly after they had gone to such trouble to make us welcome. Anyway, I knew where she was coming from because it was obvious that the aunties would have been just as stunning as their nieces if they had uncovered their hair and possibly worn clothes which were a little more revealing than their shapeless house dresses.

Later we went off to Faleh's house to settle down for the night. We didn't go out because there wasn't really anywhere to go at night, so the kids played for a while before going to bed whilst I helped Sheila organise the sleeping arrangements before getting out glasses and the rest of the paraphenalia necessary so the adults could have a drink. I say a drink, but in fact Faleh could work his way down a bottle of whiskey faster than anyone I had ever met. Zane joined him very enthusiastically whilst Sheila and I enjoyed a modest glass of wine. It had been a long day and we planned an early start the next morning, so we women went off to bed quite early. As we said goodnight, Faleh was opening a second bottle of whiskey.

We set off for the marshes early the next morning, arriving in plenty of time to see the Madan going about a typical day. The thing that struck me most were the colours – bright blue water with large tracts of green foliage in between, sun glinting on the golden reeds which were used to build the villagers' houses and flashes of colour as the many species of birds which thrived in the area were disturbed and took off into the clear blue sky. Everywhere we went we encountered big smiles and gestures of welcome; women ushered us into their homes, inviting us to see what they were like inside. I must say I was impressed by how neat and tidy they were, with bedding neatly stacked and bundles of clothing tied up and stored in corners. Naturally, the kids were more interested in trying to catch fish and angling for a ride in one of the smaller boats which were being used by Madan children, although they came running quickly enough when the cold drinks were brought out. Faleh's family was obviously well-known in the area and the local Sheik insisted that we must have lunch at his home, so when the time came we were taken to an island which was larger than the rest where the meal was being prepared. Strangely, I can't remember actually getting into a boat at all that day, although my children assure me that we parked our cars and travelled to the edge of the marshes by a large vessel. Apparently, we also travelled between the islands on a smaller one, until eventually arriving at the place where we had lunch. However, I can clearly remember the lunch.

When we arrived at the Sheik's house, our host began supervising two young men who were gutting several fish and spearing them on sticks so that they could be grilled in the traditional way. Like a western man involved in getting a barbeque going, he seemed to believe that no-one could grill fish correctly without his advice. Anyway, once he was satisfied that everything was set up to his liking, they started the fire. As we travelled around the village I had noticed that every house had a neat pile of round, flat objects stored alongside it, looking from a distance like a stack of brown Frisbees. Now it became apparent that the Frisbees were in fact used as fuel for cooking fires. As the flames rose higher, we moved nearer to watch the men expertly build up the fire, adding more fuel as required. Close up I could see that the 'Frisbees' were more like flat pancakes, but with a dry, fibrous texture which made it easy to break them into smaller pieces as required. It was no longer possible to ignore the fact that our lunch was being cooked over a fire fuelled by dried buffalo dung.

I could tell that the kids had also noted this by the muted 'OYs' and giggles which were coming from their direction, but Ali, always a finickety eater, wasn't going to let it go at that. Sidling up behind me he hissed:

'Do you realise what they're cooking that fish on? I'm not eating that'.

'Shut up, the fire will sterilize it. Just pretend to eat.'

The last thing I wanted was to offend our hosts after they had shown us such hospitality and I was determined that our spoiled kids would not let us down by their bad manners. When our host was satisfied that the fish were ready they were dished up onto large meat platters and served with hot, freshly baked bread (also cooked over the dung, I suspected). It was a simple meal but delicious; the fish had been cooked directly they were taken out of the water and their slightly smoked aroma held no trace of the origins of the cooking fuel. The meal was washed down with bottled soft drinks cooled in the river then followed by fruit, obviously brought from the nearest town, then sweet tea flavoured with cardamom. If I had any concerns over hygiene regarding the method of cooking I need not have worried because none of us suffered any ill effects after the meal. Just before we left a boat passed us, travelling fast. It carried a local woman and a young man dressed in smart but casual clothes who turned out to be the local doctor. Even though she was obviously engaged in a mission of some importance, she was not about to forget her manners:

'Welcome and peace be with you. How are you? How are the family?' before getting down to business. 'We're off to deliver a baby – why don't you come with us?' the woman called over her shoulder from the boat she was steadily propelling forward at the same time that she looked back at us. Sheila and I laughed at the notion that we could be any help in that situation and waved her on her way. We couldn't imagine that any woman's hospitality would stretch to welcoming two untrained British women whilst she was in the middle of labour, no doubt obliging her to make small talk between contractions.

Sadly, their proximity to Iran was later to contribute to the downfall of the Madan, a situation which may have been made worse by their own tradition of hospitality. Soldiers fleeing the front during the long years of the Iraq/Iran war found the marshes to be the perfect hiding place; later, when Saddam put down the uprising which took place after the war with Kuwait, the marshes again provided a haven for people fleeing for their lives. Rightly or wrongly, the locals were suspected of helping them and for Saddam, never one to worry about using a sledge hammer to crack a nut, the solution was simple – drain the marshes. It must have taken quite a feat of engineering, but drain them he did, leaving the local inhabitants to manage as best they could. Recently, the dams and canals which he built to divert the water away from the area have been removed in an attempt to re-flood it, but many of the Madan remain stranded in refugee camps in Iran and it seems doubtful whether either their traditional way of life or the rich natural habitat in which it took place can ever be revived.

# Chapter Sixteen

The following summer, at the age of fifteen, Summer was fallen in love with; the first I knew of it was when she took me aside one morning to tell me that a boy kept phoning her.

'Well, do you want him to phone you?' I responded, crossing my fingers at this unexpected and unwelcome reminder that my daughter was growing up, much as I had the time when she proudly announced that her boobs were growing and invited me to feel them.

'No, I don't, I just hang up when he calls'

'Well tell him to get lost then and if he phones you after that, I'll talk to him'.

It turned out that the boy was the best friend of Farah's brother, so he was often at Farah's when Summer went round. He went to Baghdad College and had already befriended Ali, like most of the older boys who lived nearby, but I had a sneaking suspicion that in his case he had the ulterior motive of getting closer to Summer; he had also bribed the driver of the school bus to move their pick up point to the spot where the girls waited, so now boys and girls bound for the two schools all congregated at the same bus stop every morning. Not satisfied with this, he always seemed to know when the girls were planning an outing together, probably through Farah's brother, and made sure he got there first. The boy's sister was at medical school with Nadia and his family were on friendly terms with my in-laws so I didn't want to make a big deal out of it, but Summer was finding him a bit of a pest so I told her not to go to Farah's so often, since it was just as easy for Farah to come to our house.

Deprived of opportunities to spend time in her company, the boy began a campaign which nowadays would be described as 'stalking'. We could hardly go out of our front door without seeing him passing by – he must have passed our house several times every day. In the late afternoon he would go for a stroll with Farah's brother, making several circuits of our block on the way. He would also be certain to drive slowly past our house several times in the afternoon, often using a different car each time, probably because their owners were enjoying a siesta. At other times he resorted to the bike, cycling slowly round the area as though he had lost his way but with his eyes firmly fixed on our front door. Matters came to a head when one of our neighbours, another Pauline, called round to warn me that she thought we were being watched by the secret police. 'What makes you say that?'

'Well, haven't you noticed that guy who passes by several times every day? Sometimes he's on a bike and sometimes he drives. I've even seen him walking with another boy, although he hasn't got the moustache. You must have seen him – he always seems to be looking at your house.'

Did I forget to mention that Summer's admirer sported a moustache? Although it definitely wasn't a 'twenty past eight', it might have passed for one in unenlightened circles. Anyway, it was obviously time to intervene; I had a word with Farah's Mum, asking her to speak to the boy's family. I told her that, if they couldn't put a stop to it, then I would have to do something about his harassment myself. Fortunately, his family all went off on an extended holiday to Europe soon after that – it must have been one of those windows when Iraqis were allowed to travel abroad – and they returned without the stalker, who remained in Britain. Unfortunately he returned within a few months because he was unable to get into university until the following year, but as this meant he had a lot of catching up to do at school he wasn't quite such a nuisance as before. Summer was to meet up with him again a few years later when she was herself a student in the UK and they subsequently married. Although the marriage didn't last, it produced three great kids who are a credit to their mother and enhance all our lives.

I also took the kids and travelled to Britain that summer, returning with a lively Springer Spaniel puppy to replace Tiger, who had met a premature end that spring. It happened one night while Zane and I were out with Adnan and Marita, leaving the kids at home to finish their homework before going to bed. Recently, a new house had been built on the land adjacent to the palm grove opposite; its owner, named Mahmoud, had been left a widower when his wife died of cancer, leaving him with two young children. He later re-married. His second wife was Australian, a pleasant, unassuming girl, quite different from her flamboyant husband, and they had a third child together. Mahmoud's daughter was a couple of years older than Summer, but as she went to the same school and lived nearby they became quite friendly despite their difference in age. Summer sometimes went with her to the Alwiyah Club after school and whilst she was there Mahmoud told her that Tiger was a nuisance and he intended to shoot him one day. Naturally she thought he was joking because he always seemed to treat everything as a joke, and he had a dog himself – a handsome black and white hound. We often heard its howling through the palm trees, so we didn't think he was in a position to complain and we certainly didn't take him seriously. Perhaps we ought to have been more perceptive because he had already shot a couple of the wild dogs which lived nearby. On one occasion he tied the body of one of them to the bumper of his car and drove up and down the street, dragging the dead animal behind him to the horror of everyone who witnessed the spectacle.

Anyway, when Zane and I arrived home that night the gates leading to our driveway were standing open. I got out of the car with great foreboding because it was obvious immediately that something was wrong. I have read that a menacing atmosphere frequently surrounds the spot where someone has met a violent end. I don't know whether that is true, but there was an unmistakably bad atmosphere in the garden as I hurried towards the front of the house. Tiger was lying, motionless, half on the path with half of his body slumped over the irrigation ditch and even to my inexperienced eye it was obvious that he was dead, so I skirted his body gingerly, my first concern being to check on the children. I called out as I entered the house, coming face to face with Summer and Ali – Ali was standing at the bottom of the stairs, and crying.

'Where have you been? We tried to phone you. I think someone tried to break in. They were shooting and I think Tiger's dead – he's not moving.'

Ali had heard noises and what sounded like shots and had come downstairs to investigate. He tried to make out what was going on by looking out of the window but wisely decided not to go outside but woke Summer instead. They cautiously opened the glass doors on the inner side of our front door and peered out, managing to make out Tiger lying near to where the garden path disappeared round the corner. They had lain awake waiting for our return, no doubt also waiting in fear of the gunman coming back. By this time the girls had woken up and whilst we were trying to make sense of what had happened, our door-bell rang. Zane went to answer it whilst I tried to comfort the children, but we were all drawn outside by the sound of shouting from the gate. It was Zane shouting at Mahmoud and not being over choosy about the language he used. I rushed over and Mahmoud turned to me, pointing to his chest, where his shirt was torn.

'Your dog bit me, so I shot him.'

'What do you mean, you shot him? What were you doing in our garden?' I was trying very hard not to shout myself.

'He was out in the street when I passed by and he attacked me. The gates were open'.

'And you just happened to be carrying your gun, did you?'

He was obviously lying since we never left our gates open and the children would never have gone outside and opened them, particularly when they were alone in the house. Whilst this conversation was going on I got between the two men, trying to stop Zane from hitting him. Realising that the kids were coming out behind us, Zane stopped shouting and turned towards me: 'Take them back inside. I'm going to ask the neighbours if they saw anything. I'll be back in a minute.'

The rest of the night passed in a haze, as did the following day. The children were devastated, angry and tearful, so none of us got much sleep that night. Zane reported the incident to the police first thing in the morning. They came to our house, looked at Tiger's dead body, then went and arrested Mahmoud. I let the kids stay home from school that morning and Zane and one of his men buried Tiger's body underneath the Oleander bushes next to the garden wall. Later in the afternoon we received a visit from a distant relative of Mahmoud who also happened to be a friend of Zane. He was very influential in the Baath party and he had come to ask Zane to withdraw the charges so that his relative could be released. Zane liked the guy, and helped him get a job when the Baathists were out of favour, making it difficult for him to get employment. I found him rather dour and serious but he was married to a German girl whom I liked so we socialised with them occasionally. My first instinct was to tell him to get lost, but the decision wasn't in my hands; he had come to make the request to Zane, who said he would think about it. Actually, there wasn't much to think about and I knew Zane would feel it wiser to withdraw the charges.

I have no idea what would have happened to Mahmoud if he had not done so and I didn't particularly care. Apparently there is an Arab tradition which makes it a heinous crime to harm another person's dog since it is the protector of the family, but I doubt that this tradition was incorporated into law. Nevertheless, we had the sympathy of everyone in the area. All our neighbours were outraged at the shooting and considered it right that Mahmoud had to spend a couple of nights in jail. The children gradually recovered from their fright, particularly when we promised we would bring a puppy from Britain to take Tiger's place. The day after his release, Mahmoud's wife called round to ask me whether Tiger had been vaccinated against rabies, because Mahmoud would have to undergo a series of painful injections into his stomach if he hadn't. I was very tempted to answer 'no'.

'He was bitten, you know'.

'Maybe he was, but how did our dog get out into the road? And why did Mahmoud have a gun with him?'

She couldn't answer those questions, so she left and I think that was the last time I spoke to her, which was a pity because, as I've said, she was a very nice girl. Her son didn't get off so lightly, though. Soon afterwards he was spotted by Zara riding his bike down our street. She grabbed hold of his handlebars, bringing the bike to a halt so abruptly that he fell off, then grabbed him and slapped him across the face.

'That's what you'll get if you ride past here again' she warned whilst the other kids who were playing outside all jeered and cheered. I was horrified when she told me.

'Why did you do that? It wasn't his fault. Don't you ever do that again', I warned her. Luckily she did as she was told, largely because the boy wasn't caught riding past our house again after that.

A line was drawn under the episode several weeks later when Mahmoud arrived at our house with a sweet little puppy very like his own black and white hound – presumably as a peace offering. 'I brought it for your children, it's a thoroughbred.'

'That's very kind of you, but I couldn't possibly accept it. We're off to the UK in a couple of weeks anyway, so I couldn't take on a puppy now even if I wanted to'. My response was icily polite: I was amazed at his cheek, thinking that he could so easily compensate for terrorising my children and killing our dog. He tried to persuade me to take the puppy but I was not to be moved. I was determined not to make him feel better by accepting it, apart from the fact that it happened to be true that we were leaving for England within a couple of weeks.

Whilst we were there, we bought a Springer Spaniel puppy which I had promised Tula we would take back with us. She adored animals and had been even more devastated than our other children by Tiger's death. They named him Fonzy after the *Happy Days* TV programme, which was very apt as he was quite a character. The plan was that he would travel freight on the same flight as us, but I had to drive him up to the freight terminal at Heathrow airport a few days before we left so the freight company could prepare the necessary paper-work. Unluckily, the day before we were due to leave they phoned to say that they couldn't get him on our plane so he would be sent out to Baghdad the following week. The children were disappointed, but Zane was furious when he heard the news. 'Do you think I'm going out to the airport looking for a dog? Are you crazy? Do you want to get me arrested? If you want him, you'll have to go and get him yourself.'

I'm still not sure why he thought it would be dangerous for him to go the airport freight area, but no doubt he had heard things which he hadn't passed on to me. Anyway, I couldn't disappoint the children; they were so excited and couldn't wait to see Fonzy again, so I had no choice but to drive out to the airport the following week at about two in the morning to try to find the freight section. It wasn't very difficult, I simply followed the signs round to the back, where I bumped into a cheerful young British Airways employee from the Midlands who gave me very clear directions. He even called out a warning after me, 'Make sure you take the second entrance, don't take the first one – that's the VIP lounge – you don't want to be going in there by mistake!'

I crossed over so that I was well clear of the first entrance, at the same time wondering what happened to people who went in there by mistake, then walked on until I reached the large shed where freight was off-loaded. The young customs officer confirmed that a dog had arrived on the plane from London and assured me that he was fit and healthy. 'We've given him some water, but I think he's hungry. Do you have his papers?' I gave him the necessary papers, then stood looking around while he examined them; the shed didn't appear to contain much in the way of freight.

'And his rabies vaccination certificate?'

The kennels which had arranged Fonzy's transport had assured me that dogs travelling from the UK didn't need this since the disease did not exist in Britain in those days. 'Oh, he doesn't need one; we don't have any rabies in Britain.'

'That might be true, but I can't let him into the country without one.'

We argued this back and forth but he was adamant that he could not release the dog unless he had a certificate stating he had been vaccinated for rabies. It was about 3 a.m. by then, and I really wanted to take my dog and go home. Fortunately, another, older officer came in to see what the fuss was about; I explained the situation, and his colleague explained it from his point of view.

'She hasn't got a rabies certificate; I can't release the animal without one.'

'Why not? It's a dog, not an illegal immigrant. Let her take it so we can all go home'. I could have kissed him. The young officer caved in and took me into a smaller section where Fonzy was sitting in his crate, bright-eyed and alert as if he travelled by plane every day. The officer opened the door of the crate, I clipped on his lead and left the building as quickly as I could, calling out my thanks at the door. As I drove home I thanked my lucky stars that common sense had prevailed over bureaucracy. It was getting light by the time we arrived home so I entered the house quietly and bent down to unclip Fonzy's lead before going towards the kitchen, where I planned to bed him down for what remained of the night. As soon as he was released, his tail began wagging madly, like all Springer Spaniels, and he rushed off in the opposite direction. He charged into my bedroom and leapt onto the bed where he proceeded to wake Zane by jumping all over him enthusiastically. It was a great move because Zane, who already thought of him as a great inconvenience, was prepared to dislike him on sight. Instead, he was won over by Fonzy's infectious enthusiasm and the English Springer Spaniel remains his favourite breed of dog to this day.

# Chapter Seventeen

We had been living in Baghdad for sixteen years during which time our children lived happy and free. I will always be grateful that they had the benefit of enjoying a wonderful childhood; nevertheless it was becoming obvious that we wouldn't be staying for ever. Every year, friends and acquaintances would go on holiday to Europe and not return, thus creating a brain drain of substantial proportions. The government tried various means of stemming the flow, alternating between stick and carrot methods. Periodically, bans on travel abroad were imposed on professionals such as doctors and engineers, but these bans could be counter-productive as professionals had to go abroad in order to gain post graduate qualifications. To encourage those who did so to return to Iraq on completion of their studies, they were offered special licences to import a tax-free Mercedes car from Germany. As a result, Mercedes saloons became abundant in the capital for a time, prompting me to wonder whether this was one of the reasons the secret police began to use other means of transport.

The capital continued to expand, putting pressure on existing services. It was noticeable that water pressure fell during the summer months, sometimes to the extent that the tank on the roof didn't completely fill, causing us to run out of water at the end of the afternoon. Tired of coming home dusty and weary from a day on site to find a trickle of water emerging from the shower, Zane installed a pump in the garden. Our water supply was plentiful again after that, but one of our Iraqi neighbours was very disgruntled and accused us of siphoning off water which should have gone to their house. I tried to explain to her that it didn't work that way, but I don't think she ever believed me.

One evening we were at a dinner party at Pauline's when the conversation turned to the provision of services. Munim was saying that he worried that a time would come when there would be electricity shortages in the capital because of the increased population.

'I've told the people who run our country that they ought to make plans to build new power stations but nothing's been done about it.' For once Zane couldn't stop himself from responding:

'Don't you realise you are one of the people who run our country?'

'You're joking; who listens to me?' Munim glanced around as he said this, no doubt looking for signs that one of the agent provocateurs who always attended such gatherings was taking an interest. It was the kind of remark which could easily be interpreted as a criticism which should be reported to the secret police.

And that was the problem of course. Everyone in the room understood that by 'the people who run our country' he meant Saddam. Though still nominally vice president, it was Saddam who controlled everything, making the final decision on every aspect of the nation's policies, for good or for ill. The president, Ahmed Zane al-Bakr, only remained in power because he was influential in army circles, an obstacle Saddam would no doubt find a way around in due course. In the meantime, there was a never-ending stream of directives from the vice president's office. Together with the president, he made the ultimate decisions on crucial matters such as the purchase of weaponry and other government policies, but he was not above interfering in more trivial matters. When it was announced that every household must have a portrait of the President and Vice President hanging in their living room we chose to ignore it, but many people did not. When all shopkeepers were ordered to sell goods at fixed prices and label their products clearly, he took all the fun out of shopping for Baghdad's experienced hagglers and also made the traders very grumpy. One afternoon, when I asked the owner of a fruit and vegetable stall how much his okra was, he pointed to the front of his stall, where a battered square of cardboard with a list of his prices was propped up among the onions and replied curtly: 'They're labelled'.

'But I can't read'.

He looked me up and down, then said quite rudely, 'Don't tell me that a woman like you can't read'. I decided that we would manage without okra that week and went to another stall.

Whilst he was engaged in taking the reins of the country entirely into his own hands, Saddam was also engaged in a popularity campaign, apparently endeavouring to promote himself as 'a man of the people'. There was frequent television and newspaper coverage of him spending leisure time with his children, particularly his youngest daughter, of whom he appeared to be particularly fond. He also began making unannounced calls on ordinary citizens, turning up at the door like a long lost son and making himself at home, poking around in the family's belongings and helping himself to food from their freezer. These visits were also televised and included in the evening news. It was said that the entire street and every house in it would be thoroughly searched by the secret police before he arrived for his 'unannounced visit'. I have no idea whether this was true but I do know that Mum bumped into Saddam one day while she was shopping in Karrada. He was making his way through the fruit and veg stalls surrounded by his guards, occasionally stopping on his way to speak to the people who were out shopping. One of them was Mum:

'Hello Aunty. How are you? How's everything going with you?'

'I'm well, thanks to God'. She gave the stock response.

He went on to ask her who her sons were, what they did for a living and how she found life under the current government. He also asked whether he could do anything specific for her.

She thanked him carefully, assuring him that everything was wonderful in her life, ending with ' God bless you, my son'. It was *de rigueur* by then to attribute every advantage or blessing one might receive in life as coming directly from him, including the entire product of the Iraqi exchequer. The wealth of the country was just as much in his hands as the lives of its citizens, and one family who failed to remember this were to suffer the consequences. They had been selected for one of the 'unannounced' visits and apparently, not being fans, did not make the vice president feel sufficiently welcome. Notwithstanding, he looked around their home and found the furniture in their sitting room looking rather shabby.

'You need new sofas, I'll send you some – it will be my gift to your family.'

'No, thank you, ours are fine. We don't need new ones.'

'No, I insist. You deserve nicer furniture. I'll make sure you get it.'

'No thank you, we're happy with what we've got. We don't want new furniture.'

The upshot was that the Vice President left having failed to persuade the family that they should accept the furniture. The next people to visit them were the secret police. They took the husband, wife and children away, leaving their neighbours wondering whether they were all executed or merely thrown into prison.

We saw Saddam ourselves one evening when we were driving past the presidential palace. He was walking with his bodyguards, exercise apparently recommended by his doctor following problems with his back. The group came through the gates, striding along at a brisk pace, and the sentries indicated that we should stop our car and allow them to pass. The bodyguards looked as though they were finding it hard to keep up with their boss, but he looked as though he was enjoying himself, with the trademark grin which he always wore before the cares of war and other matters wiped the smile off his face.

He was a tall, handsome man in those days and he smiled broadly as he looked into our car through the open windows. People talk about 'charisma' but I had never encountered it before until then. Even with the chassis of the car separating us we could feel the force of his personality and the kids followed him with their eyes as he disappeared briskly into the dusk, with his little band of followers scurrying behind him. From the moment he appeared I kept my face down because I didn't want him to notice me. It was rumoured that Saddam took any woman he fancied and we knew there was some truth in the rumours because he had tried to seduce the mother of one of Summer's school friends, even though she was happily married and not inclined to be unfaithful. The woman was an artist from a well-known Iraqi family and she also had the reputation of being very beautiful. Her husband had been at school with Zane, so we knew his family were decidedly 'good folk'– not the sort of people to accept lying down a scandal affecting their daughter in law. Anyway, they managed to escape the country and ended up in London. These events were quite recent and very much in my mind as I sat staring down into my lap on that particular evening. As the walkers moved away from us I looked up, breathed a sigh of relief and thanked God that I wasn't blonde.

Throughout my years in Baghdad my Arabic vocabulary continued to expand. I frequently learned new words from my children, who tended to use more formal expressions than those I had picked up in Mum's kitchen, so when I noticed that the word 'Ajim' seemed to crop up quite a lot it was quite natural for me to ask Summer what it meant. She told me that it meant 'foreigners' in classical Arabic, but it struck me that the word was being used in a derogatory way to refer to people who were of ethnic Iranian descent. Since Iraq was largely a land-locked country it was inevitable that many of its citizens' forebears originated in neighbouring countries. For example, Erica's husband was Kurdish but his family were originally from Iran.

At the beginning of the century when the British had an informal mandate over the region they had formalised the origins of every individual in Iraq by requiring the head of each household to indicate whether he considered himself to derive from Turkish or Iranian stock. I have heard varying explanations of their reasons for doing this, but whatever the motivation, every Iraqi's ancestry was still recorded as originating from one of these countries.

Zane's grandfather had registered as being of Turkish origin, although he might just have easily chosen Iran since he had no particular allegiance to either. It was lucky for his descendants that he did, as they began to realise when speeches by government officials began to include tirades about 'Ajim traitors' who were to be rounded up and sent back where they came from.

Because the Shia population of Iraq had been contained under a 'glass ceiling' by their Sunni rulers since the time of the Turkish Empire, it is often assumed that they are primarily uneducated farmer workers and labourers. Whilst it is true that farm workers make up a large proportion of the Shia-dominated south, this is because the primary industry in the south is agriculture. In the cities, however, hard-working Shia Moslems turned to the professions or to trade since they knew they were unlikely to rise above a certain rank in the army or civil service. Nowhere was this more obvious than in Karrada, where successful businessmen had built huge houses along the river from which their sons and daughters could be seen every morning emerging in their Mercedes to go to work as doctors, engineers and lawyers. The campaign of deportation was slow getting off the ground, so at first we were aware of it only as rumours. However, it soon became apparent that whole families were actually being deported and most of them were Shia Moslems. Once they had left, their homes and other assets were confiscated by the state, so it was easy for us to attribute the deportations to jealousy and greed, since we had no idea at the time of the larger, global political machinations which were at work. All we knew was that on more than one occasion when we were returning home late at night we saw open pick-up trucks crowded with people waiting outside the police station. In the months which followed, huge numbers of people were rounded up and dumped on the Iranian border. Although largely Shia Moslems, Turkoman families and people from other ethnic groups were also dragged from their homes and put on the lorries. Sometimes, the men and boys were taken away separately, leaving the women to be sent to the border on their own; it's anyone's guess what happened to their menfolk after that. Since the Iranian government under the Mullahs viewed these exiles from secular Iraq with great suspicion, they were not allowed into Iran so they had no alternative but to set up refugee camps. Some of those exiles remain there to this day. Although Saddam's crimes against the Kurdish people have been well publicised, the mass deportations to Iran did not prove quite so interesting to the world media, for reasons best known to themselves.

These events convinced me more than ever that our lives had to change, so when Pauline phoned to say that the British Council was running a TEFL course I jumped at the chance. We decided to go and apply for a place together; luckily we were both accepted and within days commenced our training to become teachers of English as a Foreign Language. Pauline had bought a box file in preparation for our training, so I thought I should do the same with the result that on the first day we arrived at the centre with the unwieldy cardboard boxes tucked under our arms looking like a couple of village idiots. About twenty women had been accepted for training, all of them British wives of Iraqis, but I didn't know any of them, which wasn't surprising because there were quite large numbers of British and other foreign women living with their husbands in Iraq at that time. In the following weeks many of these women either dropped out or were simply dropped, so only a couple of us successfully completed the course and were given work at the end. I wasn't surprised that I was one of the few because I had made up my mind to do well and in fact I took to teaching like a duck to water.

Our trainers were a British Council-employed couple named Mary and Patrick Fox; they ran all the courses at the centre which was rather grandly named 'The Centre for Higher Studies of English'. They subscribed to the theory that teaching a foreign language is done most effectively by demonstration and repetition rather than explanation, particularly at the beginners' level. I actually agreed with them and found the course very helpful, but some of the established, qualified teachers who worked there criticised their methods, saying that they were only using us as guinea pigs because they were writing a book about training teachers.

Be that as it may, I viewed it as an opportunity to prepare myself for the changes in our lives which were so obviously ahead of us, and was determined to succeed. Zane was not so enthusiastic; he put up all sorts of difficulties – how the kids were going to get to school being the main one – but I knew his main objection was the suspicion with which all foreign institutions were viewed by the government. In short, the British Council was considered to be little more than a cover for intelligence gathering, even though Iraqi government employees were routinely sent there to improve their English, so its employees fell under similar suspicion by default. When it became obvious that his objections were not working Zane simply forbade me to go and when that failed, he stopped talking to me. He maintained this campaign of silence for three months, augmenting it by making it very difficult for me to actually get to the course by denying me use of the car. Obviously, he couldn't do this on a permanent basis, since I was responsible for running the household, but when he was in Baghdad my car was needed for business purposes suspiciously often and always at times when I needed to drive across the city to get to the British Council. Luckily, I was able to find ways round this; one was Pauline, who offered to come over and get me, a journey which involved her travelling back and forth across the city in the rush hour. I even received a message via Ali from my future son in law, offering to drive me to the centre whenever I needed a lift. I didn't bother to reply, mainly because at that time I still regarded him as no more than an annoying nuisance, but also because he had recently driven his brother in law's Mercedes through the plate glass windows of the florists at the end of Mum's road. When all else failed I took a taxi, justifying the expense to myself as an investment in our future.

Although our marriage had the usual ups and downs, Zane and I had never been in the habit of sulking and not speaking to each other – blazing rows were more our style – so I found his silence very trying. Luckily, I had my work at the centre to distract me so I stuck to my guns until eventually he caved in. As it happened, I also had other things to think about because in early spring the event which everyone had been expecting for a number of years finally took place, and Saddam took over as President. The change in leadership was publicly attributed to the allegedly failing health of the President, Ahmed Zane al-Bakr, but everyone knew the real reason was that Saddam had finally gained enough influence within the army to make him feel secure. Inevitably, within a few weeks of his elevation to the top job he carried out a purge; at a televised meeting he removed such senior political figures that the country was left reeling in shock. Soon after that, Farah's uncle – reputedly Saddam's best friend – was arrested and executed, officially because he was part of a Syrian-backed plot. My Iraqi neighbour, knowing how close Summer and Farah were and no doubt influenced by her belief that we were still stealing her water, told me that she thanked God that Saddam had taken over and saved the country from a civil war like the one which was going on in Lebanon at the time. In fact, the 'plotters' were seeking to ensure that a proposed treaty with Syria went ahead in an effort to limit Saddam's power; showing a commendable ability to see into the future, they feared that the brutality he had already exhibited would eventually lead the country into chaos and possibly civil war unless it was curbed. Saddam is said to have cried bitter tears at the necessity of having so many of his trusted colleagues executed, but that didn't prevent the executions from going ahead. As for his 'best friend', political commentators have reported that Saddam found out that he was taking 'kick backs' of ten per cent on all the arms deals which he negotiated, a perk which Saddam liked to reserve for himself and his family; either reason would have been enough to seal his fate.

These events left us with a dilemma; quite often an individual's execution was followed by the arrest of many of his relatives and friends – in fact the whole object of torturing a prisoner seemed to be to find out who his friends were so that they could be arrested too. Naturally enough, this resulted in people trying to distance themselves from bereaved family members, who would find themselves isolated and alone just when they most needed moral support. Although it felt cowardly, we told Summer to stay away from Farah's house for a while until we knew what would happen. When I popped in to express my condolences, her mother told me that the only other local person who had the guts to call was the mother of my future son in law. Luckily, Farah's family did not suffer any further retribution, so far as I know. Nevertheless, I continued to worry and read hidden meanings into the most innocuous incident. One afternoon, Summer and Farah decided to walk home from school with another friend. It was quite a long walk, so on the way they stopped and changed into sports shoes. By the time they set off again they realised they were being followed by a couple of secret policemen. The girls were convinced that they were the same men they had seen standing near the gates of the presidential palace when they passed. In any case, they managed to shake them off by going into a neighbouring house, then exiting their garden by a side gate and taking a long detour before coming home.

The most likely explanation is that the men were simply attracted by three pretty young girls; it was highly unlikely that they would have known who Farah was, but still I couldn't help worrying, so when my car had a puncture right outside the gates of the presidential palace a few days later I expected trouble. One of the guards was beside me before I had even opened the boot – he didn't need to ask why I had stopped because the tyre was as flat as a pancake.

'You can't change that here, I'll get someone to help me push it.' He called one of the other guards and together they pushed the car a few yards round the roundabout whilst I steered. 'Where's your spare?' That was a very good question; I poked around in the boot of the car but I couldn't see it. I think I was probably too flustered to think straight, expecting the secret police to come out and arrest me at any moment. 'I don't know where it is, I've never changed a tyre before.' The guards looked in the boot, but it didn't appear to contain a spare tyre. 'It's no good, I'll have to go home and get my husband.' Never had I felt more feeble, but amazingly the guards let me go, leaving the car where it was. I walked down the road and flagged down a taxi.

When I arrived, I was relieved to see that Zane was at home for once. I told him what had happened and he went ballistic: 'What do you mean, there's no spare in the car, of course there is. Did you lift up the lining of the boot?' Of course, I hadn't. It was quite a new innovation to disguise the space in which a spare tyre was kept – they were normally clipped to one side of the boot in full view. 'Don't you know anything about your own car? Don't you know I'll get arrested if I go back now?' I recognised that these were rhetorical questions, and quite wisely kept my mouth shut. But there was nothing for it but to return and collect the car. 'Do you want me to come with you to drive it back?' 'No, I'll take someone else.' He had obviously had quite enough of me for one day. Whilst he was gone I walked the floor, imagining all sorts of things happening to him when he arrived at the palace. I felt quite sick with fear for him and very angry at myself for my own stupidity. Whilst I paced, I tried to think of who I should contact for help if he didn't return. Thankfully he did and nothing had happened to him. He had taken his foreman with him, they had changed the tyre and driven both cars home. So far as I know, no-one even came out to speak to them, but I can't be too sure of that because Zane was still too angry with me to talk about it. I suspect he would have made some comment to the guards about the innate stupidity of women, and they would have shaken their heads and agreed with him. One of the paradoxes of life in Baghdad was that you could get away with something which most security forces would regard as highly suspicious, then be arrested for the most trivial offence.

It was whilst we were in the midst of these events that I had my first experience of taking a class alone. This teaching practice involved each of us giving a talk on a specialist subject or hobby of our choice, with visual aids. Looking back, it seems rather a strange assignment to give us as preparation for teaching by a 'demonstration only' method. All the other student teachers were buzzing with ideas about what their talk was going to involve, but try as I might I couldn't think of any hobby which I could talk about, let alone one that the class might find interesting. One by one, they gave their talks with varying degrees of success; Pauline talked about pop music since she had the advantage of owning a large record collection, mainly brought back by Munim from his frequent trips abroad on government business. Her visual aids were record sleeves which she used to back up samples of records which had recently been in the UK charts, making hers by far the most popular talk with the class of young people. The days passed and my turn to take a class was approaching, but still I floundered around trying to think of an idea. Somebody advised me to think of my background and childhood in the UK for inspiration; I thought of my childhood school holidays spent wandering around the fields of Somerset and later, as a teenager, cycling to the beach and suddenly I had it – my talk would contrast the endless battle of keeping the desert sands away from a Baghdad household with the willingness of the British to endure long hours in the cold lying on a sandy beach. This would also have the advantage of linking in with an incident in the book we used at the centre as a teaching aid where the hero – Arthur – spends a day at the beach. My visual aids were pictures of women doing housework and people cavorting on beaches, including girls in bikinis (these were particularly well received by the men in the group). I even took in a small bag of sand. On the whole, though, I can't say that my talk was particularly well received by the students. If anything, they were slightly bemused rather than interested. In fact, if I'm honest, I would have to admit that they didn't know what the hell I was talking about. Despite this, I passed the course with flying colours and was ready to go on to the next stage, which was to take a class every day for a month before the centre closed down for the summer. I wasn't paid for this as it was teaching practice, but the students or their sponsors still paid fees, so it was a very good deal for the British Council.

It was during this teaching practice that I was driving to class one afternoon at a time when most sensible citizens were at home snoozing with the air conditioning turned up high. As I approached the roundabout in front of the presidential palace a Porsche shot out of the gates and whizzed round the roundabout before zooming back into the palace grounds again. It appeared to be driven by a child. I happened to mention this to my kids when I returned home later that day. 'Oh, that was Oday – he's got all kinds of sports cars – Porsches, Lamborghinis, Ferraris, you name it, he's got one', Ali explained with more than a touch of envy. Oday could not have been more than fourteen at the time. Because I was teaching this class, we would have to postpone our trip to England until rather later than usual, so we decided to send Summer and Ali on ahead; they left Baghdad very excited at their first trip abroad alone. Little did they know that it would be many years, if ever, before they returned to the country of their childhood.

I think it was also in the spring of that year that the British Home Secretary announced his decision to correct the anomaly which existed between men and women regarding foreign spouses. Previously, children born to non-British women who were married to British subjects automatically became British, but the children of British women married to foreign men did not. Now they were to be given the same rights as men and they could also apply for British nationality for their existing children, so long as the fathers agreed to their having dual nationality. Naturally, there was a great deal of discussion about this among the teachers at the British Council and everyone agreed that it would be far too dangerous to apply for our children and that our husbands wouldn't agree to it anyway in the current political climate. We were all lying: I don't know anyone who didn't take advantage of the offer, although they may have waited until they visited Britain to apply. Zane agreed that dual nationality might be an advantage to our kids in the future, but made it clear that he would not go to the embassy to sign the papers. Since he had no plans to visit the UK that year and I felt I couldn't wait, I decided to go and speak to the consul alone.

I had only been to the British Embassy once before in order to renew my passport; it had been much like any other consulate, business-like and quiet with polite officials going about their jobs, so I was totally unprepared for the chaos I encountered when I arrived for the second time. A service hatch had been installed facing onto the street to deal with consular enquiries. It was protected by a steel shutter and the reason was obvious – surrounding the hatch were crowds of people pushing and shoving each other as they tried to get to the front and gain the attention of staff. I couldn't hear what they were saying above the din but it was obvious that they were all enquiring about a visa for the UK. I stood there gaping, wondering whether I had the guts to throw myself into the melee, when the decision was made for me by a loud male voice yelling out in a broad Lancashire accent to 'shut that fucking shutter'. The shutter crashed down straight away, narrowly missing the heads and arms of the people at the front, and the crowd moved back to re-group and chat among themselves. I assumed it would be opened again in due course, but I wasn't sure whether I wanted to wait around for that to happen. As I milled around with the crowd I happened to bump into a British woman from Portsmouth who was there with her sister in law to apply for a visa. They were about to leave, but before they did she mentioned the contrast between this section and the embassy proper which fronted the street behind.

'Do you know how you get in there?'

'Well, if you walk round the corner and up the street you'll see the entrance'.

So that was what I did. I was after all a British subject and felt I had as much right to enter as anyone, so I walked round until I found the entrance to the embassy. It wasn't a particularly imposing building and the gardens could have done with some attention, but it did have a long driveway with a swimming pool to one side. I don't even remember seeing guards at the gates. Anyway, I went in and asked to see the consul immediately. Whilst I was waiting I witnessed an Iraqi army officer being dealt with in marked contrast to the service given to the crowds waiting by the shutters. A smartly-dressed embassy official came to speak to him by name – I remember he was a major – assuring him that his visa would be ready the next day. She could not have been more deferential and I felt very sorry for the people who were being dealt with so differently outside.

I didn't have to wait long before I was shown into a small room and immediately joined by the consul, a mild-mannered elderly man who got right down to business. 'Problems?' I explained to him that I wanted to apply for my three younger children to be made British subjects. 'Yes, that's fine, but your husband must sign the application in the presence of a consular official'.

'Well he's happy to do that but he won't come to the embassy'.

He told me that one of the conditions was that all applications must be signed by the father at the embassy, in order to eliminate forgeries. I countered by reminding him that he must know as well as I did that any Iraqi citizen who visited a foreign embassy without having obvious business there would automatically place himself under suspicion. We fenced verbally back and forth and in the end he agreed that if I filled out the applications in front of him he would allow me to take them home for Zane's signature. I wondered how many times he reached that agreement with other British mothers. The applications were duly completed and sent off and eventually the children all became British subjects, making their transition to life in Britain much easier to achieve.

The reason I wasn't prepared to wait was because I had made up my mind to leave Summer and Ali in England, at least until they had completed university. Zane and I had talked about doing this at some stage in the future, but as they were both doing well in school there was really no urgency and the truth was that we were reluctant to part with them before we had to. Now, I really felt that we had to get them away. I lived in constant fear that Summer would suffer repercussions because of her friendship with Farah, possibly even arrest and torture, or that Ali's quick wit and talent as a wind up merchant would attract the hostile eyes of Oday and his cronies in the school playground. If that happened, it wouldn't take them long to find out that he had been a good friend of the murdered boy. We couldn't tell them any of this before they left the country in case they mentioned it to their friends, so they didn't even have a chance to say goodbye to them.

I had been putting some money away in a UK Building Society each time we visited my family and we would have enough to pay boarding school fees for Ali for a while. Since Summer was a British Citizen she could live with my mother and attend the local sixth form college. She still had a year to complete before she graduated from high school in Baghdad, so the college insisted that she begin at 'O' level, even though she had covered the syllabus already. It was a sixth form college, so the other 'O' level students were re-sitting and were only allowed to take four subjects. The college would not make any exception to this, although they did allow Summer to take the classical Arabic exam since there would not be any tuition involved, so long as I paid the exam fees. Unfortunately, I had no experience of British university requirements at that time and had no idea that limiting the number of subjects she took at 'O' level would make it impossible for her to get into medical school. She had wanted to become a doctor for as long as I could remember and her excellent academic record meant that she was undoubtedly heading straight for medical school in Baghdad, so I suppose you might add to Saddam's list of crimes the fact that he deprived the country of a promising doctor.

I spent most of that summer looking for a school for Ali; I wanted it to be reasonably close to my family so he could visit them at weekends and during school holidays, so Hampshire was one of the possible locations. I obviously scandalised the admissions officer of Winchester College when I phoned to tell him that I was considering starting my son at the school in the autumn term, little knowing that parents enrolled their offspring practically at birth. In the end I found a school which was not much more than an hour's drive from my mother's house. It was just outside of Andover, housed in beautiful old buildings and surrounded by picturesque countryside. Although I was astonished by the sparseness of the boys' sleeping accommodation – it reminded me of army barracks in a *Carry On* film – I was satisfied that he would be safe there. Ali would share a study bedroom with two or three other boys so his quarters were marginally more comfortable than that of the younger boys, but I can't say he was impressed with his new accommodation. I drove him to the school a couple of days before we were to fly back to Baghdad. He had just turned fifteen at the time, outwardly very confident and at the stage when he hated public displays of affection. As we carried his things to his new room he leaned over and whispered 'I'm worried that the teachers will all be queers and perverts' – not something which had crossed my mind until that moment. As I hugged his skinny frame goodbye, I crossed my fingers and prayed that I had not thrown him out of the frying pan and into the fire.

When I arrived back at the airport in Baghdad, accompanied only by Zara and Tula, Zane was there to welcome us as usual. He had no more idea than the rest of our friends that we were returning on our own, since it would have been unwise to mention it in letters because of the censors. He greeted us with hugs and kisses, but made no mention of our two missing children until we were safely out of the airport and on our way home. 'You left them then?' It was obvious that he hadn't really believed I could bring myself to leave them behind; when we reached home the house already felt strange without them.

Early the next morning we were woken by loud clapping coming from outside – it was the signal used by Ali and his friends to indicate that one of them was out and ready for some fun with his mates; this one obviously couldn't wait to see him after the summer holiday. I got up, put on my dressing gown and went out to tell my son's friends that he wouldn't be coming home for a while. Over the next few days I repeated the explanation to friends and family: 'We thought it would be good for them to go to university abroad'. No other comment was necessary. Farah came round with a friend from school to check that the news was correct; the friend was devastated and sobbed so loudly that I began to wonder whether she was mentally unstable. In contrast, Farah was so calm and unsurprised that I suspected that she had known Summer wasn't coming back with us – I think Ali might have been in touch with friends of her brother in the UK.

The fact that we had felt it necessary to keep quiet about our plans was a reflection of the general paranoia. Since the authorities were engaged in the mass deportation of Shia Moslems at that time, one might think they would be grateful that we had saved them the trouble in the case of our own two children. However, you never knew how the secret police would react and added to that, it was never wise to let them know that you had funds abroad, however small the amount. It was perfectly possible that they might decide to arrest Zane and try to beat a 'confession' out of him as to why we sent our children abroad.

It was strange not to have boys in the house. We had been used to Ali and his friends surging in, looking for drinks and snacks after a game of football, while the girls to wrinkled their noses and opened all the windows to let out the smell of dusty teenage sweat. We missed their music, too. Summer loved the Carpenters and was a devoted Abba fan, whilst Ali's favourites alternated rather confusingly between James Brown, Tom Jones and Englebert Humperdink. Not that Zara and Tula were quiet and retiring, far from it, it was just that their friends were all girls now that they were both in high school, so once Ali's friends had come to check that he really wasn't coming back they had no other reason to call round. Zara and Tula's musical tastes were still developing, but they loved the film *Grease* and wanted to see the sequel in Britain that summer. Unfortunately, it had not been released before we left, so they were very excited the day they returned from school to tell me that the new *Grease* film was on at one of the local cinemas in Baghdad.

I rarely went to the cinema in Baghdad; we usually watched the latest films at the engineer's club, where you could sit outside in the summer enjoying dinner and drinks whilst the kids played with friends until the film began. However, I knew that there were several categories of cinema in the city. The best and most expensive were the places where people tended to go with the family. They were cleaner, the seats were more comfortable and a man could relax and enjoy the film in the knowledge that his wife and daughters would not be ogled by unattached males. There were others which were cheaper but not so luxurious and they tended to be choice of single men, although there was no reason why women could not go to them. The one which was supposed to be showing *Grease* was not one of the better ones, but I was determined that life should go on as near to normal as possible for the girls, so I promised to take them after school.

As soon as we arrived at the cinema I could tell from the hoarding outside that the film was not the *Grease* sequel, but an Italian film. It was obviously about teenagers, however, so I thought we might as well give it a go. We bought our tickets then started up the flight of stairs which led to the auditorium, with Zara rushing excitedly ahead: she was still convinced that the film showing was the sequel to *Grease*. There was a pair of heavy velvet curtains at the top of the stairs in place of the usual fire doors, so Tula and I each pulled one back and walked through just in time to see Zara disappear – she simply vanished. I stood there for a second, trying not to panic as my eyes adjusted to the dark and my ears tried to identify the clicking sound coming from the darkened room around us. Within seconds all became clear as several dozen cigarette lighters were held up at arm's length to reveal Zara lying spread-eagled on the floor below us. It turned out that there was another flight of steps going downwards on the other side of the curtain. Hardly any of the lighter-holders even bothered to turn away from the screen, so film-goers falling down the stairs must have been a regular occurrence at that cinema. Once we had assured ourselves that Zara wasn't hurt we made our way to the nearest vacant seats and collapsed onto them, helpless with giggles. At intervals throughout the film, mental pictures of Zara lying flat on the floor illuminated by the flickering flames of the lighters recurred and Tula and I would be convulsed with laughter, making it almost impossible for me to follow the plot. That was difficult enough because the sub-titles were in Arabic, but from the little I did understand it was obvious that the film was complete rubbish. Nevertheless, whenever I see recordings of a pop concert with fans holding lighted candles aloft the memory of that cinema visit comes rushing back to me and I still can't help laughing.

The new term started at the British Council. I was now a paid employee with my own classes to teach, so I was entitled to free transport. Staff who lived near to the centre were transported by mini bus and there was also a car which picked up the stragglers who lived further afield. I could have used the latter service, but I had already tried it once during the summer. The driver insisted on using side streets rather than keeping to the main roads, and seemed to deliberately choose the dustiest, most bumpy ones. He also tended to accelerate then brake sharply for no apparent reason except when he came to bumps in the road, in which case he always speeded up. By the time we arrived my head was spinning and I was feeling so sick that I decided to drive myself in future.

Apart from the teachers, the other staff who worked at the centre were a mixed bag; there were locals who had worked there for years, some in the library, others doing clerical work and so on. Most important of these was Hamza, nominally the caretaker, who had a hand in everything from making tea and coffee to ensuring the classrooms were laid out properly and set up with the correct equipment. He was indispensable and ensured that everything at the centre functioned efficiently. There were also three or four other British ex-patriots working there in addition to the Foxes: one was the Director of Studies but I was never clear what the others did. Of course, all the teachers and the secretary were British too, but as we were married to locals we were very obviously considered to be in a different category to them. The Organising Tutor fell into this group; she was a lively Irish girl named Margaret Zane with large blue eyes, a shiny dark bob, a wicked sense of humour and boundless energy. She always wore bright red lipstick and very high heeled stilettos which didn't prevent her from running up and down the stairs like an athlete (there were several flights of these at the centre). I had been working there for several weeks before I realised that she was the girl who used to read the television news in English when we first arrived in Baghdad. Tragically, years later she appeared on TV screens again, this time all over the world, when she was taken hostage and later murdered following the invasion of Iraq.

The students were also a mixed bag. Some were foreigners working in Baghdad, including diplomats and their wives, but there were also substantial numbers of government employees who were sponsored by their departments. In addition, most classes included quite a large quota of young people who paid for themselves and were obviously keen to improve their English, although the opportunity to mingle with people of the opposite sex was clearly a motivating factor too. The students all tended to be good-humoured and friendly, but some of them stick out in my mind. One is the Japanese student whose spoken English was so poor that the class would all hold their breaths when he was required to speak in case they erupted into laughter. The English words would burst from his mouth like bullets from an automatic weapon, without any inflexion or variation in pitch which might have made them even remotely comprehensible. Because his pronunciation was so poor, I used to make him repeat sentences more frequently than most of the other students, but I don't think he ever improved. On the plus side, I don't think anyone ever laughed either. Another character was an Italian engineer called Gino, who frequently interrupted our work in the middle of a lesson to ask:

'Mrs Khafaji, why you don't come to my house and I maka you the real Italian spaghetti?'

Needless to say, I never went.

There was also an Iraqi teacher of primary English who never managed to master the use of the personal pronoun. I would try to catch him unawares, suddenly picking up a book to ask 'Whose is this?' then follow up with more of the same. He rarely got it right but would throw wild guesses at me. 'It's hers. It's mine... It's yours?' This would go on until one of his classmates would put him out of his misery and tell him the correct answer. However, there is one student who I remember most for the simplest of reasons – he was the handsomest man I've ever seen. He was a Syrian film director and it was perfectly obvious from the moment he entered the room that he had captured the heart of every female there; he simply couldn't help it. He was also very likeable and never gave any indication that he was aware of the effect he had on women. He always rushed into class at the last moment without his book, so naturally all the girls would offer to share with him, but he never showed any favouritism. Each time he would sit next to a different girl, waiting politely for other students to budge up so that he could squeeze in. His even-handedness was fascinating and I couldn't help wondering what thoughts were going through the mind of the lucky girl who had been chosen that day.

The classes at the British Council were always full, so teachers were used to being asked to 'put a word in' for someone who hadn't managed to secure a place. I learned very early to say that I didn't have any influence on admissions, which happened to be the truth anyway. A further complication was that government-sponsored students all preferred to attend morning classes because their working day was usually from 8.00 a.m until 2.00 p.m. Thus, a morning class allowed them to miss work whilst an afternoon class meant they had to work all morning then go to classes in the afternoon. Because of this, State employees were always angling to swap their classes over, so in order to prevent abuses it was British Council policy to insist on signed permission from a ministry before a student could transfer to a morning class. Naturally, when one student said that his boss required him to change to a morning class but was too busy to write the necessary letter, his teacher's suspicions were aroused. She conferred with Margaret Zane who agreed. 'Tell him I can't change his class unless he brings permission from his boss. Tell him I'm not allowed to'. But the next time the student arrived he told the same story: 'I can't ask my boss, he's a very busy man.' Knowing what the answer would be, his teacher was adamant. 'There's no point in my asking Mrs Zane again, she can't transfer you unless you get a letter. If your boss wants you to change to another class, there must be someone in your department who can authorise it.' The student sighed. 'I'll try, but my boss is a very, very busy man.' The next evening his teacher was at home watching the news on television. As usual, the main item was what the president had been up to that day. The cameras showed him greeting some official, his trusted bodyguard close behind him. The new president rarely went anywhere in public without this man at his shoulder. He was usually dressed in military uniform and was beefy rather than muscular but very tall – tall enough to see over Saddam's shoulder. Because of this, his face was almost as familiar to Iraqi citizens as Saddam's. There were other bodyguards following on behind. They formed a semi-circle around him, but they didn't get quite so close to the president. For some reason the cameraman decided to zoom in on them, enabling the teacher to recognise one of them as the student whose boss was too busy to authorise his transfer to a morning class. I think it was decided that, under the circumstances, the need for the normal letter of authorisation would be waived.

That student wasn't the only person at the centre whose work brought him close to Saddam. One afternoon I happened to be alone in the staff room because the bus bringing the other teachers was late arriving. I was going over my lesson notes before class when Margaret Zane came in, pulled a face as she flopped down on a chair and groaned: 'I hate today.

I've got to go to the presidential palace in a minute.' I don't know which surprised me more, hearing where she was going or the fact that she was being so negative, because it was out of character for her to moan about anything. 'Oh, you're honoured. Why are you going there, then?' 'I've got to go and give the president's sons English lessons – I go every week. It's part of the Organising Tutor's job.' That came as a surprise; up until then, I had assumed that her job was solely to do with organising the students and teachers into classes, carrying out the admin connected with exams and so on.

'Why don't you like going there?' I was imagining her being strip searched, or subjected to

Some other humiliation from the tone of her voice.

'They're just so badly behaved: they're insolent and have no respect for anybody and they're not interested in learning anything. They're uncouth and ignorant and all they want to do is throw their weight about. They're completely different from Ahmed Zane al-Bakr's kids. They were polite and really wanted to learn – I didn't mind teaching them.' I wasn't surprised by what she said but I was surprised at her outspokenness; by that time it was generally taken for granted that 'even the walls had ears', especially in a place like the British Council. I suppose she felt at home there because she had worked at the centre for quite a long time.

By then, the term was well advanced and Christmas was approaching; we all really missed Summer and Ali, especially Zane. He felt badly about the fact that he hadn't said a proper goodbye to them before they left for Britain, so he decided to invent a reason to go abroad on business so that he could go and see them.

"Well if you're going, I'm coming with you. I want to see them too.' Zane felt this was unnecessary, as I had spent nearly three months with them in the summer but I insisted, so in the end we went together, leaving the girls with their aunty. We were relieved to find them both fit and healthy, if unaccustomedly pale from the lack of sunshine. Ali hated the discipline of boarding school, where nearly every minute of the boys' time was filled with prescribed activities. These didn't prevent him sneaking up to the main road in the dark with his new-found friends to pick up pizzas which they clandestinely ordered over the school telephone. The older boys were allowed to go into town one afternoon a week and Ali apparently led the way into the cinema to see a new X-rated film. He was quite proud of this achievement since he was still two and a half years short of the required age for admission.

Summer had also made new friends as well as becoming a member of the Venture Scouts, which she seemed to enjoy tremendously. This may not seem a big deal but it was a new departure for her because Zane had always discouraged our children from joining even the scouts or guides because of the inevitable political implications. Since they enjoyed so much freedom when school was out they had generally been happy to go along with him, apart from Zara, whose stubborn determination to do her own thing was very worrying to Zane. She insisted on joining the girl guides, much to his irritation, although initially their activities seemed to be confined to wearing the uniform to school for the Thursday 'raising the flag' ceremony, which seemed to me to be perfectly harmless.

The schools were all on their Christmas break in England, so we spent most of the holiday driving around the countryside doing touristy things, and of course we spent Christmas with my family for the first time in about sixteen years. I didn't enjoy it as much as I should have because I felt unaccountably tired all the time. Whenever I sat down I would begin to doze off on the settee, and couldn't wait to go to bed at night. My brother accused me of being a party pooper with some justice, but I couldn't help myself, particularly as I was also having blinding headaches. By the time he drove us back to the airport, with Summer and Ali beside me on the back seat trying valiantly to be cheerful, I was pretty sure I knew what the problem was. A few days after we arrived I was certain – I was pregnant again.

So far, I haven't said anything about abortions, but it was one of the paradoxes of Iraqi society. Although Iraq was essentially a secular country, most people kept more or less to their faith – some more, some less – whatever that faith might be. I don't recall ever hearing anybody questioning the existence of God and it went without saying that life was sacrosanct. Despite this, abortion appeared to be regarded as a necessary evil; women would speak quite openly about having a 'curtache' – obviously derived from the medical term 'Dilate & Curretage'. Several of my friends, neighbours and acquaintances underwent the procedure, some more than once, and although abortion was illegal except on medical grounds, there were plenty of doctors willing to do the honours for a small fee. I even knew of one young doctor who terminated the unwanted pregnancy of her own middle-aged mother. When my family came from England to visit us I was just recovering from an abortion myself – it was in the days before the invention of the mini pill.

Anyway, after the usual soul-searching undergone by women facing this decision, I decided that it would be better for all of us if I terminated the pregnancy. There was no secrecy involved; the husband of one of my friends was a Psychiatrist and he offered to phone a gynaecologist friend and give his view that another child would threaten my mental health (how right he was!). I duly paid a visit to the gynaecologist's clinic where he confirmed this diagnosis, recommended a termination and booked me into a private hospital for later that week. Erica drove me there, passing the time by telling me how she had become pregnant when she was a young girl in Germany. The German method of terminating pregnancy at that time had been to insert a pellet containing the necessary chemical into the neck of the womb, a procedure which apparently caused the patient hideous pain. This drug would cause contractions to begin and the foetus would eventually be aborted. Erica told me that she writhed in agony throughout this experience and vowed never to put herself in the position where she was likely to need the treatment again. I imagine most patients felt the same and there seems little doubt that it was intended to act as a deterrent. It certainly did the trick in Erica's case.

Buoyed up by this girlhood memoir, I stepped out of her bright yellow VW Beetle, leaned over the seat to pick up my overnight bag and entered the hospital. Luckily my experience was quite different from hers – I went into the operating theatre pregnant, came out not pregnant and had a good night's sleep for the first time in weeks. I felt only relief that my life was not going to be further complicated by another baby, and couldn't wait to get home and get on with it. Typically, Zane had not thought it necessary to stay in Baghdad whilst this was going on, so he arranged for the young son of his business partner to collect me from the hospital the next morning and drive me home. I have no idea what he thought was the reason for my being in hospital. The only person who seemed to disapprove of the procedure was Ali. I don't know how he found out, but he obviously worked it out from snippets of overheard conversation, because for quite some time afterwards he used to tell people that I had killed his brother.

Now, just a few years later, I couldn't believe that I was faced with the same dilemma and this time I found it much harder to come to a decision. I dithered and agonised over the options for as long as I could, but really it was a foregone conclusion: on the surface we seemed to be carrying on as normal, but by then we lived with the constant feeling that we were losing control over our own lives. Now that my worries over our eldest children had been reduced to concerns such as whether they might be homesick, I was constantly fearful for the safety of our younger daughters. Although we never formally agreed that we were leaving for good, in my heart I knew that we would not return from our next trip abroad. It was this knowledge which made another baby out of the question, so despite my reluctance I set about putting an end to the pregnancy.

First I paid another visit to the gynaecologist who had helped me before, but I was devastated to find that this time he was not so accommodating. The phone rang just as I entered the consulting room, so he gestured to me to sit down whilst he answered it. It quickly became obvious that it was Zane's voice on the other end of the line – he always shouted when he was calling long distance – and I sat and watched the doctor's expression change from professional courtesy to solemnity as he listened. Finally he spoke: 'I don't know what she wants, I haven't spoken to her yet'. I understood immediately what was going on: Zane had suffered a pang of guilt at not being around when I needed him and this had prompted him to phone the gynaecologist to encourage him to carry out the termination. I have no doubt it was intended as a gesture of support, but it was a bad idea, as he would have realised if he had taken a moment to think about it. They had not met before so the doctor had no way of knowing who was on the phone – he might have been anyone, possibly someone from the secret police checking that he wasn't breaking the law. Anyway, he wasn't prepared to take that chance, and who could blame him. He listened in silence while I explained that I was pregnant and gave my reasons for feeling that I couldn't go through with the pregnancy. The expression on his face was not encouraging but I plodded on, near to tears, until he took pity on me and brought my faltering explanation to an end: 'I'm sorry, I can't help you. It's against the law to carry out an abortion for social reasons in this country.'

As I drove home my feelings see-sawed between relief that the decision had been taken out of my hands and anger that the practitioner who had been so accommodating just a few years ago had sent me packing on this occasion. I wasn't about to give up that easily, though. As soon as I got home I went back to our psychiatrist friend to explain what had happened, omitting the part Zane had played. His response was immediate and I was oddly comforted at being reassured by a man that I was doing the right thing.

'Of course you don't want to be pregnant now, it would be a disaster. Don't worry, I'll speak to him, he'll understand'. The next day he called in on his way home from his clinic to tell me to go back to the gynaecologist the next day. 'I've had a word with him; he wants you to go back tomorrow to arrange when you can have the operation.'

And that was that. I went back to the hospital where the doctor explained that I would not have to stay in hospital overnight as there was a new 'suction method' of carrying out the procedure which was quicker and also shortened the recovery period. We exchanged a few pleasantries and shook hands before I left; neither of us mentioned my previous visit. Two days later I took a taxi to the hospital after dropping the girls off at school and Zane collected me later in the afternoon. This was a welcome affirmation of his role in my life, although I would have preferred it if he had come on his own. Instead, he arrived with our two young daughters in tow, thus exposing them to the sight of their mother dragging herself out of bed in a blood-stained hospital gown. As I made my way to the bathroom to dress I tried to hold the gown together over my exposed and no doubt similarly blood-stained backside, but the way they wrinkled up their noses and exchanged horrified looks left me in no doubt that I hadn't succeeded.

# Chapter Eighteen

There were several reasons why I felt this increased sense of urgency about leaving the country. One of the most obvious was the campaign against 'foreigners' which had been stepped up to a frightening degree. We were used to Erica's histrionics, so I rarely concentrated on what she was saying, but when she turned up in tears and told me that her two sisters in law had both been summarily divorced by their husbands earlier that morning she had my full attention. The odds of that happening were so unlikely that I didn't know quite what to say. The men were both army officers and although their action was unexpected their grounds were unequivocal – the announcement that army officers married to 'foreigners' must either divorce their wives or resign their commission. I'm sure that they reached this apparently heartless decision after considering the underlying implications of the directive. No doubt the desire to safeguard their families was an important factor, but if that was their motivation it was a useless gesture because within days the teenaged sons of the elder sister were dragged from their home and taken off to an unknown destination.

Naturally, the whole family was devastated, but Erica's eldest son, an awkward, rather clumsy thirteen-year-old who was usually rather quiet around adults, told me in a voice seething with rage, 'I hate this country; I'm going to leave as soon as I can and when I do I'm never coming back.' That summer he left to continue his education in Germany and so far as I know, he has kept his word. Erica's relatives were not the only people we knew to be affected. When we returned to work after the Easter break, several of the Iraqi employees at the centre had

321

simply disappeared, together with one of the teachers. No-one asked what had happened to them, so far as I know.

Up until then, foreign wives of Iraqis enjoyed certain privileges simply because we were foreign. During those times when Iraqis were banned from travelling abroad we were free to leave the country whenever we wanted to, subject only to gaining our husband's permission. We were also able to take our minor children with us when we went, an advantage much envied by some of their friends. As a British subject I was entitled to hold dual nationality, but I had never seen any reason to apply for Iraqi citizenship up until then. Moreover, before I left to go to Iraq for the first time I had promised my father that I would never give up my British nationality. He believed that a British passport was a talisman which afforded its bearer protection anywhere in the world, and although I was not altogether convinced he was right I intended to keep my promise. This presented me with a bit of a dilemma when the searchlight which seemed to be always on the move, sweeping the country and seeking out citizens it had yet to annoy, settled on wives like myself.

In a nutshell, we were no longer going to be able to live in the country on an extended residence permit, nor were we allowed to have dual nationality: if we wanted to stay we had to apply for Iraqi nationality within a fixed period of time – I can't remember how much time we were given. In addition, our minor children would not be allowed to leave the country unless their mother had already applied for Iraqi nationality. Little else was talked about in the 'foreign wives' community for the next couple of weeks; the more we thought about it, the more potential problems we could see arising from this new decree in the future. What if someone had a parent or other relative taken seriously ill at a time when Iraqis were forbidden to leave the country? What about those of us whose offspring lived abroad? Strangely enough, I can't remember anyone asking 'What if there was a war?'

Someone suggested that any foreign passports surrendered to the Iraqi government would have to be returned to the appropriate consulate, at which time we could simply ask for them back, but nobody really knew whether this was true or not. Mary Fox offered to try to get a Consular official to come and explain to us exactly what our position would be, but the visit never materialised. For their part, the Iraqi government stated that they were not so heartless as to refuse to let someone leave the country to visit a sick or dying relative; I don't think anyone found this reassuring. In the end, it became obvious that there was nothing for it but to bite the bullet and do as we were told. In my case, I did so only because I wanted to take the girls with me and leave for England in the summer; neither Zane nor I had any clear idea of what would happen after that.

Despite having lived in Iraq for nearly eighteen years, I had never actually been to the residence department because Zane always renewed my residence permit for me. However, I was certain that my application for citizenship would involve endless bureaucracy, so I was dreading going there. I kept putting it off until Pauline phoned to say that Munim had arranged an appointment to process her application and if I went with her I could apply at the same time. We arranged to meet the next morning and off we went, expecting special treatment because of Munim's position. Unfortunately, only Pauline got that. There was always a crowd of people gathered outside of government departments because anyone on official business had to make a formal written application, set out in a specific format. The stock answer to any citizen making an enquiry to a government official was 'Write an application'. Consequently, outside of every government department you could find professional scribes stationed at the small folding tables which they set up every morning. They knew the correct wording to use in any official correspondence and for a small fee would write out an official application for any citizen who had been referred back to them.

When we arrived, several policemen cleared our way through the people waiting for their applications to be written by using the magic words, 'Let the minister's wife pass'. I trailed along behind her as she was shown into a large room where an officer asked if he might see her residence documents and passport, after which she was asked to sign her application. I don't remember that she was asked any questions at all, apart from whether she would like a glass of tea. Whilst she was occupied one of the policemen turned to me quite rudely and asked; 'Who are you, her sister?'

'No, we're friends – I've come to apply for Iraqi nationality too.'

'Well you can't; your husband will have to come with you and you'll both have to answer some questions before we decide whether you can apply or not.' Clearly, a Minister's influence only extended so far.

A week or so later, Zane and I went together to make my application. The thing I remember most was the abruptness, bordering on rudeness, of the officers who were processing applications; it was so different from the way Iraqis usually behaved. Whilst we were waiting, two young men arrived to enquire about some documents which they were waiting for; they were told very roughly to 'come back next week'. This was from one of the security people who seemed to outnumber the police officers permanently employed in that department. As the young men left, he turned to one of the officials and said: 'They can go to hell, they're Ajim'.

When my turn came, the procedure was quite straightforward, involving providing documents such as birth and marriage certificates and filling out an application form. I then had to answer a few questions: 'Have you ever been a member of a political party?'

'No' – Zane jumped in here before I could answer that one.

'How do you know?'

'How could I not know, she's my wife'.

'She might have joined a party before she met you. Let her answer'.

I duly confirmed that I had never been a member of any political party. 'Not even the Labour party?' I didn't know whether membership of the Labour Party would have been considered a good thing or not, but I was able to answer quite truthfully that I had never been a member of any political party whatsoever. When the interview was over I was handed a receipt confirming that I had made my application and we left. That receipt was as precious to me as my passport, since I wouldn't be able to leave the country without it. I couldn't wait to be clear of the crowds who were pushing and shoving around the entrance door so that I could stow it safely away in my handbag.

Whilst these events were taking place, my teaching career was getting off the ground. June, a local friend who taught English at a school in Mansur, had been asked to find someone willing to take classes for parents of children attending the International School. The objective was apparently to improve their English so that they could help their children with homework. The classes took place two or three times a week and would fit in with my commitments at the centre, so I jumped at the chance. I'm so glad I did because, apart from gaining valuable experience, the majority of the students were from countries which were then part of the Soviet Bloc – people who were rarely encouraged to socialise with locals whilst they were working abroad. Because of this they were generally thought to be churlish and unfriendly, so it was a pleasant surprise when they turned out to be charming and unfailingly polite; they were also very serious about improving their English. I enjoyed taking those classes and at the end of the summer they threw a tea party for me at which I was presented with various small gifts, including beautifully hand-embroidered tablecloths which I keep at the back of a drawer to this day.

I was really starting to enjoy my work, but Zane, who had always loved civil engineering, was not having such a happy time. He had been requested to return to work at the state contracting company, something he was not able to do even if he had wanted to because he had just started a new construction contract of his own. I was too preoccupied with my own fledgling career at that time to give this much thought, and he typically did not tell me that intermediaries had been sent to put pressure on him to go back. However, one afternoon when I answered the phone to someone who asked for Zane but managed to make it sound like an order, omitting the 'please' at the end, he had my full attention. Now Zane is naturally olive-skinned and he became even darker in the summer months because much of his working day was spent outdoors, so it would have been hard not to notice that the colour drained from his face whilst he was on the phone. The conversation was short, and by the time he hung up he was actually pale. 'I've got to go out; I'll be back later'.

'Wait, what's wrong? Are you OK?'

'I'm fine; it's just work.'

This was hardly the first time he had cancelled our plans at the last minute, but I was concerned by his appearance, which suggested something disastrous had taken place. Once, on one of his first jobs, one of the men had been killed when a large bank of sandy soil which had just been excavated collapsed on top of him. Although Zane wasn't in charge of operations and no-one was at fault, he was very upset by the incident and always dreaded something similar happening while he was in charge. 'Has something happened?'

'No, don't worry, everything's fine.'

'I might be late back, though.' This last comment was added as an afterthought as he went out of the front door. I was used to these mini crises as Zane was taking on quite large civil engineering projects by then, so I thought no more of it at the time. He didn't tell me until a few days later that the phone call had been from the central security headquarters, ordering him to attend for questioning immediately. It was the summons every Iraqi dreaded, no doubt conjuring up visions of torture, mutilation and heaven knows what else: no wonder he had paled when he received the order. When he did get around to telling me what had happened, it was clear that he was dealt with in a way which would instil maximum humiliation; thankfully this did not extend to actual physical abuse in his case. This is how he described his experience: He had driven to the area which was known to house the central intelligence offices, where he was flagged down by a guard demanding "Where do you think you're going?'

'I don't know, I've been told to report to the central intelligence headquarters.'

'What's your name?' After consulting a list the guard went on: 'Park your car, then walk down that road and take the first left, then go to the third house on the right.' Zane set off with great trepidation but then realised that, because he was so nervous, he hadn't taken in the directions, leaving him with no option but to return and ask the way again.

"What's the matter with you, are you stupid? I told you – walk to the end of the road, turn left then go to the third house on the right.' Everything was said with maximum aggression; if a citizen wasn't afraid when he was first sent for, they made sure he would be by the time the questioning began. Zane set off again, this time managing to find the correct building. Once again he was greeted in a manner that fell far short of the traditional Arabian welcome: 'What do you want?'

'You sent for me'.

'What's your name?' His reply was met with: 'Oh yes, you're the traitor'.

'I'm not a traitor' – he was beginning to recover his nerve a little.

'You're a traitor and a criminal. Bend over,' the man opened a drawer as he spoke.

'What do you mean, bend over?' I imagine these words would strike fear into the heart of any red-blooded man

'Bend over I tell you'. The man leaned forward and clipped some sort of tag onto Zane's jacket. 'Now go in there".

He was sent to wait in a room where several other people were waiting to be interviewed. Some were obviously Christian – one he recognised as a man who sold alcohol in the central market – he was probably suspected of smuggling. There was a makeshift reception area manned by yet another scowling interrogator. 'What's your name?' After answering once again, Zane was told to sit down on one of the plastic chairs. Another man entered and called out a name, ordering a man in traditional Arab dress to rise. Apparently he was a brick manufacturer. 'You're a traitor. You sell bricks at inflated prices, driving the price up in the market'. That particular individual had probably spent all his life in the building trade. He looked tough and not easily intimidated: 'I make them in my factory and sell them for the going rate. That's business.'

'Sit down' His interrogator left the room only to return within minutes.

'Where's the traitor and criminal, Zane Toma?'

'I'm not a criminal or a traitor'

'Stand up. Why have you refused to serve your country by working for the state contracting company?'

'I am working for the country. I've just started a new project under contract for the Irrigation Department'. The man left the room and went outside, leaving Zane standing to attention. When he returned he re-entered the inner room so Zane sat down again, relieved to have some clue as to why he had been summoned. Whilst all this was going on the other people in the room sat in silence: there was none of the usual waiting room chit-chat. Zane was worrying about what would happen to his children if he were thrown into prison and no doubt the others were similarly preoccupied. After a while the door to the inner room opened and the second man came out. 'Stand up the traitor and criminal, Zane Toma. Come in here.' Zane followed him into a small room which was piled high with desks and plastic chairs. It appeared to be some kind of store room. 'Why are you a traitor? Why do you refuse to work for our country?'

'I do work for our country. I'm working on a government contract at the moment'.

'Leave it and return to the State contracting company'.

'I can't just leave it – I've signed a contract.'

'They'll release you. I'll write to them and order them to release you from your contract.'

'I don't want them to release me. I worked for the State contracting company before – I left because I wasn't happy there.'

'You weren't happy because you're a traitor and a criminal. You are not allowed to take any more contracts – an order will be sent to all government departments. Leave here now and come back with a signed and notarised guarantee that you will not run away. In the mean -time, someone must guarantee you for the amount of ten thousand dinars. Go'.

Ten thousand dinars was a huge amount in those days; Zane drove away from the security headquarters with his head buzzing. Who could he possibly ask to take such a risk? He consulted a relative who suggested he ask another distant relative who also happened to be a party member. That man was apparently well-connected in the party and reputed to be a good mate of Saddam; he agreed immediately and unconditionally. 'No problem – let's go and do it straight away.' They set off together and the guarantee was drawn up, signed and notarised in record time. Zane knew he should go back to present the guarantee at the security headquarters immediately but the stress of the past few hours suddenly caught up with him and he felt so unwell that he came home and went to bed instead. He still hadn't told me what was going on when he returned to the security area the next morning. This time he knew exactly where he was going so he arrived at the building where he was first interviewed quite early in the morning. The officials on duty hadn't changed, nor had the procedure: 'Stand up the traitor and criminal Zane Toma. Why didn't you come back yesterday?' 'I wasn't well. You made me ill, sending for me like that.'

'Have you found a guarantor?' Zane handed him the document which he read carefully, glancing up at Zane as he noted who had signed it. Sometimes it was an advantage to live in a city where everyone knew everyone else. When he had finished reading, he shouted to the guard manning reception: 'I want a policeman in here now to accompany this traitor and criminal to the offices of the State Contracting Company and deliver him to the Director.'

A police officer appeared, took charge of his prisoner and the two of them set off as ordered, with Zane driving them both in his own car.

When they arrived at the company they went straight up to the director's office where they were informed by his secretary, whom Zane knew well, that the director was at a meeting but was expected to return at any time. In the meantime, the secretary contacted the deputy director who signed the warrant carried by the policeman to the effect that he had taken delivery of the traitor etc, etc. At that point the policeman duly handed him over and left. The director, whom Zane also knew well, returned and made a big show of being surprised and pleased to find him waiting there. At first he tried to treat the events leading up to Zane being brought to his office as a joke, but Zane rounded on him furiously, convinced that he must have known about the involvement of the secret police. At that point the director began to bluster, denying that he had any hand in it but Zane knew better – the director was an opportunist who would stop at nothing to further his career. He didn't pull any punches in telling him so and he also repeated his determination to see his project through to completion. The upshot was that the director asked him to go away and think about it but instead of thinking he discussed it with his partner, who agreed that the best thing would be to take as long as possible to complete the current contract and hope that the matter would blow over. It was remarkably generous of him as they both lost money as a result, but that was what they agreed to do.

The main reason Zane had left the company in the first place was that he knew he would not be able to implement orders which would go against the grain professionally; he was convinced that this would eventually lead to his imprisonment, or worse. It was a common dilemma under Saddam's government, affecting not just engineers but doctors, journalists and many other professionals. A good example was a dam which was to be built in the north of the country. For some reason, Saddam didn't like its proposed location and decided to move it. Although he was warned that the new location was unsuitable and might eventually threaten the safety of the local area, he was adamant – in all things he felt he knew what was best for the country. Inevitably, the dam was built where he wanted it and has needed regular repairs ever since. I understand that there are currently fears that at any time it might collapse and flood a large area in the north of Iraq, potentially submerging the city of Mosul. Saddam was also in the habit of appointing his trusted cronies to senior positions even when they had no relevant experience: when one such friend became director of the ministry of industry he called a meeting of senior management and started it off with the announcement: 'I know nothing about industry. All I know is that I'll hang anyone who doesn't do a good job.'

Added to Zane's fears was the potential loss of income just when he was beginning to make serious money as a contractor, and of course as a government employee he would lose the freedom to travel. This was not in itself a concern for him since he rarely accompanied us on our summer visits to Britain, but things were different now that our children were living abroad. Whilst I was mulling over this latest development, my Iraqi neighbour called over to see me. This was unusual because, although we had always been on friendly terms, despite her annoyance over the water pump, our relationship mainly consisted of chats over the garden gate since, like Mum, she left home every day to visit one of her sisters or other relatives as soon as she had finished her housework.

'I need to talk to you; my husband told me not to tell you, but I think you should know that the secret police came to our house asking questions about you.'

'About me? Why would they be asking about me? What did they want to know?'

'They asked about your morals, whether you're a loose woman, if you have affairs, stuff like that. I told them that your behaviour is always impeccable, even better than that of an Iraqi woman'. I was touched both by this accolade and by her obvious concern; I told her not to worry, explaining that it was probably part of the campaign to force Zane to go to work for the government. I imagined that they were looking for something they could blackmail him with, but I have no idea whether that was the case – I might have been under consideration for some Mata Hari type role for all I know. If I was, I obviously didn't have the right qualifications, because I heard no more about it.

# Chapter Nineteen

Whilst we were preoccupied by these personal concerns, large numbers of people continued to be arrested on suspicion of being connected to the Dawa party. Anyone who showed signs of being overly religious ran the risk of arrest. At the same time there were reports of bombs going off in public places and these were also attributed to Dawa party plots. Possibly in an attempt to divert the attention of the nation away from these dark events, it was announced that a huge party on the lines of those put on by communist China was to take place, with large numbers of young girls moving together in a synchronised dance. I think the party was to celebrate Saddam's birthday, although I'm not absolutely certain, but I do remember that dignitaries from abroad were expected to attend along with high ranking party members. The girls would be drawn from organisations such as the young Baathists and the girl guides, and that's where Zara came in. As a member of the guides she had no choice – she had to take part in the celebration.

Rehearsals began in preparation for the big event: initially they took place at school, but later it became necessary for all the performers to practise together so the girls were taken off to the football stadium where the performance was to take place. There was no prior warning to parents – buses would simply turn up at all the girls' high schools to collect the girls and whisk them off. When they arrived at the stadium the whole operation was directed by a number of young security men. They herded the girls around, putting them through their paces until they performed their manoeuvres with almost military precision. Whilst they were doing this they were scanning the performers, looking out for the prettiest ones.

Later on they would compete to assist them back onto the bus, chatting them up and allowing their hands to linger on the girls' backsides or other interesting parts of their anatomy. At thirteen Zara had a very well-developed figure, so I didn't pass this piece of information on to Zane because he was already fuming over the fact that she had been coerced into taking part, but even if I had told him there was nothing he could do about it.

The rehearsals coincided with the weather getting hotter as the summer approached. Zara would arrive home rosy cheeked and sweaty from the long bus journey needed to drop all the girls back to their various schools. Her black curls bounced on her shoulders as she hurried up the garden path, eager to tell me about the latest incident to occur at the rehearsal. She had already witnessed a young boy being beaten up and dragged away by secret policemen when she went to the cinema with a couple of her friends one day. The incident started whilst they were queuing to get their tickets. A security guard accused the boy of pestering a girl who was waiting in the queue. He started to protest his innocence, but within minutes the argument attracted the attention of other secret police in the crowd who ran over and jumped on the boy, punching and kicking him into unconsciousness. Zara was convinced that the argument had started out of jealousy because the girl had chatted to the boy after ignoring the secret policeman's advances. 'They really beat him, I think he was dead when they dragged him away', she told me in hushed tones later that day.

Anyway, one afternoon she was going to a friend's house straight after school and was getting a lift back with her friend's Dad later. There were rehearsals nearly every day by then and I remember that I was sitting with Erica enjoying a cup of coffee in the balmy spring afternoon when Zara was dropped off at the garden gate. The door to the terrace was open, giving us a clear view of her arriving much earlier than expected and I could tell immediately from her face that something momentous had happened. Despite the events which had been unfolding all around us I was totally unprepared for the tale she was about to say.

She stopped short when she realised where we were sitting and grasped the edge of the door for support: 'Five bodies, laid out in a row', she managed to gasp before dashing through to the kitchen. She was back in seconds bearing a bottle of water icy cold from the fridge. Ignoring the years of constant nagging to use a glass, she upped the bottle and took a long draught then wiped her mouth on the sleeve of her school shirt: 'Bombs. They thought the party was today. They tried to blow it up on the wrong day'. And that was the story in a nutshell; someone had planned to set off bombs and disrupt the celebration. Whether they had genuinely got the date wrong or whether deliberate disinformation about the date had been publicised I have no idea, but on that particular day five people were killed in the explosions – I don't know how many were injured.

I think there must have been students among the people who had been killed, because a few days later there was to be some kind of demonstration held at the university, which was located in the same area as the British Council. I was due to go to the centre that morning to join Mary Fox and a couple of the other newly-trained teachers in a planning exercise. For some reason there were no classes going on that morning, possibly because it was the Easter break, so the centre was unusually quiet when I arrived. We went into one of the upstairs classrooms and sat down to discuss exactly what we hoped to get out of the morning but we had hardly got started when we heard the sound of shots and shouting coming from outside. We all jumped up to look out of the window, but the street below was unusually quiet – normally there would be students hanging about outside, so we shrugged and went back to work. Not for long, however because within minutes there was a series of loud bangs which sounded like explosions, prompting us all to rush back to the window to have another look. Whilst we were peering out an army officer rushed into the room waving a gun and yelling, 'Move away from the windows, stand back against the wall over on this side!' He rushed off again once he was satisfied that we had retreated from the window and crossed over to the other side of the room. As we were speculating about what might be happening, Patrick Fox rushed into the room shouting, 'Everyone get down on the floor'. We looked at each other very sheepishly; but no-one made a move to lie down and I certainly wasn't going to be first. Instead, feeling rather foolish, we all remained standing by the wall like a row of sunflowers until someone came up to tell us that we should all go home as quickly as possible – I think it was one of the mysterious ex-patriot British employees.

We all hurried downstairs to where everyone at the centre, including the library and clerical staff, were being bundled into the minibus, leaving the Foxes, who had their own driver, and me standing by the door. Unfortunately, I didn't have my car with me that day, but one of the Foxes had already offered to take me with them. We got into their car and were driven up the side street to where a couple of policemen had been stationed, forcing the car to slow down. Mary Fox turned to me and instructed: 'Ask them where you can get a taxi. Go on, ask them,' she urged when I responded with stunned silence. I had assumed that they intended to make sure that I was safely clear of the area but they obviously just wanted me clear of British Council premises. 'I don't need to ask, you can normally flag a taxi down on the main road. I don't know if there will be any taxi drivers still operating with all this excitement going on, though'. 'Well, ask him where you can get one,' my boss urged, pointing at the policeman who was giving us a cursory inspection through the car window, so I did.

'At the end of the road'. The officer looked at me as if I was stupid then nodded his head in that direction as he moved away, waving the driver on. He drove rather cautiously towards the end of the street and immediately he turned into the main road he was directed by the Foxes to stop and let me out of the car.

I couldn't believe it, they couldn't wait to abandon me and hurry off to the safety of their nearby home. For all they knew, I could have found myself in the middle of a gun battle. Thankfully, although the traffic was lighter than usual it appeared to be moving along as normal. My stomach was churning as I stood on the pavement but to my immense relief I was able to stop an empty cab without having to wait too long. I can't say I felt at ease even when I got into the car, though, and I didn't relax fully until I had crossed the bridge which took us out of the university area.

A couple of days later we were all due back at work; when I arrived at the centre there were secret policemen stopping people and searching everyone's bags. A couple of them stepped in front of me as I was getting out of my car: 'What are you doing here?'

'I work here; I'm a teacher'. 'What have you got in there?' I handed over the large leather bag I used to carry my books, overhead projector transparencies, tapes, lesson notes and such like, then waited whilst they inspected each item one by one. 'What's this? And this?' One would have thought that they had never encountered a tape recorder before. I explained what each article was used for, but I couldn't help noticing that they were spending a lot more time with me than anyone else. Whilst they were going through my things I was relieved to see the caretaker, Hamza, striding down the driveway with Margaret Zane hot-footing it behind him. 'Why are you searching her? She's a teacher here'. The men looked at each other, then by some kind of unspoken agreement they let me through, rather reluctantly, I felt. I fell in beside Margaret and as we walked up the driveway towards the building her serious expression dissolved into her usual smile, 'We saw them stop you from the office window. You're lucky, that spoilsport Hamza wouldn't let them frisk us'.

Over the next few months it seemed as though there would never be any good news again; there were constant rumours of arrests and tales of the bodies of torture victims being flung over garden walls during the night. Everyone assumed that this method of disposing of victims was intended to maximise the horrific effect on grieving relatives when they stumbled upon the mutilated remains the next morning – it certainly helped to spread fear among the general population. One British wife sent her husband out to buy bread for the family lunch; he never returned and his wife and children don't know what happened to him to this day. Zane came home one night and asked me to give up my work at the centre, saying it was getting too dangerous to be associated with a foreign organisation. I have no idea what prompted his request but I refused anyway; with my children growing up and two of them far away I needed something to fill my days, particularly as our stock of friends was dwindling more and more as people left the country. We hardly ever went out any more, so preparing lessons and writing letters to Summer and Ali were welcome distractions, even though the need for strict self-censorship probably made my letters very stilted and boring.

One had to be equally careful what one said during telephone conversations, but at least a direct dialling system to the UK was now up and running, although I had several failures when I first tried using it because no-one had told me that you had to omit the first zero of the UK number. Frustrated by my failure to carry out what everyone else assured me was the simplest of procedures, I had been forced to resort to dialling the operator and asking for help; once I was infuriated when the operator mocked my accent, asking me whether I was Kurdish – something Zane liked to do when he was in an annoying macho mood. On another occasion, an operator put me through to Summer as requested, but phoned me back the next morning for a chat. I have no idea whether he was just bored and wanted to practise his English, or whether he was carrying out a security fishing exercise. Either way, I simply hung up the phone. When I did at last manage to place a call to Ali at his school a grumpy house master answered, demanding to know whether I realised that it was nine o'clock in the evening. 'I didn't realise, I'm phoning from Baghdad, please get my son on the phone as quickly as possible.' I put on my haughtiest voice. This seemed to do the trick and he went off to fetch Ali, who came on the phone to ask in a hushed voice, 'Mum, what are you doing in Saudi Arabia?'

'I'm not in Saudi Arabia, I'm at home, why are you asking me that?'

'Oh, my teacher said that you were phoning from Saudi Arabia'. One could only hope that he wasn't the geography teacher.

Whilst all this was going on I noticed that there were more foreigners to be seen around the city than usual, not workers from the eastern bloc or foreign wives but casually dressed, prosperous-looking male foreigners, and some of them had American accents – not something we were used to hearing in Baghdad. I don't know whether it was a coincidence that a state supermarket for the sole use of foreign customers was opened around this time, but we were delighted to find that you only had to look foreign to be allowed in. The store wasn't large by western supermarket standards, but we could buy things there which were just not available elsewhere and it was also cheap. Naturally, when we shopped there we made sure that we didn't speak in Arabic, just in case.

I began giving some of the kids' possessions away, things which we wouldn't be able to take with us, like Ali's large collection of model cars. I gave those to a friend's little boy under the pretext that Ali had outgrown them, although the reality was that he would probably have kept them forever if he could. We couldn't tell the girls that they wouldn't be returning to Baghdad until school was over for the summer in case they let it slip to one of their friends; there was always the fear that word would get out and we would be stopped from leaving. We didn't tell anyone else either, not even Erica, who had been an almost daily visitor to our home for the past eight years: in return, she didn't tell us that her eldest son was going to remain in Germany when she returned from her summer visit.

Once the school holidays had started and the girls were safely away from their friends, I told them that we were leaving for good; Tula was devastated and refused to go, saying that she would not leave her beloved dog, Fonzy, behind. It took all my powers of persuasion to convince her that Zane would find a very good home for him once we had left, plus a promise that we would get another Springer Spaniel puppy as soon as we could after we arrived. Zara was also upset, mainly because two of her friends had given her money and asked her to bring them back something from the UK. Obviously, she couldn't return the money before we left without arousing suspicion, especially since she was convinced that the father of one of the girls was in the secret police. I tended to agree with her after she attended a birthday party at the girl's home. Her family had recently built a new house which was unusually large and luxurious, so when the kids arrived for the party they naturally wanted to look around. Their proud hostess led the way as the girls wandered around the ground floor, admiring the ornately-furnished rooms, until they reached a corridor which obviously led to a separate wing. 'No, no, you can't go down there, no-one's allowed to go there'. The party guests turned to look at her in surprise, then turned back again as the stern voice of the girl's father demanded: 'What are you doing here?' He had emerged into the corridor from the nearest doorway and was glaring at his daughter's guests in what Zara felt was quite a menacing way. They all retreated to the staircase and made their way upstairs to investigate some of the bedrooms. Zara was ahead of the others, so she took the opportunity to whisper to one of her friends, 'What was that all about?' The girl giggled, 'Perhaps that's where he keeps all his money'. The bedrooms were also beautifully fitted out but Zara's eagle eye immediately spotted their most unusual feature – they were all fitted with an intercom. 'Why d'ya need those, then?'

'They're connected directly to the front gates. In case we have visitors after we've gone to bed.'

'But why? Do you go to bed really early or something?' The girl was beginning to look quite uncomfortable, and Zara for one was beginning to feel the same way. By that time they had reached the birthday girl's bedroom, and they all collapsed onto her bed, trying to recapture the party mood, but the door flew open and her father announced from the doorway that 'everyone must go home'. There was a general flap as the guests tried to contact their parents or organise lifts, but no explanation was offered nor was there any apology. Added to that, there was no hint of any refreshments being in the offing, let alone a birthday cake. Zara was never invited to visit that friend's home again, nor would we have allowed her to go. Nevertheless, she was a nice girl and they remained friends, but since it was obvious that her father was no ordinary citizen she kept the money, hoping to be able to return it later; to date this has not been possible – something she still feels guilty about.

The plan was that I would leave with the girls on 1 June 1980 and Zane would follow shortly afterwards. We weren't certain that he would be allowed to leave, but we were counting on the fact that he still hadn't completed his contract and was therefore still a businessman, which was normally accepted as a reason for having to make a trip abroad. He wasn't planning to stay in the UK at that time, he just wanted to spend a little time with Summer and Ali before returning to Baghdad to complete his contract – he had no intention of leaving his partner in the lurch. He would then try to wind up his affairs and return to the UK as soon as he could. We were resigned to the fact that it might take quite a while.

During the few days remaining before we left, I cleaned the house from top to bottom and, with the help of Zara and Tula, packed all our bedding and other possessions into cupboards and wardrobes. We had to leave most of our clothes behind, but I ironed the girls school uniforms, leaving them hanging in a row of crisp white shirts and navy blue skirts – I had a crazy notion that the secret police might break into the house and search it, so I hoped that the sight of the uniforms already prepared for the autumn term would serve as evidence that we intended to come back. The night before we left, we all went round to Mum's to say goodbye. We found her and Dad outside, the teapot in its customary place on the primus; Mum was sitting on the long garden swing seat with Layla and Dad was pottering about in his garden as usual. When we told them that we weren't coming back there were emotional hugs and kisses all round, but Mum didn't cry: 'You'll come back, things will get better, you'll see.' Perhaps they will one day, but sadly, my parents in law didn't live to see that time. I wonder how they would have felt if they knew that practically every one of their children, grandchildren and even great grandchildren would soon be scattered all over the world, part of the new diaspora which has replaced the wandering Jews.

I hardly slept that night; I lay awake dreading that something would happen to prevent us from leaving. I couldn't wait to get on the plane, and was showered, dressed and ready to leave by the time the alarm clock went off. As we drove along the tree-lined dual carriageway which led to the newly-built airport, I reflected on how much Baghdad had changed during the past few years. New roads and hospitals, modern hotels and government buildings had sprung up everywhere, and the city itself had spread outwards to make room for them. Despite this, the new had somehow been incorporated into the old without sacrificing any of the city's charm, either by large amounts of luck or good planning.

Zane always hated saying goodbye, so he wasted no time in dropping us off at the airport, where we checked in and followed the signs towards the departure lounge. It was much bigger than the lounge in the old airport, but I didn't waste any time admiring the new building – I was too busy trying to make sense of what was going on around me. There was the usual glass cubicle positioned by the gate which was processing non-Iraqi passport holders. There were relatively few passengers heading in that direction and the gate appeared to be operating in the normal way. In contrast, there were large numbers of Iraqi passport holders; as they came through most of them stood looking around uncertainly because there were a couple of security men at the entrance yelling at everyone to go to the right queue. It turned out that 'the right queue' was the one which was labelled with the first letter of an individual's name. Behind them, on the far side of the room, there were about a dozen more security men. They stood in a line about two yards apart looking rather like a row of birds of prey. They remained still for the most part, their eyes on the passengers who were gradually filling up the room, but whether they were looking for someone specific was anybody's guess. Occasionally one of them would move forward to check a passenger's papers following a query from one of the passport officers, who each had a large black book on their desk containing a list of names beginning with a particular letter. If your name was in that book, man, woman or child, you weren't allowed to leave the country. I could tell, not only from the size of their moustaches and the smartness of their suits but also the demeanour of the officials when they spoke to them, that these men were from the higher echelons of the security services.

It was chaos; the queues were getting longer and longer as people entered the room and realised what they had to do next, shepherded on by the security men. I gave each of my daughters her own passport and made sure they were in the correct queue before very reluctantly leaving them and going to present my own passport to the waiting passport officer. Within minutes I had passed through, but instead of going ahead into the departure lounge I took up position on the other side of the desks alongside the security men and waited for my girls; if they were banned from travelling they would be stranded at the airport since Zane had already left for the site and there was no public telephone system. In any case, there was no way I was leaving the country without them so, just like the unfortunate passengers who had been herded into the queues, I had no option but to wait, and it was obviously going to take a long time. Because Zara was approaching fourteen she was about the same height as the other female passengers so I could see her most of the time as the queue slowly advanced, but at eleven Tula was quite a lot smaller. She kept disappearing for minutes at a time as the queue ebbed and flowed and I was terrified that she would be pushed over and either lose her passport or be trampled underfoot as the queue was forced forward by the people joining it from the rear. On the plus side, there are fewer Iraqi names beginning with Gh than with Z so she was making better progress overall than Zara, whose queue just seemed to get longer and longer.

I checked the large clock on the wall; it confirmed what my watch was telling me – only ten more minutes before our plane was due to take off. As I did so a member of the BA cabin crew came through to remind the world in general that the plane to Heathrow was due to take off shortly, and that the passengers really needed to board the plane. No-one took any notice so he went away again only to be replaced a few minutes later by the pilot: 'I'm due to take off in five minutes; where are my passengers?' he demanded of the line of secret policemen. Since they were more accustomed to questioning people than answering them, no-one bothered to reply. In fact, they barely glanced at the irate pilot as they continued to scan the lines of waiting passengers. He hesitated, probably mentally counting to ten, then blew his top: 'Right, that's it. I'm taking off in five minutes, with or without my passengers'.

My heart nearly exploded as he stormed off – neither of the girls was anywhere near the end of her queue. If we missed the plane and had to come back next week there was no guarantee that we wouldn't be listed in the black books ourselves. There was nothing for it: I had to do something. I walked towards the nearest secret policeman, who was well over six feet tall and very fit-looking. I stood right in front of him so he couldn't ignore me. 'Excuse me, can you help me?' His face, which was dominated by a very large 'twenty past eight' moustache, was expressionless as he looked at me and waited for me to continue. 'My plane's due to take off in five minutes, but my little girls are still in the queue; I can't leave them here. Can you help me?'

He looked at me again, summing me up. 'Come with me. Show me your daughters'. For all I knew, he might have been planning to throw all three of us out, or possibly into prison, but I had to take that chance. Tula was nearest so I pointed her out first, then moved down the Z queue until I spotted Zara determinedly holding her place as people were being pushed forward by others joining the queue behind them. 'That's my other daughter'. He beckoned her to the front of the queue then took her passport and handed it to the official at the desk. 'Check it'. Once it was confirmed that Zara wasn't on the list, the three of us moved towards Tula's queue. She lost no time in coming to the front, where she was also given the thumbs up. I put an arm around my daughters' shoulders, 'Thank you so much for your help', but he was off, back to his job of examining the crowd, so we hurried though to the departure lounge where we were immediately shepherded onto the plane. Once we had boarded and settled ourselves I looked around at the empty seats and silently gave thanks to my unlikely helper. He might have been a member of Saddam's dreaded secret police but he was also a gentleman. What more can one say?

I am ashamed to say that I have no idea whether many people were pulled out of the queues that day – I was too busy willing my daughters to pass safely through to the departure lounge. Once we were on the plane I remained on tenterhooks, my stomach churning, until the plane had safely taken off and passed over the border. I can't remember the rest of the journey, I only remember being in my brother's car and passing Ali in a telephone booth near to our house. He had somehow managed to persuade his school to let him leave a few days before the end of term. When he arrived to find an empty house he went to the phone booth to try to find out from family members where we were.

The next day I set about finding a school for the girls so that it would be familiar to them when they went back in September. I also started looking for a job and it seems incredible now that when Zane arrived a week later the girls had settled into their new school and I already had a job, teaching English to two large classes of Libyan government-sponsored students in a small private college. If I expected admiration for my efficiency I was disappointed. 'What's the hurry?' was his reaction and I realised for the first time that he had not entirely come to terms with the fact that we were staying in the UK for good. Like Mum, in his heart he was still hoping that the situation in Iraq would somehow improve and we would all be able to return to Baghdad. In the meantime, we spent a few days together, trying to recreate the family as it had been before.

Unfortunately, the dynamics had changed so it wasn't an easy task; Summer and Ali had grown into very independent adults who were used to doing exactly as they pleased. Summer already had a boyfriend, a nice ginger-haired lad who turned up and presented me with a large box of chocolates the afternoon after we arrived. This came as a bit of a shock to Zane. Although he was resigned to the fact that he couldn't make our kids follow the strict codes of behaviour still expected of teenagers in Baghdad, he hadn't expected what he considered the rot to set in so soon. On top of that, for the past year Zara and Tula had no longer been the junior members of the family, always vying for attention. With Zane away so much and our social life in decline, they had been my constant companions and had got used to having my undivided attention. We were still trying to work through these issues and become comfortable with each other as a family again when we awoke one morning to learn the most shocking of news. Perhaps we had been naïve, or wilfully blind because the signs must have been there had we chosen to read them. We did not, so it came as a complete surprise to learn that the unthinkable had happened – the two neighbouring countries of Iraq and Iran, both ancient civilisations sharing the same religion, if not the same culture, were at war.

And as everybody knows, that was the day when the trouble really started.